MW00669387

Additional praise for

# Governance, Risk Management, and Compliance

## It Can't Happen to Us—Avoiding Corporate Disaster While Driving Success

"In this complex and perilous global marketplace, it is vital that corporate leaders—senior officers and board members—put the highest premium on being smart about managing risk. Richard Steinberg has written a superb resource not only for strengthening your governance, risk management, and compliance practices but also ensuring they lead to competitive advantage."

**—James Kristie, Editor, *Directors & Boards***

"A practical and commonsense approach to corporate governance from someone who knows the subject well!"

**—Richard Koppes, former Deputy Executive Officer and General Counsel of CalPERS, founder of the National Association of Public Pension Attorneys, and board member of the National Association of Corporate Directors**

"This compelling work by Rick Steinberg enables even experienced senior managers and board members to fully appreciate how governance can and should work. Filled with critical analyses of how major companies have stumbled or failed, with clear lessons to be learned of what needs to go right, this book should be required reading for all of us striving to see our businesses thrive and grow shareholder value."

**—Scott Eston, former Chief Operating Officer, GMO**

# Governance, Risk Management, and Compliance

# Governance, Risk Management, and Compliance

## It Can't Happen to Us—Avoiding Corporate Disaster While Driving Success

RICHARD M. STEINBERG

**WILEY**

John Wiley & Sons, Inc.

Published by John Wiley & Sons, Inc., Hoboken, New Jersey.
Published simultaneously in Canada.

Some content in this book was originally published in columns by the author in Compliance Week, an information service on governance, risk and compliance. For more information, visit www.complianceweek.com or call (888) 519-9200.

For general information on our other products and services or for technical support, please contact our Customer Care Department within the United States at (800) 762-2974, outside the United States at (317) 572-3993 or fax (317) 572-4002.

Wiley also publishes its books in a variety of electronic formats. Some content that appears in print may not be available in electronic books. For more information about Wiley products, visit our web site at www.wiley.com.

*Library of Congress Cataloging-in-Publication Data:*
Steinberg, Richard.
  Governance, risk management, and compliance : it can't happen to us—avoiding corporate disaster while driving success / Richard Steinberg.
       p. cm.
  Includes index.
    ISBN 978-1-118-02430-0 (hardback); ISBN 978-1-118-10255-8 (ebk);
ISBN 978-1-118-10256-5 (ebk); ISBN 978-1-118-10257-2 (ebk)
  1.  Corporate governance. 2.  Risk management. 3.  Compliance.
4.  Business planning. I. Title.
  HD2741.S7636 2011
  658'–dc22                                                          2011012036

Printed in the United States of America

V10003071_081018

*This book is dedicated to my wonderful wife, Lana, without whose love and support it never would have been written.*

# Contents

# Foreword

I N THE AFTERMATH OF the worst economic and financial crisis in the United States in decades, policymakers, journalists, investor advocates, and others have been hard at work trying to identify those responsible. Commissions have met and studies have been undertaken, and people are beginning to reach their conclusions. But at the very core of this crisis was not a single set of actors. The problems stem significantly and systematically from the failure of governance, oversight, and risk management at the corporate, legislative, and regulatory levels.

Those in position to imagine, identify, and reduce the possibilities of failure simply did not do their jobs. As Richard Steinberg makes clear in these pages, the price of inattention or inaction by managers, regulators, and board members could be measured not in the hundreds of millions of dollars, but in the hundreds of billions of dollars. He explains how reputations and corporations were shattered in a matter of weeks and months, because individuals and institutions had no means of checking and correcting their market assumptions and their culture of risk-taking. In short, not enough people were asking: "What could go wrong?"

This failure in governance pains me deeply, primarily because as a regulator throughout the 1990s I was able to see many of these same failures play out once before in corporate America and our regulatory infrastructure. Many of the biggest changes in corporate governance were launched just after the Enron, WorldCom, and other major scandals of the early 2000s. And the resulting reforms, especially Sarbanes-Oxley, have had deep and lasting impacts.

In the immediate aftermath of those scandals, we saw a revolution in thinking about governance. Most boards are now majority independent—and key committees are now entirely independent, except at some controlled companies. Most companies have a lead independent director and/or a separate chairman. Boards meet more frequently—both as a whole and in executive session without the CEO—and are under significant scrutiny by shareholders. What's more, SEC rules have enabled shareholders to interact with each other more freely, and shareholder proposals have been effective in forcing removal of classified boards and other takeover defenses at many public companies. Majority voting is now the standard for director elections at many public companies, and shareholders are not hesitating to engage in proxy fights or withhold vote campaigns. While there are clear examples of boards failing to take their responsibilities seriously, many appear to be working better than they once did, and are doing a better job. What is clear is that while these measures were important and necessary, they were not enough. Like the challenge of developing a regulatory scheme to match the fast-moving nature of financial markets, governance standards will have to constantly be updated to take account of the way corporations operate.

I would suggest two significant areas of effort. The first is within the corporate structure itself, in the requirements set for board membership, the bylaws of corporations, the way compensation is structured, and the manner in which shareholder proposals are handled. The other is within the regulatory structure.

Within the corporate realm, our bias should always be toward transparency and accountability. Basic improvements, like giving investors greater access to the proxy, would push boards to be more proactive and more sensitive to investor concerns. But being more accountable is easier when you have the right expertise, and independent board members often don't have the base of knowledge they need. When an executive working every day inside a corporation is presenting information and analysis to the board, there will always be a gap between what they know and what the board knows. This gap exists but it need not be permanent.

Board members have an obligation to ask every question, and push in every possible way, to understand the financial and operational position of the company they are pledged to help lead. Yet in many cases, board members simply lack the expertise to do this job well, with this lack particularly notable when companies look to engage in financially complex transactions. These transactions can be a significant source of hidden risk, which, as we have seen, can reveal itself in ways few anticipated. I would like to see boards include individuals with financial market experience, and especially expertise in understanding, pricing, and managing risk. With even one such member regularly raising challenging questions and issues, boards would be able to press management to think more creatively about issues such as counterparty risk, operational risk, and so on. Corporate boards should disclose to shareholders their ability to handle such matters, referencing their past work in those areas. Large institutional investors should insist on such board expertise; otherwise, they have no cause for complaint when the companies they own stumble.

I would also favor that boards take a more aggressive approach to compensation. There are proposals on how to implement advisory votes on compensation, and for boards to better effect pay for performance and to set hard caps on income. These are all appropriate ideas. I would urge board members to hold themselves to the same standards and compensation rules. This is not merely for symbolic purposes. Unfortunately some board members are only too happy to draw their substantial salary, ask few questions, and believe they earn their keep just by showing up. But board service of course is not an entitlement for retired executives, politicians, and others. It's a responsibility, and compensation should be earned for meeting that responsibility. Board members should be expected to work harder for their compensation, which should be paid in a balanced cash-and-stock package that incentivizes them to think about the long term. And if executives are subject to clawback provisions, the board should be as well. Further, if we think of board service as a difficult and time-consuming job—which it is, when done well—then let's pay board members accordingly. That means compensation equal to expectations for performance, where board members see their financial fortunes tied to the long-term health of the company.

Of course, none of what is done in an individual boardroom will have broad impact unless improved corporate governance is mandated, in certain clear ways, by Washington. For all the headlines on compensation, a real problem is with lack of disclosure and meaningful transparency. Boards may have some success, on a piecemeal basis, in probing management and forcing out meaningful details about their business. But only Washington can have a lasting and broad impact on corporate America, by setting stronger standards for disclosure and transparency, including what are now considered non-material events and issues. These are matters investors need to decipher and understand: issues like how companies manage risk in their operations, use leverage, and monitor loan performance, including such key performance metrics as plant utilization, store sales per square foot, and revenue generated from new products and per employee, except where giving competitors undue advantage. Reality is that no companies will offer this information unilaterally—so Congress may need to take such action. Some suggest that the SEC should create stronger disclosure rules forcing company boards to describe how they fulfill their shareowner stewardship roles including oversight of corporate strategy and executive succession to supplement rules on risk management. Such disclosure would focus board energies around such issues and lay bare to investors potential weaknesses in governance.

The guiding principle behind these proposals is this: Managements can't overinform their boards, and companies need to better inform investors. Except in situations where disclosure would compromise a significant competitive advantage, boards should press management to issue more information to the marketplace, thereby improving transparency into its operations and permitting the marketplace to properly assign value.

But Washington can improve governance not just by requiring greater disclosure and setting higher standards for transparency. It also needs to focus its energies, both in Congress and in the executive branch, on dealing with systemic risk, too-big-to-fail, and other macro-issues. While financial regulatory reform addresses these issues, I fear that important work has been left undone, and our financial system remains exposed to the ills of moral hazard and systemic risk. For all the failures of corporate governance during the recent financial crisis, a key failure was in regulatory oversight that led to the problems we now are dealing with. In addition to failure of governance of individual businesses was failure of governance of government.

We have seen, for example, regulators who were supposed to be overseeing Fannie Mae and Freddie Mac say they did not do their jobs. That is no surprise to anyone. But what needs to come out is why they didn't do their jobs. There were, for example, artificial restrictions placed on the regulator community by both Congress and the White House. When regulators fail to do their jobs, blame also falls on those who were supposed to be holding the regulators accountable and empowering them to do their work well.

Those who were overseeing the regulators were being lobbied and pressured, and gave into that pressure. They pulled the regulators back in certain notable cases. Reasonable regulation of derivatives, for example, got shelved. Regulatory efforts to keep banks from taking on too much risk were jammed. We had good people in the regulator community trying to do their jobs, but they were not allowed to. We had standards-setters in the accounting profession who were being browbeaten to change the way mark-to-market rules affected bank income statements. We had career SEC investigators who were not allowed to set fines and penalties on corporations unless politically appointed overseers gave their okay—which created an avenue for those same corporations to avoid meaningful punishment. We had bank overseers making reassuring statements about banks they knew to be fundamentally unhealthy, just to avoid further credit panics. The fundamental architecture of our regulatory system was deeply compromised, and we paid a heavy price.

This book, and the thinking behind it, will help America's boardrooms and C-suites avoid repeating the mistakes of the past decade. It covers the processes of governance, and also focuses on the underlying daily challenges of building a corporate culture that welcomes self-reflection, values-driven business practices, and an openness to course correction. Richard Steinberg's work is a tonic to the complacency which afflicts every corporation that has avoided scandal and crisis. Governance failures can happen everywhere. Those who have been fortunate to avoid them either have worked at it, or simply have been very lucky—many have been lucky.

I would caution those who have been lucky to take the lessons of this book to heart and initiate a governance revolution in their own boardrooms. Whether you are a manager, a board member, or an investor, you need to press for more transparency. You need to elevate on your boards the importance of financial market expertise, especially the ability to evaluate risk. You need to look for the gaps in your own awareness of potential crises. This compelling and literate treatment of the serious issues confronting today and tomorrow's business community leaves no doubt as to the way forward.

**Arthur Levitt,**
Former Chairman, Securities and
Exchange Commission

# Preface

YOU'RE A CEO, SENIOR manager, or board member watching your once-great company brought to its knees. You imagine yourself on the deck of the *Titanic*, your world coming to an end—your once-confident self embarrassed in front of colleagues, competitors, friends, family, and the larger communities in which you once thrived and were held in such high esteem.

You know the names of the recently failed former icons. Investment banks Bear Stearns and Merrill Lynch were sold at fire sale prices, as were mortgage generators Washington Mutual and Countrywide, and Lehman Brothers no longer exists. AIG is government-owned and selling off assets, while General Motors and Chrysler, having emerged from bankruptcy, continue to work toward regaining their footing. Toyota's reputation for safety and quality has been badly tarnished, and BP has found it necessary to sell major chunks of corporate assets.

While facing different circumstances in different industries, common themes underlie why these and other once-great organizations have seen their fortunes sink, while others withstand economic turbulence and hazards to continue to grow and reap the rewards of success. Yes, successful companies have outstanding leaders, strategies, people, resources, organization, and more. But this book is not about those things, at least not directly. And it's not solely about how to avoid disaster. This book is about ensuring that your company has the right infrastructure to enable the organization's positive qualities to lead to success. This includes what's needed to avoid the kinds of disasters that can befall any organization, but also essential to identifying opportunities and being positioned to seize them for competitive advantage.

Time and again we see successful business leaders who have seen competitors fail think, ªIt can't happen here.º To get to where they are, these CEOs, senior management teams, and directors have experienced long-term success, and gained the inner confidence that justifiably comes along with it. Consciously or otherwise, many believe they're smarter or at least more savvy than those who have fallen, so just as they always have done before, they and their team will be able to deal with any problems and move forward.

A related trait at the top is optimism. Successful CEOs typically develop great strategies to grow the business and enhance return on investment, focusing like a laser execution. But their passion for building the business too often gets in the way of looking at what might go wrong.

I've worked with many CEOs and their senior management teams and board members of major companies, many successful and some who stumbled badly. One chief executive whom I met in passing—we shared the podium at a governance conference—had headed accounting and consulting firm Arthur Andersen. I was amazed and impressed that he kept his commitment to the conference sponsors, since his firm had gone under just weeks before. When we sat together at lunch, he shared some of the background of what had caused the debacle, with considerable openness at his time of extreme difficulty. There was no doubt the failure of the firm weighed heavily on his soul, and as I thought about that and other companies—and why some succeeded while others failed—a seed was planted: the idea of writing this book to help others avoid finding themselves in a similar position, and instead continue to achieve success.

Any chief executive whose ship is sinking, with the lights dimming and music fading, is likely to ask, "How did this happen? How did I allow myself and my company to end up like this?" Directors of once great companies also find themselves asking similar questions. "Did I and my fellow directors do what we needed to do in carrying out our oversight responsibilities?" "Could we have obtained the information we needed to see it coming and steered the company out of harm's way?"

This book is about answering those questions in advance—or rather avoiding having to ask them at all. In reading this book you'll better understand the factors that comprise the infrastructure of every organization, and how to get these elements right to avoid disaster. Importantly, you'll also have a better handle on how getting the infrastructure right will enable you and your company's personnel to readily seize available opportunities for continued success.

As you read on, you may recognize that, unlike other books, this one is not aimed solely at senior managers or solely at members of boards of directors. It's directed to both, with an added objective of providing insight into the interface between the two. Reality is that working relationships between a CEO and senior team on the one hand, and the board of directors on the other, are very different in different companies, and experience shows there are techniques for enhancing those relationships for corporate success. Indeed, getting that right is absolutely critical to arriving at the right strategy and creating the environment necessary to establish the processes, organization, and technology to drive effective implementation toward a company's established goals. As we move forward, I trust you'll recognize where you can enhance that relationship in your company in order to further enhance shareholder value.

# Acknowledgments

HAVING LEARNED A GREAT deal from so many smart people, I'd like to offer my thanks to each and every one of them. That, of course, isn't feasible in the space available here, so I'll need to be selective, beginning with some of the individuals whose names appear on the pages of this book. I've had extensive experience with some and only limited contact with others, but each has helped enhance my knowledge of some element of governance, risk management, and compliance.

I thank you, in alphabetical order: William Allen, Director, NYU Center for Law and Business and former Chancellor, Delaware Chancery Court; Betsy Atkins, venture capitalist and corporate director; William Chandler, Chancellor, Delaware Chancery Court; Cynthia Cooper, consultant and former Vice President of Audit, WorldCom; Peter Drucker, professor, author, and consultant; Charles Elson, the Edgar S. Woolard, Jr. Chair in Corporate Governance and Director of the John L. Weinberg Center for Corporate Governance at the University of Delaware and corporate director; Margaret (Peggy) Foran, Chief Governance Officer and Corporate Secretary, Prudential and corporate director; Holly Gregory, Partner, Weil, Gotshal & Manges; Robert Herz, former Chairman, Financial Accounting Standards Board; Richard Koppes, former Deputy Executive Officer and General Counsel of CalPERS, founder of the NAPPA, board member of the NACD and corporate director; James Kristie, Editor, *Directors & Boards*; Jay Lorsch, Louis E. Kirstein Professor of Human Relations at the Harvard Business School, author, and corporate director; Patrick McGurn, Executive Director, Institutional Shareholder Services; Ira Millstein, Senior Partner, Weil, Gotshal & Manges and Executive Director of Yale's Millstein Center for Corporate Governance and Performance; Nell Minow, Editor, The Corporate Library; Harvey Pitt, CEO, Kalorama Partners and former Chairman, Securities and Exchange Commission; Neil Smith, CEO, SmithOBrien; and Leo Strine, Vice Chancellor, Delaware Chancery Court.

Thank you also to my many partners at PricewaterhouseCoopers (PwC), including, to name just a few, in alphabetical order: Scott Eston, valued colleague as a partner and beyond; Miles Everson, for whom early in his career I served as a mentor and then watched as he became an outstanding consultant and GRC leader of the firm, and who was kind enough to look over the manuscript for this book and provide valuable input; Michael Garrett, who was and continues to be a trusted source of legal and business advice and counsel; Bob Herz, who generously offered me the opportunity and encouraged me to start up and run a board-level corporate governance practice; Jim Hogan, who early on gave me invaluable advice to roll up my sleeves and take a significant hands-on role with a major advisory client; Dennis Nally, who put his trust in me by asking that I take on a consulting project with the firm's board of partners; Vin O'Reilly, who put his trust in me by giving me a leadership role in developing the COSO internal control report; and to so many of my other partners who provided knowledge, inspiration, and friendship during my career at PwC and beyond, including those who provided perhaps the highest compliment by later engaging Steinberg Governance Advisors, Inc. to consult with their companies.

Thank you to the many clients whom I served when at PwC and in my own advisory firm, for allowing me to work with you and your colleagues on your governance, risk management, and compliance initiatives. I follow the general practice of not naming names unless authorized; you know who you are and I hope you realize how appreciative I am.

I thank the folks at John Wiley & Sons, including Production Editor Laura Cherkas, Developmental Editor Stacey Rivera, Executive Editor Sheck Cho, and Vice President and General Manager Jeff Brown, for your initiative and support in the book's development.

A special thank you to Scott Cohen, publisher of *Compliance Week*, for generously allowing me to use content from my columns in formulating this book. The support you have provided over the years, along with that of Editor-in-Chief Matt Kelly, is appreciated. Also, I thank Open Pages (an IBM Company) CEO Mike Duffy, Vice President of Marketing Gordon Burnes, and Director of Product Marketing John Kelly for our working relationship and for allowing me to use content of work developed for you.

And I owe a debt of gratitude to Arthur Levitt, former Chairman of the Securities and Exchange Commission, for writing the Foreword to this work. The gift of your time and wisdom is deeply appreciated.

You all have directly or indirectly contributed to this work, and your contributions are appreciated. And of course, regarding any errors or omissions, or as I sometimes say, if I've misspoken, the responsibility is my own.

# What Is GRC, and Why Does It Matter?

I F YOU'VE SEEN THE movie *A Few Good Men*, starring Jack Nicholson, Tom Cruise, Demi Moore, and Kevin Bacon, you'll likely remember the courtroom scene where Bacon's character asks a witness if a military manual includes the term "code red." He receives the desired reply: "No, sir," indicating that a code red—a punishment allegedly used on a soldier—doesn't exist. But Cruise's character counters by asking where the manual provides the location of the mess hall or other realities of military life, also receiving the desired response: "Well, Lieutenant Kaffee, that's not in the book either, sir." Cruise successfully makes the point that although there's no specific, tangible place to look for a code red, this does not mean that a code red doesn't exist.

Why this diversion to Hollywood? The same applies to the term *governance, risk management, and compliance*. You've probably never seen any company with a unit or function called governance, risk management, and compliance, or GRC for short. But certainly that doesn't mean GRC doesn't exist.

Indeed, it does exist and has tremendous impact on a company's ability to succeed. It may sound extraordinarily boring, conjuring up thoughts of insignificant plumbing deep in the recesses of an organization. But that's just not the case. GRC, in fact, is extremely important to every company, influencing virtually everything done from strategy formulation and implementation to every kind of operational decision.

 ## WHAT IS GRC?

Few of us have the patience for dealing with technical definitions, so if you'd rather skip to the next section, no problem. But if you've heard about GRC[1] and would like a better a sense of its genesis and what it is, read on.

Some months ago I spoke at a conference where the moderator turned to me saying, "GRC is an acronym used by many people, but with many different meanings—what does it mean to you?" Here's my response.

GRC originated in the management consulting world several years ago. Technology firms and others quickly picked it up and used it to describe available services and software solutions. And while sometimes the term is used by compliance officers, risk officers, or internal auditors, it is rarely used by line executives or board members.

As for what it means, GRC is a combination of related although somewhat disparate concepts. The term *governance* traditionally has been used in the context of a company's board of directors. A definition of governance I particularly like is: *the allocation of power among the board, management, and shareholders.* But today the term is used also to encompass an array of actions taken by management in running a company, from senior levels down throughout the management ranks.

The R is for *risk management.* This term is used in many different ways, from a simple risk assessment to a full-blown enterprise risk management process. The C stands for *compliance,* initially meaning adherence to applicable laws and regulations, though many users now include adherence to internal company policies as well.

I refer to these pieces as "disparate" because GRC isn't really one end-to-end process that companies employ. While the elements of GRC relate to a company's strategic and other business objectives, they also pertain to activities and processes at different levels of an organization. Indeed, there's significant overlap, in that risk management can and should be designed to address compliance as well as other categories of a company's objectives.

Okay, leaving terminology for now, let's look at why GRC is truly relevant.

## WHY GRC MATTERS

As you look over the following chapters, you should get a good sense of exactly why GRC matters to every organization. Let it suffice here to highlight a few key points.

A critical element of GRC is a company's culture, including the oft-used term *tone at the top*. Inherent in culture is the extent to which a company and its people embrace integrity and ethical values. Why is this important, especially so in today's environment? Because companies operating from a base of integrity and ethics not only stay out of trouble, they build on that foundation to drive success. Such companies attract the best people to their organizations, as well as the most desirable customers, suppliers, financiers, and business partners. And the opposite is also the case.

No, we've not seen empirical evidence put forth in academic studies, but we do see anecdotal evidence. Take Johnson & Johnson, for example. Back in the 1980s when the Tylenol scandal hit, J&J's culture of integrity and ethics drove a quick decision—to pull every last unit of Tylenol off drugstore shelves. The action was costly, but it positioned the company extremely well in the consumer marketplace, providing tangible dividends for decades to come. But the recent travails of J&J have been quite different. When Tylenol, Motrin, and other products of its McNeil Consumer Healthcare Products unit were found to make people sick, the company was accused of failing to report and investigate the matter, and its reputation has taken a hit.

Another company suffering charges of not doing the right thing is Toyota, which has had numerous recalls due to vehicle safety issues and allegations of failing to inform regulators. Toyota has lost market share to competitors, and we can surmise that while some customers simply are concerned about safety, others have stayed away due to anger at the company's failure to be forthcoming in reporting the dangers.

In the Preface to this book I mentioned Arthur Andersen; that firm represents another good illustration of how integrity and ethical values are perceived in the marketplace. Andersen did not implode from doing a bad audit of Enron, an allegation that was never proven in court. Rather it was brought down because of a Department of Justice indictment on alleged illegal destruction of evidence—the famous destruction of documents related to its Enron audit. After the DOJ action, Andersen's clients no longer wanted to be associated with the firm. There also were concerns about whether the firm would be around to complete critical audits, and key personnel saw what they perceived to be the handwriting on the wall and left to join other firms. But the problem began with an unethical—not illegal, as the U.S. Supreme Court ultimately decided—lapse in judgment.

In the coming chapters we look more closely at how and why these and other companies suffered while others continued to succeed. I think you'll find what's coming easy to digest. Although you might not be intimately familiar with GRC—if you were, you probably wouldn't have picked up this book—you will recognize key elements. And of course this isn't rocket science. I've no doubt you'll find what's in the coming chapters not only relevant but easily understood and readily implementable.

 **NOTE**

1. In some circles, GRC stands for governance, risk, and compliance, leaving out management for brevity.

2

# Culture, the Critical Driver

W E KNOW THAT A unique culture exists within every organization, and seasoned executives recognize that shaping a company and its people to a desired culture plays a major role in how an organization is run and how successful it will be. In this chapter, we look at the relevance of culture, its effect on corporate behavior, and what works in its formulation and enhancement within an organization.

 ## WHAT IS CULTURE?

The dictionary says culture is the professional atmosphere of a company, along with its values, customs, and traditions. A well-recognized risk management report adds substance and context:

> An entity's strategy and objectives and the way they are implemented are based on preferences, value judgments, and management styles. Management's integrity and commitment to ethical values influence these preferences and judgments, which are translated into standards of behavior. Because an entity's good reputation is so valuable, the

standards of behavior must go beyond mere compliance with law. Managers of well-run enterprises increasingly have accepted the view that ethics pays and ethical behavior is good business. . . .

Ethical behavior and management integrity are by-products of the corporate culture, which encompasses ethical and behavioral standards and how they are communicated and reinforced. Official policies specify what the board and management want to happen. Corporate culture determines what actually happens, and which rules are obeyed, bent, or ignored. Top management—starting with the CEO—plays a key role in determining the corporate culture. As the dominant personality in an entity, the CEO often sets the ethical tone.[1]

The effect of culture can be seen in any company, and German engineering company Siemens is worth a look. Reports say corruption at the company was far reaching, driven by a culture where employees believed bribes were not only acceptable, but implicitly encouraged. Reflecting on Siemens' reaction to the bribery scandal, a founder of Transparency International says: "There are new processes, new people, and new procedures, but that does not make a difference in the world unless there is a change in culture." An executive brought in from General Electric as the company's new anticorruption cop understood the challenges inherent in his new role, saying, "Healthy compliance cultures depend on a more values-based leadership, where people don't need to look at the rule book, where they know intuitively what the right thing to do is."

Still relevant is the example from Chapter 1 of Johnson & Johnson, clearly a company that knew the right thing to do when the Tylenol package tampering scandal hit in 1982. Because the company's culture put the customer first—regardless of short-term profit pressures—management pulled the product from shelves and maintained and strengthened its positive reputation in the marketplace. Because of the shared values within the organization, the decision was a no-brainer: There was no choice but to do the right thing for customers. As we've seen, today's culture appears to be different, at least in J&J's McNeil unit.

 ## MORE CULTURAL FAILURES

Although the list of companies experiencing disaster from cultural deficiencies is too long to include in any one book, we can look at some of the failures inherent in the recent financial system meltdown.

- *Mortgage generators.* It's become all too clear that many banks, mortgage brokers, and other generators of home mortgages developed a culture of "get my money now, damn the customer." Putting buyers in homes they simply could not afford—either initially or when adjustable rates were to ratchet up—certainly helped the companies' bottom lines in the short run, but resulted in disaster for both the companies and home buyers alike.

- *Credit card companies.* The next shoe to drop in the mortgage-led economic downturn was the credit card industry, which sent pre-approved applications seemingly to anyone who could breathe. Providing credit to people unable to afford further debt, along with policies of charging exorbitant interest rates for one-day-late payments or jacking up rates on new balances, surely does not put the customer first, and bad debts are now overwhelming these organizations. The Dodd-Frank Act and ensuing regulations are intended to deal with these practices.

- *Investment banks.* Of course we can look to the investment banks and other financial institutions slicing and dicing collateralized debt obligations and selling them off as gold-plated securities. Another fair question is to what extent they knew these securities didn't deserve the triple A ratings bestowed by the credit rating agencies. Not only did pension funds, municipalities, and other investors get burned, the financial institutions were left with toxic securities in their pipelines and too much leverage, bringing these firms to their knees and threatening the entire financial system. If you're interested in a deeper look at causal factors of the financial systemic near-meltdown, you might want to jump to Chapter 5.

Another massive failure of several years ago, briefly touched on in Chapter 1, is relevant to this discussion—that being the demise of Arthur Andersen, then one of the Big 5 auditing firms held in high esteem within the profession and marketplace. There are differing views of what went wrong at Andersen. I see the failure as centering on the firm's urgent drive to grow the business, based in part on losing its highly successful and profitable consulting arm in a high-profile court case, after being awarded the lowly sum of $1. Andersen then instituted a policy where the engagement partner—rather than the national office technical accounting and auditing experts—was authorized to have final say on all professional decisions. An implicit objective was to bring engagement partners closer to clients, apparently with a main reason being to better position engagement partners to grow a new consulting business. So with this policy in place—and I believe Andersen was the only one of the large firms to institute such a policy—when a national office partner disagreed with the partner leading the Enron engagement, guess who won? And we know what transpired thereafter. This wonderful firm let its culture shift from embracing the highest integrity and professional and ethical standards to one allowing critical audit decisions to be left to one field individual.

## COMPANIES THAT GOT IT RIGHT

There's no quick recipe or silver bullet for developing the right corporate culture. But I'd like to share a few of my experiences with chief executives whose actions have had a dramatic and long-lasting positive effect on their organizations, shaping their corporate cultures for years to come.

- *Insurance company.* This major firm got caught up in a scandal involving improper sales practices and was working diligently to strengthen its system of internal control to help prevent future failures. It learned that a group of customer-service call-center employees needed to obtain requisite licenses to continue being paid on a commission (rather than salary) basis. Looking to do the right thing, the CEO announced that the group's personnel would immediately begin the necessary steps to register for and take the tests for licensing, and in fairness to those employees, commission-based payments would continue during the transition. Although he had good intentions, after discussion the CEO realized that the message received by the company's personnel was that continuing to break the rules is okay as long as there's a plan to come into compliance. Recognizing how the initial decision was being interpreted, he quickly changed tacks, shifting the group to a straight salary until licenses were secured. This company's culture soon reflected the message that not only is it necessary to work toward doing the right thing, but also to take what might be an unpopular action in order to do what is right at all times.
- *Professional services firm.* A manager passed over for partnership in one of this firm's highly profitable business units requested that this decision, made at the local level, be reviewed. Following a thorough file review and interviews with the manager and the unit's partners, it became clear that this female manager was eminently qualified in all respects for admission to the firm. The problem turned out to be the unit's managing partner,

who apparently had a history of discriminating against women's advancement in the firm. The CEO met with a leadership group, listening to one recommendation after another on how to deal with the matter. The CEO—a former Marine and highly principled no-nonsense guy—then asked the question: "What is the right thing to do?" After a brief period of silence, the general counsel answered that not only should the manager be admitted to the partnership, the managing partner should be removed. Those actions were quickly implemented and became well known throughout the organization, and the decision to do the right thing became embedded in the firm's culture.

■ *Consumer products company.* This company's CEO and leadership team decided to move forward with plans to design and implement an enterprise risk management process. Following a diagnostic review of the current state of risk management in the organization, it became evident there was a risk focus in only a few small, contained units, while the "tough guy" culture of the broader organization essentially prohibited personnel from speaking about risk. Anyone doing so would be viewed as going against the company's can-do philosophy and style, and perceived as being negative, weak, and lacking in leadership. Recognizing the importance of an effective ERM process, the CEO realized that the company's culture needed to change. By initiating an in-depth risk analysis at the next strategic planning and budgeting meeting, the CEO made clear to his direct reports that discussing corporate risks would be not only tolerated but mandated. He followed up in meetings with the next management level and videos to the entire organization, and within months the culture embraced the concept that smart, tough guys indeed do focus on risk in making action-oriented decisions to move the company forward.

There's little doubt that what a CEO does is quickly noticed and his or her behavior is imitated. Delta CEO Richard Anderson, for one, put it well: "Everything you do is an example, and people look at everything you do and take a signal from everything you do."

Experience shows that culture has a strong and pervasive effect on a company, either positively or negatively. Top management usually has an accurate picture of an organization's culture, but reality is that a significant number of CEOs learn too late that they were badly mistaken. Among the most critical roles of a CEO and senior executive team is to have an in-depth and accurate understanding of the company's culture, determine what changes are needed, and take quick and decisive action to mold the culture to what's needed to bring about the company's successful future. But changing a culture isn't easy, as noted by Starbucks CEO Howard Schultz: "Turning a culture around is very difficult to do because it's based on a series of many, many decisions, and the organization is framed by those decisions. . . . Everything matters—everything. You are imprinting decisions, values, and memories onto an organization. In a sense, you're building a house, and you can't add stories onto a house until you have built the kind of foundation that will support them."

 ## BEING LEGAL, HONEST, CANDID, AND . . .

Critical to a corporate culture founded in integrity and ethical values is how people within the organization communicate with one another as well as with external parties. We all know there's a significant difference in providing technically accurate information versus communicating in a way that provides a true picture of what's really relevant.

Several years ago a business columnist noted, and I'm paraphrasing, that honesty has been downgraded to mere compliance with contracts and laws, a demand too easily satisfied, as opposed to candor, which is bluntly facing the facts and exhibits the qualities of light in a dark room. Taking a look at the dictionary, we find that *candid* means "honest or direct in a way that people find either refreshing or distasteful and free from prejudice or bias."

Certainly when we are involved in discussions with our own company's personnel and others, we want people to communicate using the characteristics of candor. Unfortunately, too often that doesn't happen. You may recognize some of the following interactions:

- *Employee to manager.* How many times have we seen an inexperienced employee bring forth what he or she considered a great idea, working hard to sell it upstream in the organization? The facts are accurate, and there's no blatant dishonesty in presentation. But there's bias, in omission or skewed emphasis and focus. Getting personal for a moment, I'm sure in my early days as an associate in the firm I joined I was guilty of such communications.
- *Communicating with external parties.* How often have we fallen prey, in talking with suppliers, customers, potential customers, and recruiting targets, to the desire to shade the truth? It might be viewed as putting

the best light on an issue, or putting our best foot forward, but we knew in our hearts that we were withholding information that was relevant and important to the other party.

■ *Communicating with shareholders.* Have we always been entirely straight in communications with shareholders and the investment community? Certainly it's appropriate not to disclose information that should be kept confidential for appropriate regulatory or competitive reasons. But we don't commonly see examples like the forthright letters that Warren Buffett writes at Berkshire Hathaway each year.

■ *CEO to the board.* Have we encountered instances where a chief executive presented a picture of past or expected future performance or a new strategy or initiative designed to evict a specified response—namely, approval from the board, or at least the absence of disapproval? I've personally seen such circumstances, and my guess is that those of you who have spent time inside a boardroom or have prepared presentations for the board have as well.

The effects of these behaviors vary greatly based on the persons or groups on the receiving end of the communications. There are, however, some commonalities. One is that the essence of such behavior almost always becomes known over time. Whether it's a manager, customer, target, shareholder, analyst, or board member, he or she gets a good sense of whether a person or company is truly being candid. And when there's a sense that the communications are otherwise, the effect can be and often is dramatic.

With that said, there's a word that brings the concept of candor to a still higher level. That word is *forthcoming*. By this I mean being not only honest and candid, as just described, but also being willing to talk or give information.

We've all been in situations where a person seemed hesitant to tell us the whole story. And you'll remember your reaction. Some people are more adept at withholding information, and we sometimes don't immediately pick up on it. I believe, however, that people with whom we are trying to communicate will trip up sooner or later, and we'll recognize that we're not getting the information we need and expect in order to be positioned to make informed decisions.

We don't want to have to pull teeth. We want the person to tell us the information that he or she knows and we need to know. We want them to identify clearly what's fact and what's opinion and the basis for and against their opinion. When we communicate with someone who's forthcoming in providing appropriately complete, honest, and unbiased information, we immediately trust not only that information, but also the individual or institution, with respect to information that we will need in the future.

Beyond complying with the law and being ethical, honest, and candid, we want and expect those we deal with to be forthcoming. Those who are gain the trust and respect that builds meaningful, long-lasting, supportive alliances.

Looking further at the scenario of communication between a CEO and board, let's say a CEO presents a new strategy. The facts in the presentation are accurate—the marketplace and competitive conditions are accurately portrayed, the positive effect on earnings and returns is properly calculated, and the supporting rationale is outlined with depth and precision.

While the presentation might look good on the surface, experienced directors begin asking pertinent questions to elicit critical information that is absent: What are potential disadvantages of this new strategy? What is the downside? What are the associated risks? What needs to go right for this strategy to succeed?

And then the really insightful board members will ask: Are your direct reports fully committed to the proposed strategy? Where is a fully developed implementation plan? Are related processes, organization, resources, and investments in place to make the strategy work? And equally important, what alternative strategies were considered and discarded, and why?

Clearly, a board that needs to ask these questions views its CEO differently from one who builds the relevant information into the strategic planning presentation in the first place. The trust one gains by being candid is a critical element in gaining and keeping the board's support, especially when times are tough.

This is not to suggest that information going to external parties should be as comprehensive as that going to the board. But the concept of being candid with the information that is appropriately communicated is similar if not the same. If one wants to attract the best employees, customers, and business partners, honesty—and we can add candor and being forthcoming—are most likely to produce the desired results.

Boards have a right to expect the CEO to be forthcoming, even about a personal matter that could affect the CEO's ability to perform his/her duties. A recent example involves the 10-year CEO of Horace Mann Educators who, according to a police report, on Memorial Day 2010 was driving drunk and hit another vehicle. He's said to have told some company personnel in July about his arrest, but he didn't inform the board of directors until *after beginning to serve a 60-day sentence* in September. After being placed on leave, the CEO resigned and was replaced. Asked by a reporter whether the CEO should have informed the board, my response was "absolutely 'yes,'" adding that there's no question the board needed to be immediately apprised at the very least of the charges and the possibility that he would not be available for work, and also to enable the board to deal with the potential surrounding publicity. Paul Hodgson, a well-known governance guru of the Corporate Library, is quoted as saying about this incident, "The board should have been notified immediately and it is completely unacceptable that such a delay was allowed to happen. . . . [The delay] makes the board look stupid and the executives duplicitous." And Jay Lorsch, a well-known Harvard governance professor, reportedly noted, "It's material information because it goes to the question of [the CEO's] judgment and his stability."

Yes, there are different schools of thought regarding how much about a CEO's life, such as health issues, needs to be disclosed to the public as it relates to the concept of materiality, but informing the board is a no-brainer.

One more instance of an executive being less than forthcoming is worth a look. You've likely seen the media reports on what happened at none other than Berkshire Hathaway, where David Sokol, a senior executive and possible successor to Warren Buffett, is said to have misled Buffett on Sokol's purchase of shares of Lubrizol before recommending that Berkshire Hathaway buy that company. The Berkshire audit committee since issued a report saying that Sokol's "misleadingly incomplete disclosures to [CEO Buffett] concerning these purchases violated the duty of candor he owed the company." The report also indicates that Sokol may have broken the law and that Berkshire is considering legal action to recover damages. And for good measure, Buffett reportedly called the SEC's enforcement division, which is looking into possible insider trading violations. This case illustrates well the problems caused by an executive being less than forthcoming—for the company as well as himself.

 ## INTEGRITY VERSUS SPIN

It's fascinating to see just how many companies have had serious problems related to cultural issues and lack of honesty. We've touched on just a few— the tip of the iceberg. To get a sense of how pervasive these problems seem to be, we can look at news reports about three well-known companies from just one day late in 2009. And as you think about what happened at these companies, you'll want to also consider the public relations spin they tried to put on what had occurred.

## General Electric

On this day came news of General Electric's $50 million settlement with the U.S. Securities and Exchange Commission over allegations of repeated accounting improprieties, with a corporate eye toward "making the numbers."

The story refers to a priest who worked for GE years ago after obtaining a degree from the University of Pennsylvania's Wharton School. When informing a GE executive that results were coming in low due to overseas losses, the employee was told, "Just reverse a few journal entries," because headquarters would be displeased if his unit missed its numbers. Further, his boss told the man that he "was taking those accounting courses too seriously" and directed him to "squirrel away excess earnings in fake accounts with made-up names," to be used when earnings went down in later months.

Well, as often happens, history repeats itself. GE's accountants ultimately found "misstatements and secret side deals, and more senior executives telling [staffers] to sign off on the books anyway." Further, the SEC states that GE executives failed to give relevant information to the auditors (although the company says it did so later on). Interestingly, links to what transpired at Enron are indicated, with accounting violations in a scheme to inflate profits with fake sales. But even more fascinating, the SEC says that while GE's local external auditors at KPMG consulted with the firm's national office, the engagement personnel signed off on the financial statements "without telling the national office what was going on." This happened in 2003, after the Enron–Arthur Andersen debacle was in full view! Was anybody home?

And here comes the PR spin with the news reports. The company issued a statement that "the errors at issue fell short of our standards, and we have implemented numerous remedial actions and internal control enhancements to prevent such errors from recurring." Use of the word *error* is telling—as in "Gee, it was only an honest mistake."

And the spin continued, with the company telling a journalist he was wrong to view these violations as "indicative of some larger problem in GE's overall culture, its finance function, or compliance practices. GE is committed to the highest standards of accounting and good corporate governance. We are confident in our controls and culture, which have been made even stronger through the process that we've just completed."

## American International Group

On the same day in 2009 came reports of former AIG chief Maurice (Hank) Greenberg's settlement of SEC charges that he oversaw accounting fraud at the company. Greenberg is paying $15 million, where restatements of $2 billion were reportedly called for. Despite the standard prohibition against defendants making public denials or statements that the accusations were without merit, Greenberg immediately declared that he had "no responsibility" for the fraud, and the vast majority of the restatement "was unnecessary."

Media reports went on, noting that despite Greenberg's frequent past statements that AIG never had an underwriting loss, the SEC contends that AIG actually did have those losses but Greenberg decided to keep them secret. Greenberg and Howard Smith, the company's CFO who also settled with the SEC (for $1.5 million), allegedly devised a scheme to mask the underwriting loss as an investment loss by using an offshore shell company and lending investors money to hide a related loan. AIG reportedly then pretended to have sold bonds at a profit when it had not, and invented distributions from hedge funds.

The public relations and legal people seemed to be working overtime, with Greenberg's lawyer saying his client "appreciates the SEC's recognition that he personally should not be charged with any fraud," and "the settlement is recognition of his lack of responsibility, even as a control person, for the vast majority" of AIG's accounting improprieties.

We know what ultimately happened to AIG, but there were other reasons, and that's for another chapter.

## Société Générale

Rounding out the day was news of Jean-Pierre Mustier leaving his job at the beleaguered French bank Société Générale (Soc Gen). Mustier, a member of the executive committee and former head of the investment banking unit (and seen as a potential chairman someday), reportedly received grievance letters from French regulatory authorities related to insider trading of company stock. So did Robert Day, a nonexecutive director at Soc Gen.

Reports indicate that Day sold Soc Gen shares less than a week before news of the now-infamous $7.2 billion loss related to unapproved trades made by rogue employee Jerome Kerviel. Soc Gen says Mustier (who sold shares earlier) and Day deny all accusations.

Following the Kerviel fiasco, this tells us much more about the corporate culture at Soc Gen, where the Chairman-CEO put all the blame on Kerviel, calling him "mentally weak" and a "terrorist"—and said nary a word about the bank's culture, management, or controls. In spinning its message, the bank essentially said that Kerviel was a bad person and the bank bore no responsibility for his actions—and certainly could not have seen anything like this coming! And long after that argument, two directors departed under an insider-trading cloud. Hmmm.

## Culture and Spin

We can surmise a few points about all three companies from this news. First, all evidence points to flawed cultures, with tainted tone at the top set by the actions of senior executives. What may be surprising is that this occurred at these brand-name institutions. Clearly, if it can happen there—as looks to be the case—it can happen anywhere.

Second, experience shows that how an organization reacts, in the form of public statements, can actually exacerbate a cultural problem. We understand that spin doctors—some well-meaning PR and legal professionals—try to keep the names of their companies from being further tarnished. But the truth is that few people, inside or outside the business, believe such statements. Perhaps most damaging is how company personnel react, with some thinking, "Well, management says this wasn't so bad, and things are fine now, so it's business as usual."

Some years ago I was working with a financial services client that got caught in a major scandal. Top management's first reaction was to classify it as a "PR problem," calling for the best legal and PR people to make things right. Well, after extensive discussions with the client, the CEO accepted the reality that something was terribly wrong within the organization, and significant action was needed to make it right. Statements soon were put out to the public acknowledging that a good deal of work was necessary to get the company where it and its customers needed, and expected, it to be.

That change in direction and attitude ultimately cut the cost related to regulatory actions, judgments, settlements, and corrective actions significantly. Above all, the culture of the organization was transformed, becoming centered on integrity and ethical values with a strong control structure in place. Since then and continuing today, this company's brand shines brightly in the consumer and financial marketplaces.

The message is twofold. First, top management must set the right tone not only with words, but also with its actions—before a crisis hits, and also when it does—along with sound organization and management processes. And second, spin is seen for what it is: It doesn't fool anyone, sends the wrong message, and is counterproductive both within and outside the organization.

 **SPEAKING THE SAME LANGUAGE**

Before leaving these cultural issues of honesty, integrity, and spin, let's look at another relevant issue critical to effective communication—using words whose meanings are understood throughout the organization. We know the importance of effective communication, in both formal and informal settings, to get our messages across as intended. But how many times have we been misunderstood, or have we not understood a thought someone else was trying to convey? We say one thing, and business colleagues, directors, lawyers, auditors, regulators, or others hear something very different. The consequences of bad communication range from simply extending a conversation to gain clarity to talking at cross-purposes resulting in bad business decisions. Yes, tone of voice and body language are important in sending the right message, but using the right words is often critical.

The governance, risk, and compliance realm is not exempt from lousy communication, and indeed seems to lend itself to misunderstandings—both inside a company and outside. This is about saying what we mean and meaning what we say. Exhibit 2.1 shows some examples of miscommunication. I apologize in advance for what might be perceived as nitpicking, and if you'd rather jump to the next chapter, please do so. But if you're interested in how precision in GRC wording is particularly relevant, you may want to take a look at the exhibit.

**EXHIBIT 2.1**  Talking at Cross-Purposes

---

- **Is it really the control environment?** One of the most common errors in communication involves misuse of the term *control environment*. My guess is that we've all used the term more times than we can count, but I can assure you, speakers often mean different things. Too frequently when someone refers to the control environment, the speaker really means to say *internal control system*.

   The control environment actually refers to one of five components of internal control (*internal control* is an acceptable shortcut for internal control system). The control environment is critically important to effective internal control, dealing with such things as the integrity, ethical values, and competence of an organization's people; management's philosophy and operating style; the way management assigns authority and responsibility and organizes and develops its people; and the attention and direction provided by the board of directors. It encompasses the tone at the top of the organization and serves as the foundation for the other internal control components. These definitions are from COSO's *Internal Control—Integrated Framework*, which is what companies and auditors use in connection with Sarbanes-Oxley Section 404.

   Why is this relevant? There are numerous instances where a speaker is trying to focus attention on the whole of a company's internal control system, but recipients of the message think the intent is to look at only one component. Or, a problem might exist in other internal control components but be misrepresented as occurring in the control environment

*(continued)*

**EXHIBIT 2.1**   (Continued)

component. These misunderstandings can have, and sometimes have had, serious consequences.

- **Let's talk governance.** The terms *governance* and *corporate governance* are so overused it's almost humorous, except that such usage contributes to misunderstandings. These terms now seem to be applied to virtually anything that comes to mind, often for self-serving purposes. That is, because governance is a good thing, the word now is applied to many different areas by those with a particular interest or agenda.

  For example, we hear a great deal about IT governance. Speakers sometimes use the term for anything from strategic use of IT in an organization, to more mundane management of IT control activities, to a board of directors' responsibilities in overseeing where and how IT is used. We hear about management's role in governing the organization, including how senior management runs the business and extending far downstream to all managerial activities in a company. *Project govern-ance* now is used to describe how a discrete project is organized and managed. Sometimes the term is used for the shareholders' role in governing an organization. These are just a few examples of how use of the term *governance* has spread.

  I believe "governance" is most appropriately applied to the allocation of power between the board of directors, management, and shareholders. If memory serves, this definition was coined by Canada's Dey Commission; in any event, it captures how the term was traditionally used before being extended far beyond. Communication is enhanced when we use the term *management* to mean what management does, and leave *governance* to what happens at the board level and the board's interfaces. But if used otherwise, it's important to communicate exactly which meaning is intended.

- **Looking at risk management.** The terms *risk, risk management,* and *enterprise risk management* are used in many ways, often interchangeably. Without getting into painfully detailed definitions, suffice it to say here that COSO's *Enterprise Risk Management—Integrated Framework* is probably the most authoritative and generally accepted source of risk-related concepts and terminology. Having led development of the framework, I'm somewhat biased, but that report is widely looked to for guidance and a common language around the topic of risk management.

  Misuse, however, is rampant. For example, one writer said: "It's important to deal with risks proactively, not reactively." Well, that's great advice in terms of the intended meaning, but the words make no sense. Because risk relates to uncertainty—an event that has yet to occur—it's simply not possible to react to risk any other way. On the other hand, it's perfectly appropriate to suggest that risk management

**EXHIBIT 2.1** (Continued)

---

involves being proactive by taking prudent action before a potential event occurs.

How often have we heard someone speak of *risk assessment* when later it turns out that he or she really meant *risk management*? Risk assessment is a part of risk management, but it's just one part. A risk assessment is a snapshot, taken at one or more points in time. Risk management involves a number of integrated activities, including identifying risks, analyzing them, and taking action to manage the risks on an ongoing basis.

We sometimes hear it said that a risk assessment is equivalent to having an enterprise risk management process, but an ERM process actually takes dealing with risk to a significantly higher level. In differentiating risk assessment from ERM, one supposedly knowledgeable person was quoted as saying, "I don't know a large percentage of companies out there that actually perform true ERM." But a company doesn't *perform* ERM—rather, an ERM program or system is designed and embedded in the organization.

- **Key controls.** This term has been used in connection with Section 404 of Sarbanes-Oxley, referring in most instances to those controls that, if absent or working incorrectly, would result in a material weakness in internal control over financial reporting. On a hunch I searched the SEC's SOX 404 guidance to management and the PCAOB's AS5, and found no use of "key controls." It's interesting that this term was first used years ago by at least one large accounting firm to refer to those company controls on which an auditor planned to rely in determining the nature, extent, and timing of substantive tests. In that context, the universe of key controls is much smaller than the number of controls that could result in a material weakness in internal control. This is due to audit efficiencies in performing substantive tests in certain areas rather than testing related controls.

---

Using the right words is not about precision for its own sake, but about ensuring that we're communicating effectively. Because we need to be sure we're getting our messages across as intended, words really do matter.

* * *

The effect of culture on every organization indeed is pervasive. If not already evident, you'll see its impact more so in the next chapters on compliance, ethics, and risk management programs, and in following chapters with respect to every aspect of how companies are managed and governed. We'll also see how the effects of culture come full circle, as the actions of management and the board, in turn, continue to directly and often dramatically impact an organization's culture.

 **NOTE**

1. COSO, *Enterprise Risk Management—Integrated Framework*, (2004). COSO is the Committee of Sponsoring Organizations of the Treadway Commission, which also issued *Internal Control—Integrated Framework*, used as the standard for measuring companies' internal control systems and referenced by senior management and auditors in public company annual reports to shareholders. For full disclosure, I was a leader and principal author of both of those frameworks.

# CHAPTER THREE

# Cost-Effective Compliance Programs

VERY COMPANY MUST STRIVE to comply with laws and regulations applicable to its organization and activities. This *compliance* is the C in GRC. We'll come back to the R and G later, addressing them in depth. But let's look now at compliance programs. Although they are viewed by many as a necessary evil, we'll see in this chapter that they can have associated benefits.

Certainly companies are finding legal and regulatory compliance costs soaring while effectiveness declines, giving rise to huge fines, penalties, awards, and settlements—often in the billions of dollars. Policies and procedures build with each new law and regulation but are disparate, duplicative, and fail to comprise an effective compliance program.

Yet some companies have not only made their programs effective and efficient, but have also gained tremendous business benefit. Understanding the rationale for ever-expanding legal and regulatory requirements, they recognize the underlying marketplace drivers and align strategic initiatives to gain market share, profit, and return. By aligning business objectives and building compliance programs into existing management and business processes, responsibility and accountability are put where they work best, increasing effectiveness, reducing cost, and providing senior management and the board of directors with the information they need.

What's the state of your company's compliance program? Is it truly effective, and are you satisfied with its costs and benefits? Have senior executives in your organization said things like:

- "We're fine, because we've never had a major compliance problem."
- "The kinds of problems our peers suffered couldn't happen here—we're better and smarter than that."
- "We already have a code of conduct, whistleblower channel, and other elements of what's required for compliance."
- "Our general counsel has responsibility for ensuring we're fully compliant with all laws and regulations, so we're covered."

If you're an experienced compliance professional reading this, you're probably cringing at these so-called positive expressions of satisfaction. But whatever your corporate responsibilities, if you're concerned about the cost and effectiveness of your company's compliance program, please read on.[1]

## THE BACK-BREAKING COSTS

Leaving program effectiveness for a bit later, let's look at the tremendous costs of dealing with compliance, which can be viewed similarly to those automobile motor oil ads of long ago: "You can pay me now, or pay me later"—a few dollars now, or thousands later, although here the later numbers are much larger.

Surveys of cost information vary in their estimates, but they provide at least directional insight. One survey of several years ago shows that for every $1 billion in revenue, the cost of compliance programs comes close to $6 million.[2] Another shows the cost of Sarbanes-Oxley compliance alone averaging $4 million for companies with $5 billion in revenue, and $10 million for companies with $10 billion and more in revenue. More telling is that for companies with more than $1 billion in revenue, compliance costs strikingly equaled the salaries of 190 full-time-equivalent employees.[3]

And when we consider one of the highly regulated industries—the U.S. securities industry—compliance costs for each firm averaged a whopping 13 percent of revenues.[4] And this is before the financial system's near meltdown and the resulting Dodd-Frank Act and regulatory reaction now underway.

From a broader perspective, a 2010 report says the cost of complying with U.S. federal laws and regulations came to an estimated $1.75 trillion in 2008, totaling 14 percent of U.S. national income. The cost to business is stated to be $970 billion, with state and local governments paying the rest.[5]

When looking at the cost of a compliance failure, the numbers take on even greater significance. One of the studies found that $1 billion–revenue companies with just *one* compliance failure incurred $81 million in costs—consisting of settlement fees of $64 million, lost business of $14 million, and fines, remediation, and business interruption costs of $3 million.[6]

Unfortunately, those numbers pale in comparison to compliance failures suffered by many companies—each running in the billions of dollars. Looking at just a handful of those companies, media reports show the following payouts:

- American Home Products, diet product: $3.75 billion
- Bank of Credit and Commerce, fraud: $17 billion
- BAT Industries, tobacco settlement: $73 billion
- Cinergy, pollution: $1.4 billion
- IBM, age discrimination: $6 billion
- Johns Manville, asbestos: $3 billion
- Philip Morris, tobacco settlement: $9 billion
- Prudential Insurance, sales practices: $4 billion
- Texaco, interfering in merger: $3 billion
- Time Warner, accounting practices: $3.5 billion
- Visa, anti-competitive business practices: $2.25 billion

Loss of market capitalization often is dramatic, with examples including Merck's Vioxx product liability cutting $40 billion in market cap and Marsh's bid rigging causing a reduction of over $10 billion.[7]

So, while the cost of implementing a compliance program may seem high, it's clear that not putting an effective compliance program in place can be significantly more expensive.

The already high and growing cost of complying with laws and regulations to which companies are subject has gotten the attention of senior management and boards of directors. Drawing significant focus is the reality that while costs continue to rise, the effectiveness of compliance programs doesn't necessarily keep up and may in fact deteriorate. So, with costs becoming virtually unsustainable in the context of other business pressures, senior management teams and boards are looking at ways to make compliance programs both more efficient and more effective.

## BEYOND THE DIRECT COSTS

We should make no mistake—compliance is up there with strategy and risk management in boardroom discussions today. It's not just the significant costs but also program effectiveness that have captured attention, for good reason. Directors are well aware of the myriad laws and regulations to which their companies are subject. As a brief sampling, these include broadly applicable requirements related to product safety, employment, workplace health and safety, employee benefits, pensions, securities laws; those cutting across a number of industries dealing with information privacy, anti–money laundering, and appropriateness of product to customer profile; and industry-specific mandates for government contractors, pharmaceuticals, and health care, tobacco, and telecom companies.

Just as eye-catching are enforcement and related regulatory actions for noncompliance. These include ongoing and renewed activity by the U.S. Securities and Exchange Commission and Department of Justice, each of which says it takes a carrot-and-stick approach—being more lenient where a compliance program is strong and tougher when it is not, although some lawyers question whether those statements are supported by reality.[8] Then there are the Delaware Chancery and Supreme Court cases, which underscore board responsibilities for ensuring effective compliance programs. Also having gained critical notice are the federal sentencing guidelines, which deal with criminal misconduct and a company's programs for assessing and reducing the related risks.

Experienced executives and directors know well that a major compliance failure can not only cost billions of dollars in direct costs, but also bring a company to its knees. At a minimum, it steals the time and energy of top management, detracting from the day-to-day running of the company and new initiatives to grow the business. And damage to a company's reputation, which takes years to develop and can be destroyed overnight, affects relationships with customers, suppliers, alliance partners, bankers, and investors, as well as retention of key human resources and ultimately long-term success.

 ## MAJOR MISTAKES AT
## PLATINUM-BRANDED COMPANIES

We know that Toyota and Johnson & Johnson went afoul of regulators, as well as the consumer marketplace, in high-profile compliance failures. Let's take a closer look at what happened.

## Toyota

Toyota Motor Corporation was long known for the high quality of its automobiles and resulting loyal customer base, which became the envy of car manufacturers around the world—but recently Toyota stumbled badly. You know the story. This once-proud company with the superb brand is now viewed by many as producing defective cars. Compounding the problem, it also is seen as failing to inform car owners of life-threatening flaws in accelerators and brakes.

Regulators and industry observers say the company reacted much too slowly to dangerous safety issues, making changes in parts for new vehicles without advising existing customers of flaws in cars they were currently driving. Media coverage of the crisis suggests a clear and troubling pattern. Years ago, Toyota had an excellent approach to dealing with problems; somewhere along the way, that attitude changed for the worse. For example, when troubles first appeared in early Lexus models back in 1989, the company arranged to go to owners' homes to pick up the cars and make the fix. And since? Well, reported problems include:

- In 1996, Toyota found problems with the steering mechanism in its 4Runner model, but for some reason began to put a design change only into new models. Not until 2005 did the company finally decide to recall the older cars still on the road. At that time the Japanese government stepped in, ordering the company to revamp its recall system.
- In 2002, customer complaints flooded in saying car engines became clogged with sludge. Toyota promptly claimed it had done nothing wrong; rather, car owners simply weren't changing their oil often enough. The company finally agreed to extend warranties, but after customers found the claims filing process too challenging, a class-action lawsuit was filed.
- In 2007, the now well-publicized problem of accelerators in Camry and Lexus models sticking under floor mats arose. That led to a relatively narrow recall that later expanded to a much larger one.
- In 2008, a new problem surfaced with accelerator pedals sticking. Here, too, Toyota made design changes only in newly manufactured automobiles. Only months later, under fierce consumer, regulatory, and political pressure, did it agree to recall millions of vehicles.

More recently we've seen problems with the brakes on Toyota's highly touted Prius hybrid model. Ordered by the Japanese Transport Ministry to investigate, the company said it fixed the problem on newly built cars—and was then pushed by the U.S. National Highway Traffic Safety Administration to enact a recall.

With these disclosures, along with additional problems resulting in recalls of Tacoma pickup trucks for driveshaft problems and Corollas for steering malfunctions, many once-loyal customers have become disenchanted. Compounding the problem with customers, regulators have been furious with Toyota's reaction. According to media reports, in a closed-door meeting with U.S. regulators, Toyota executives admitted that when they blamed accelerator problems on floor mats, the company had known for more than a year that the gas pedals had problems as well.

So, what do we see here? Some would say Toyota is a highly centralized company with a secretive culture, acting independently and with contempt of regulators. A Japanese automobile industry academician recently said: "At Toyota, all information flows to headquarters. It's that kind of company." And the company executive in charge of quality reportedly said, "We did realize that it was not good that pedals were not returning to their proper positions, but we took some time to consider whether we needed to take market action."

The spotlight now shines powerfully on these serious problems and how the company reacted to them; company president Akio Toyoda and other company executives were grilled by a number of Congressional committees. In that setting Toyota pulled back on prior statements that the electronic systems were not at fault, subsequently saying the repairs might not totally solve the sudden acceleration problem and that the company was examining whether that is the case. And it's not just the 8 million cars that have been recalled (6 million in the United States), but ongoing questions of just how safe Toyota cars are and how much the company really cares about the well-being of its customers.

Having recalled millions of cars, agreeing to pay the maximum $16.4 million penalty, and becoming the subject of multiple lawsuits, the company seems to be trying to put itself in a better light. When its Lexus GX 460 SUV was found to be subject to a high risk of rolling over—as reported by *Consumer Reports* magazine—the company quickly confirmed the problem, halted sales of the model, and said it would provide loaners to current owners.

Soon afterwards the company announced that 1.53 million more cars had flaws in brakes and fuel pumps, accompanied by an interesting assertion that "each time we announce a recall, that is a step toward increasing quality." A skeptic might simply call this a public relations spin. It didn't help that late in 2010 the company recalled 100,000 Sienna minivans with brake light problems.

Recalls had reached 11 million vehicles worldwide, and U.S. fines $48.8 million, when in January 2011 the company recalled another 1.7 million vehicles due to defective fuel lines and high pressure pumps, and the next month 2 million more for accelerator sticking issues. Perhaps more important, Toyota faces billions of dollars in lawsuits—the company recently settled just one for $10 million—and while GM's U.S. sales rose 6.7 percent in 2010 and Ford's increased 15.2 percent, Toyota's were down 0.4 percent, the only full-line auto manufacturer to show lower sales for that year. Maybe Toyota has learned a lesson, but the jury will be out for a while. With its reputation for quality having taken a huge hit, and ongoing questions about its integrity, we'll have to wait and see to what extent it can regain its place in the market.

## Johnson & Johnson

Johnson & Johnson set the gold standard in crisis management nearly 30 years ago when it addressed the threat of poisoned Tylenol products by quickly pulling the product off drugstore shelves. This textbook case (literally—J&J's behavior is taught in business-school textbooks) notes how the company's mission statement, and indeed its culture, made the decision extraordinarily simple: It was the right thing to do for its customers. Customers continued to have confidence in the company and its Tylenol product, and we continue to see the benefits today in the safety-wrap packaging of pharmaceutical products.

But something seems to have gone wrong along the way. When batches of J&J's Tylenol, Motrin, and other products recently made people sick, we would have thought the company, with its sterling reputation for handling such matters, would have immediately pulled every such bottle from the shelves. It didn't.

Instead, according to the Food and Drug Administration, J&J's McNeil Consumer Healthcare Products executives knew of the problem in early 2008 but made only a limited investigation. "When something smells bad, literally or figuratively, companies must aggressively investigate and take all necessary action to solve the problem," said the FDA's Office of Compliance. The company has been warned by the FDA for violating manufacturing standards and failing to report and investigate the problem in a timely manner.

Interestingly, the very same day in 2010 when this matter hit the headlines, the media also reported that Johnson & Johnson was accused of breaking the law by paying kickbacks to a large nursing home pharmacy, violating the federal anti-kickback statute. There ensued a whistleblower suit against J&J and two subsidiaries, Ortho-McNeil-Janssen Pharmaceuticals and

J&J Health Care Systems, claiming tens of millions of dollars in payments. The company denied any improper activity.

But back to the product that made people sick. Why is the company now accused of failing to report and investigate the matter? Has there been a fundamental shift in corporate culture, taking compliance less seriously? Is there no institutional memory? Or is this a case of a subsidiary with a different culture than its parent?

And what about fixing the sources of the underlying causes of the product defects? In December 2010 the McNeil unit recalled millions of packages of its Rolaids brand antacids, following consumer reports of finding metal and wood particles in the products. A company spokesperson said the product was manufactured for McNeil by a third-party manufacturer, suggesting to some that this somehow removes some of the onus from McNeil. An FDA spokesperson then said what both professional and consumers alike know very well: "McNeil is responsible for the quality of its products even if they contract out the manufacturing." The McNeil unit doesn't seem to have finished with problems. In early 2011 it recalled millions of units of Benadryl, Sinutab, and Sudafed due to problems with maintaining clean equipment. And some in Congress continue to question McNeil's 2009 "phantom recall" of less-than-effective Motrin, when the company engaged contractors to surreptitiously buy the product from pharmacies' retail inventories. Recently the Attorney General filed a lawsuit on behalf of the state of Oregon alleging the company misrepresented the product's quality, saying "They did not want the negative publicity that would come with admitting they had a defective product, the negative publicity that comes with any recall." Interestingly, a McNeil spokesperson is reported to have said the unit's actions "were consistent with applicable law." One would think there would be a standard higher than legal compliance, and J&J CEO William C. Weldon did much better when testifying before a Congressional committee, saying "This episode was not a model for how I would like to see Johnson & Johnson companies approach problems with defective products when they arise."

And it seems when it rains, it pours, with other J&J units issuing product recalls, one for hip implant devices and another for soft contact lenses. Not surprisingly, sales of a range of J&J products are off sharply.

Also, the company recently admitted that it had bribed European doctors, with SEC enforcement director Robert Khuzami saying the company long tried to cover up its illegal activities by "using sham contracts, off-shore companies and slush funds." To its credit, J&J is said to have self-reported the activity and cooperated with the investigators, resulting in a reduced civil and criminal penalty of only $70 million. On the same day, it was reported that J&J "agreed to pay $7.9 million to settle bribery allegations with the United Kingdom Serious Fraud Office . . . and it admitted as part of its deferred prosecution agreement with the United States government to having paid kickbacks to the Iraqi regime of Saddam Hussein under an oil-for-food program that were found to be riddled with fraud." Regarding the bribery activities, an agreement with the Justice Department reportedly requires J&J to perform risk assessments and audits of its compliance program. CEO William Weldon came forth saying "We went to the government to report improper payments and have taken full responsibility for these actions," adding, "We are deeply disappointed by the unacceptable conduct that led to these violations."

A group of shareholders recently filed a lawsuit against the company's directors in federal court, claiming they received "years of red flag warnings of systemic misconduct" but that disregard for "their fiduciary duties including permitting and fostering a culture of systemic, calculated and widespread legal violations has destroyed J&J's hard-earned reputation." One wonders about the likelihood of this kind of suit ultimately being won by the shareholders, but meanwhile the board has to deal with it.

J&J reportedly has restructured quality control processes, and responsibility for quality control is now fixed with a senior manager reporting directly to CEO Weldon. Nonetheless, the spotlight is shining ever more brightly on J&J's manufacturing processes. It's been reported that the McNeil unit recently reached agreement with the FDA, soon expected to receive judicial approval to hire an independent expert to examine three plants and determine whether they meet federal standards and whether quality controls systems are up to par. Indeed, one of the plants is prohibited from reopening until the expert is satisfied and regulators sign off on its own inspection. Also, the FDA has authority to halt manufacturing or institute recalls—what some are saying is akin to a trustee-ship. And for good measure, federal criminal investigations are continuing.

## Lessons to Be Learned

What can we glean from these two proud companies that previously had some of the finest reputations for product quality? Here are a few important lessons:

- Reputations take years to develop, but only days (or hours) to damage. In the case of Toyota, the damage accumulated over many years, with the ensuing effect on customer loyalty, earnings and market share significant. With J&J, we don't know whether there will be long-term effects. In any event, reputations for product or service quality must be carefully nurtured and protected; they are too valuable to do otherwise.

- It is not in a company's interest to mess with regulators. Yes, a company might be able to fend off a regulator's inquiry for a while and continue on the company's predetermined path. But usually it's not in the company's, or its customers', long-term interests to attempt to stonewall an investigation or strong-arm a regulator. Lawsuits and resulting judgments, directives, or settlements can be burdensome, both in the short run and the long term. And while turnover in regulatory staffs can be high, memories are long. Getting on the wrong side of the sheriff unnecessarily can be a costly mistake.
- The desired corporate culture—based on a foundation of integrity, ethical values, customer sensitivities, and compliance with laws and regulations—must permeate an organization. This doesn't happen by edict, but rather with the right actions and processes accompanying the right words with compliance a priority. That includes drilling down to every subsidiary and business unit in an organization, as well as to sourcing and other partners whose actions can and will reflect on the company.
- A corporation's culture evolves over time. As employees turn over and new leadership rises, along with different strategies and mind-sets, the tone at the top and culture of the organization indeed will change. Company leadership cannot take for granted the positives of what once was in place; they must work to ensure the desired focus on integrity, ethical values, and the fabric of the organization is strongly held in place.
- While work can be outsourced, responsibility and reputations cannot. It's essential that third parties to whom production or other work is contracted are viewed as being a part of the company's business process, with appropriate compliance and other efforts being well controlled.

For these two great companies, which have enjoyed sterling reputations and market and financial success, the effects of these missteps may well be overcome in time. Right now, Toyota seems to have a longer road to recovering its reputation than J&J, but hopefully both are considering what fundamental changes may be needed. Indeed, the leadership of every organization may well think about lessons that might be applicable to their company, and they should take necessary actions to protect its assets and future prospects.

 ## HOW COMPANIES GOT WHERE THEY ARE

To see the best way forward, it's worth taking a quick look at some of the factors that caused many companies (though not necessarily those just named) to get to the untenable position they are now in.

- Companies typically have in place a number of policies and procedures directed at legal and regulatory compliance, including a code of conduct, whistleblower channel, educational programs, and annual employee sign-offs. In some large companies, depending on the industry, there is a designated chief compliance officer and staff, whereas in others the general counsel or other corporate lawyer serves in the role. But too often these are disparate elements that fail to function effectively as a true compliance program.
- Also typical is a buildup over time of layer upon layer of policy and procedure, each dealing with various aspects of legal and regulatory requirements. For each new law or regulation, new internal procedures are designed to deal with specifics of the rule. Unfortunately, often each is freestanding without consideration of existing protocols in the organization that may already address the new requirements.
- Responsibility for compliance rests with one senior manager. From the perspective of a company's chief executive, it's desirable to be able to look to one individual with the authority and accountability to achieve desired performance. This of course holds true for business operations as well as for such areas as finance, technology, and human resources. Responsibility for compliance is placed with the company's general counsel or chief compliance officer, and this individual is charged with ensuring the organization adheres to all legal and regulatory requirements to which it is subject. This approach also is embraced by boards of directors that see benefit in such central assignment of responsibility. While in some respects appealing, the reality is that this approach places responsibility for effecting compliance in the wrong place.

Another factor is viewing compliance solely as a necessary evil, and a costly one at that. Certainly, the thought goes, it's a drain on resources that could otherwise be used to grow the business and enhance profitability. This philosophy, however, can be counterproductive from a business perspective.

## KEYS TO GETTING IT RIGHT

Some companies have avoided these pitfalls and succeeded not only in reducing compliance costs, but also in enhancing efficiency and gaining real business benefit. Let's look at how they've succeeded in getting this right.

### Strategic Perspective

Moving from seeing compliance as a costly but necessary evil, forward-looking management teams see the bigger picture, beginning with the realization that

new laws and regulations arise from corporate actions that caused damage—
to consumers, employees, investors, or the community. Each legislative or
regulatory reaction raises the performance bar in such areas as product safety,
human resource discrimination, information privacy and security, the environment, sales practices, and financial reporting. These insightful corporate
leaders recognize that despite raising of the bar, the marketplace sees these
new standards as a minimum, with consumers looking for those products and
services that meet their higher expectations.

Successful managers get it, and their companies reap the benefits in
terms of market share, profitability, and return. One can look to the auto
manufacturer that has long been a leader in gaining better mileage performance, or another that has been a leader in vehicle safety. Companies that
recognized the demand for healthier food products—both retail and restaurant based—have gained market share. And an airline instituting a passen-
ger bill of rights continues to achieve high customer satisfaction ratings, gain
market share, and lead competitors in profitability. Companies with fair and
forward-looking HR programs attract and retain the best personnel, and
those with reliable and transparent financial reporting are viewed by the
investor community as lower risk resulting in lower cost of capital. These
companies recognize that legal and regulatory requirements indicate a
demand for better performance, and they have met the challenge by exceeding minimum requirements.

## Building into Business Processes

Recognizing the underlying motivations behind legal and regulatory requirements and related marketplace expectations, forward-looking companies
align their compliance process with the company's business goals and objectives, and build it into existing business processes. As such, responsibility for
compliance rests not with a compliance officer, but rather with each and every
line and staff manager in their spheres of responsibility.

Certainly a chief compliance officer is critical to ensuring a compliance
program is well designed and provides the necessary support to the management structure for its implementation. This responsibility includes ensuring
that what often are disparate elements are crafted into a cohesive compliance
program. More on this in a moment.

The take-away point here is that administrative costs soar if compliance
is superimposed on top of existing procedures. When built into the management process, compliance is both more effective and efficient. Looking at one

simple example, a broker-dealer seeking to comply with requirements for ensuring suitability of investment products to customer profile added costly monitoring procedures from an independent compliance group. Another, however, placed primary responsibility with local managers—who are closest to the action and know well the nature of local customer circumstances and needs and review what products are being offered by local sales personnel. Not only is compliance more effective, it is also more efficient, even when accompanied by ancillary monitoring on a test basis by compliance or internal audit personnel.

## A Program Founded on Ethics and Integrity

To be truly effective, the compliance program must be grounded in a culture based on integrity and strong ethical values. A company's culture is based first and foremost on the actions (more so than, but including, the words) of top management as well as managers cascading throughout the organization. Without integrity, a compliance program will have form but not substance, and over time will fail to do what it's designed to do.

Central to an effective compliance program is an ethics policy designed to meet the activities and culture of the company. The policy needs to be sufficiently comprehensive, but also organized and written to be understandable and readily accessible as needed to deal with day-to-day real life issues. The same holds for all policies, which need to have a business owner and be kept current and responsive to changing conditions. A recipe for disaster is having policy material that is too long, written in legalese, outdated, and hard to locate—such that noncompliance is virtually assured.

With integrity as a hallmark, a compliance program must engage the company's employees. They need to understand the reasons behind the rules— for the benefit of the company, its personnel, customers, and others. The reality is that employees who don't know why they're supposed to do something will go through the motions with a checklist mentality, if at all. So, educational programs should be in place—not just upon hiring, but ongoing—coupled with on-the-job reinforcement by unit leaders.

With whistleblower channels in place—dealing with any potential wrongdoing, not just what's required by Sarbanes-Oxley—personnel need to know that using those channels is fundamental to a culture of integrity and ethical values, and it is in the company's best interest and their own. The channel needs to be truly user-friendly, such that there is no uncertainty in reporting any concern, with an ombudsman or other support personnel ready to answer questions and facilitate communication. And of course, appropriate follow-up action with no possibility or concern of reprisal is a key. More on this in Chapter 4.

## A Risk-Based Approach and Clarity around Responsibilities

Companies sometimes set a zero tolerance approach to compliance, which indeed makes sense in terms of instilling an appropriate mind-set in an organization's personnel. Ignoring small wrongdoings can send an unintended message that compliance isn't really important. With that said, reality is that some rules carry more significance than others, and resources always have limitations.

Accordingly, risks need to be identified as to where and how noncompliance can occur, the likelihood of occurrence, and the impact on the company if it does occur. And with needs targeted, resources must be placed where they will do the most good, bringing the risks down to acceptable levels.

As noted, responsibility for compliance is best placed with line and staff managers who run operating business and staff functions. This involves more than simply assigning responsibility. It also distinguishes design, execution, and monitoring activities, including interfaces between operating and support units and the compliance and central monitoring functions, and clear handoffs with overlaps avoided. When roles are understood and built into HR processes, accountability can be established and performance measured over time.

## Technology

For mid-size and large organizations, central to an effective compliance process is sound use of technology. Done well, IT facilitates such matters as ensuring the code of conduct and other relevant policies are readily accessible, supporting the ongoing education process, facilitating employee certifications, and providing a user-friendly means of providing information or addressing concerns regarding potential noncompliance.

Recognizing that the regulatory environment continues to increase in complexity, leading organizations have moved away from manual-based methods for compliance, deploying technology to centralize and manage the full range of compliance activities. As a critical enabler, technology supports established compliance management process and methodology, but does not define them.

Among the benefits are:

- Providing real-time data management and decision support to ensure that senior management and the board of directors receive accurate information on causes, financial impact, and mitigating actions to control risk of compliance failures
- Enabling policy life-cycle management to create, approve, maintain, store, monitor, and automate tasks based on company policy requirements
- Delivering policy training and awareness, surveys, and related testing feedback
- Establishing automated workflows to establish employee accountability
- Automating and streamlining processes and information retrieval, including control testing, surveys, certification, and regulatory reporting
- Supporting measurement and reporting through a central repository of policies, procedures, risks, and controls

These capabilities are used to fix responsibilities for required actions by managers or monitors, and to track activities and enable inquiry from and to senior personnel. Real-time messaging and reporting capabilities provide the necessary information for use throughout the managerial ranks and the compliance function, with tailored dashboards and drill-down capability to home in on matters of particular interest.

## Strong Compliance Office

As noted, critical to effective compliance is a designated chief compliance officer, a position that, depending on the company's industry and size, can be part-time or full-time with dedicated staff. This individual must ensure all the necessary pieces are in place and brought together to be truly effective.

For instance, managers in the organization must receive information on existing and new laws and regulations relevant to their operational responsibilities. They all have "day jobs" and can't be expected to know what's required unless the legal or compliance function provides them with needed information in a form that's easily implemented. Importantly, the compliance officer needs to be sure any new requirements are considered in the context of existing procedures, to avoid adding unnecessary layers. In many instances, existing protocols may already address new rules, or require only minor tweaks to get them where they need to be. Overreacting can be as debilitating as under-reacting, as scarce resources are wasted on unnecessary procedures.

The compliance officer must ensure close coordination between the various activities that drive compliance, including monitoring of program effectiveness with the internal audit function, and interface with legal counsel (if separate from the compliance office) and top management.

The compliance officer can also promote and facilitate communication throughout the organization. For instance, messages on integrity need to be ongoing and reinforced. Information on potential issues of noncompliance must be communicated through regular managerial routes or separate channels, such that appropriate action and follow-up can be initiated. Information needs to flow not only up and down the organization but across as well, changing what might be a silo mentality into one where managers at every level throughout the company communicate as needed.

In this context, there needs to be clear and timely reporting in meaningful form to top management and ultimately the board of directors. Metrics on instances of noncompliance, along with severity and patterns and underlying causes, are needed to enable inquiry and corrective action. Reporting should become more summarized going upstream, although enough depth is needed to allow full understanding.

 ## THE COMPLIANCE OFFICE

The chief compliance officer role is increasingly expanding to a full-time job. Financial services firms, pharmaceutical companies, and other heavily regulated organizations have long devoted significant resources to a compliance office, typically with a full-time chief compliance officer and strong support staff. Multinationals have embedded part of the compliance function locally, typically with reporting to both the central compliance office and local management. But now studies indicate that for companies not facing heavy regulation, even large ones, which have struggled in deciding what compliance resources are needed, a full-time role is becoming more common.

One study from the Open Compliance and Ethics Group shows 75 percent of respondents have a chief ethics and compliance officer or similar title with "top-level oversight of compliance." And 40 percent said the compliance chief has no other role in their company; for companies with over $1 billion in revenue, the number is 55 percent. Where the title is shared, it's with the company's legal department 23 percent of the time. Another survey, conducted by the Society of Corporate Compliance & Ethics, shows 97 percent of respondents have a designated compliance or ethics officer, with 36 percent having no other title. Of those with another role in the company, 20 percent share responsibilities in the legal department. As with the OCEG study, other shared roles include the chief audit executive, CFO, and head of human resources, among others.[9]

Also indicative of the relative importance of the compliance officer role are the reporting relationships. A critical factor is that a chief compliance officer, wherever he or she appears on the company organization chart, has the ability to bring relevant information directly to the chief executive and, where necessary, to the board of directors. Depending on the nature of identified noncompliance events or associated risks, such access is essential. Also relevant are amendments to the U.S. Sentencing Guidelines, which call for the compliance officer to report regularly to upper management and the board of directors or audit committee.

Reporting relationships indeed are rising to high levels. The SCCE study, for instance, shows the chief compliance officer reporting directly to the CEO in 55 percent of the organizations. The compliance officer provides reports to the board of directors or a board committee, both in writing and face-to-face, in 80 percent of the companies.

With a more senior role comes higher pay. The OCEG study shows the most common level of compensation (36 percent) is between $150,000 and $250,000, with 20 percent reporting pay at $350,000 and above, not counting bonuses, stock options, or other forms of pay. As we might expect, pay in larger companies is at the higher end, with companies with more than $1 billion in revenue showing 23 percent with total compensation at the $450,000 level or higher.

Another factor is clarity around a compliance office's scope of responsibility. Is it responsible for establishing a process for effecting compliance with all relevant laws and regulations to which the company is subject? That's a good start. Does the scope include compliance with internal policies? That's typically the case as well, and makes sense. But do the CEO and board think the compliance office can possibly ensure compliance? We know it can't. As noted, the compliance function needs to focus on process and protocols, with direct responsibility for effecting compliance resting with line and staff unit leadership. Clarity around responsibility is essential. Amazingly, some company boards are looking to the compliance function to also take on responsibility for enterprise risk management! Fortunately, chief compliance officers have fought the attempt, for good reason.

Also important are the compliance office's relationships with the legal and ethics functions, if separate. Certainly compliance processes must adequately reflect the legal and regulatory realities, and we know there's often a fine line between—and sometimes a forerunner or impetus for—unethical behavior crossing over to illegality. So clearly there must be close coordination to ensure information flows, policies, procedures, and reporting mechanisms are in sync. Of course, each company needs to determine organization, reporting, and responsibility for compliance to fit its own culture, management style, and personnel.

 ## MAKING IT HAPPEN

How do you move to the desired compliance process? The way is straightforward, although as with any change initiative there are potential pitfalls. Among the tried and true approaches is a multistep sequential process that looks at what currently is in place, determines where you want to be, and crafts an action plan for getting there. Also important is dealing with senior managers who might want limited resources devoted to other important business initiatives. With that in mind, here's a brief five-step outline of what experience shows works well.

1. *Make the business case.* Get a rough estimate of current costs involved in dealing with compliance matters, including the risks and costs associated with noncompliance events. Relate this to a streamlined process built into business operations, together with support personnel and the cost of the change initiative. It's important to include the benefit of enhanced program effectiveness and anticipation of fewer and less costly noncompliance events, and senior management and the board to have better information and greater comfort. Because CEOs and boards usually already recognize shortcomings of existing compliance efforts, they are generally receptive to a thoughtful rationale for building a truly effective and efficient compliance process.
2. *Assess where you are.* Consider the current or *as is* state, including an inventory of compliance policies and procedures—both written and unwritten—and authorities and support functions to get an in-depth understanding of the compliance activities.
3. *Design the desired process.* The future or *to be* state must be developed. Importantly, design must reflect the corporate culture, including such factors as the organization structure, management style, and other embedded cultural features reflecting the desired tone at the top based on a foundation

of integrity and ethical values. In this context and as discussed, the compliance process is designed to be built into the business and management processes, with established responsibilities, accountability, and communication protocols. The process is principles- and risk-based, with details of specific procedures left to managers throughout the organization who will have operational responsibility, developed with support of the compliance office.

Consideration also must be given to such associated parties as outsource organizations, third-party networks, alliance and joint venture partners, and merger or acquisition targets, whose actions can affect how the company is perceived and held accountable. While important, extending to third parties can itself involve considerable effort—Tyco, for example, deals with literally thousands of suppliers, distributors, agents, and others in over 60 countries, while just one GE unit is said to work with 480 distributors, dealers, sales representatives, catalog sellers, resellers, equipment manufacturers, and procurement firms.

4. *Establish communication, reporting, monitoring.* Critical information flows are established—with two-way communication—and analyzed data is captured for upward reporting to senior management and the board. Technology support is selected, tailored as necessary, and embedded to enable risk analysis, accountability, and communication. Monitoring protocols are established, with clear responsibilities among the compliance office and internal audit function and their interfaces with line and staff units.

5. *Rollout and implementation.* The newly designed process is rolled out to the business, either starting with selected units or broadly across the enterprise. Training and education are critical, along with change management techniques to ensure employees fully understand what is needed, and why—that is, how new protocols will benefit every unit and the company as a whole. Personnel must truly buy in, coupled with integration into HR objective setting and performance assessment processes. Because compliance is built into existing business and management processes, new responsibilities are brought to the fore within the management structure in individual units, making implementation relatively straightforward.

## THE REWARDS

Change is never easy. For most companies, however, continuing along the same compliance path is not a viable option. Costs are soaring, instances of noncompliance rising, and the risk of a devastating failure is all too real.

Getting to a truly effective and efficient compliance process is attainable. Some companies have already gotten there, realizing the tremendous associated business benefits in understanding that the marketplace—consumer, work force, investor, and societal—sees legal and regulatory requirements as a minimum standard, which when exceeded significantly enhances market share, profitability, and return. When one considers the current costs and lack of effectiveness, together with the upside potential, a decision to get this right becomes evident. Those companies that do get it right position themselves to reap the associated rewards.

 **NOTES**

1. This chapter derives from the author's paper, "The High Cost of Non-Compliance: Reaping the Rewards of an Effective Compliance Program," published February 2010 by OpenPages.
2. OCEG 2005 Benchmarking Study.
3. META Group research conducted on behalf of PricewaterhouseCoopers.
4. Securities Industry Association Compliance Report, 2006.
5. Small Business Administration report, "The Impact of Regulatory Costs on Small Firms," W. Mark Crain, 2010, as reported by *Compliance Week*.
6. META Group research conducted on behalf of PricewaterhouseCoopers.
7. Holland & Knight, 2006.
8. A recent report by the Ethics Resource Center, Ethics & Compliance Officer Association, and the Society of Corporate Compliance and Ethics requests the Department of Justice to provide information related to the extent to which and how it takes a company's compliance program into account in enforcement actions. Information sought includes descriptions of specific (unnamed companies') cases where ethics and compliance programs mitigated enforcement actions, specific elements of ethics and compliance programs that affected enforcement decisions, and information about how corporate programs can enable a company to avoid prosecution entirely or specific sanctions. In several recent improper payments cases—Noble Corp, Universal Brazil, and Global Industries—there are clear indications that existing compliance programs served to soften the Justice Department's sanctions. While commending these actions, legal observers seek more specificity about the extent to which identified elements of companies' compliance programs provided benefit in enforcement cases.
9. As reported by *Compliance Week*. Both the OCEG and SCCE studies were published December 2009.

# CHAPTER FOUR

# Ethics Programs: Another Foundational Block

I N CHAPTER 2 WE looked at culture in the corporate environment and how some companies got it wrong and others right, and focused on the relevance of integrity in internal and external communications. Chapter 3 dealt with compliance programs—where some companies stumbled badly, and what constitutes effective programs. Here we build on those foundations, looking at ethical values and their impact on an organization, critical elements of effective ethics programs, and the role of the board of directors, including lessons learned from the recent events at Hewlett-Packard.

No, we don't see an E in GRC. But we know ethics is a critical underpinning of a company's culture and every aspect of governance, risk management, and compliance. Many companies now have ethics programs in place, either as part of or separate from their compliance processes. Some organize ethics activities as part of the legal counsel's office, some are separate. Companies may have a chief ethics officer and a chief compliance officer, some combine the two, and some have neither, with responsibility perhaps resting with the general counsel. Of course, as with most things, one size does not fit all, and each company must organize its activities as it sees fit.

With that said, we'll consider here what experience shows makes an ethics program truly effective. But before we do, let's return to a critical feature—a company's tone at the top.

**TONE AT THE TOP**

We've seen how ethical values drive a company's culture, and we understand the relevance of the tone coming from the top of the organization. What is the right tone? The answer to that question is similar to the often paraphrased 1964 indecency opinion provided by U.S. Supreme Court Justice Potter Stewart, who said that we can't define pornography, but we know it when we see it. Trying to define the right tone at the top presents a similar challenge. Nonetheless, in order to set a common base for this discussion, let's go out on a limb and say the right tone involves *a shared set of attitudes where employees maintain high ethical values and act with integrity, thereby complying with laws and regulations and behaving in a principled manner.*

The tone of an organization can be difficult to grasp. When you walk into a company's offices or its manufacturing, distribution, or other facilities and observe activities and talk with personnel, you quickly get a pretty good sense of what the organization is about. But to truly understand the tone at the top and how it influences behavior throughout the organization, you need to go deeper. One might think this concept is too abstract to recognize even when making an in-depth examination, but in fact it is doable. Indeed, managements of every U.S. public company need to consider this as part of the control environment when reporting on its system of internal control over financial reporting as required by the Sarbanes-Oxley Act. And the auditors of companies other than those defined as small businesses have to include this control environment within their audit scope in reporting on the effectiveness of the company's internal control system.

Businesses deal with ethics in a broader sense by using a number of standards and guidelines. In addition to the COSO framework on internal control, which is the basis for reporting under Sarbanes-Oxley, and the COSO framework on enterprise risk management, the New York Stock Exchange in its listing standards mandates a code of conduct and ethics. And whistleblower channels have become the norm, with Sarbanes-Oxley among the drivers.

 **PROBLEMS AT DAIMLER**

How many companies have brands that stand for quality more than Mercedes Benz? Perhaps surprisingly, the company found itself in the middle of a scandal, with media reports saying Daimler admitted to having engaged in a massive and pervasive bribery scheme and agreed to pay $185 million to settle charges. And this wasn't information the company volunteered, but rather the result of a lengthy government investigation.

According to the reports, this wasn't just a one-time event—not by a long shot. Rather, hundreds of bribes totaling tens of millions of dollars were paid in no less than 22 countries over a 10-year period. In a number of instances so-called cash desks were used to pay currency directly to government officials. In other instances the company used foreign bank accounts of shell companies to hide payments. Daimler reportedly also jacked up invoices for cars to generate still other payments.

What's perhaps most disturbing is that the reports say this wasn't a lower and middle management activity, but that it involved important executives including heads of overseas sales divisions and, more unsettling, even the company's internal audit office. The Department of Justice complaint speaks to Daimler's longstanding violations of bribery rules and a "corporate culture that tolerated and/or encouraged bribery." The reports also say the complaint points to "a lack of central oversight over foreign operations."

It's well known that the United States Justice Department is pushing hard on possible Foreign Corrupt Practices Act violations, and European regulators are increasing rule making and enforcement as well. And internal controls to help deal with the risk of improper payments are well known. But if senior managers are turning a blind eye or, worse yet, encouraging such payments, then all bets are off. That is, if the ethical values of a company are flawed, especially when emanating from senior personnel, then all of governance, risk, and compliance is undercut and becomes suspect.

##  ELEMENTS OF AN ETHICS PROGRAM

Large companies typically have in place a range of elements dealing with ethics and compliance, including a code of conduct encompassing ethics, a whistleblower channel, an ethics or compliance or other officer overseeing the program, and possibly an ombudsman to provide additional support. There may be training for personnel when the policy is enacted or changed, and usually the program is monitored or audited by the ethics officer and the internal audit function, with direct reporting to senior management and oversight by the board of directors.

This sounds pretty good, doesn't it? The reality, however, is that many companies with all of these elements do not have truly effective ethics programs. We need only to look at companies that have had major ethical failures with disastrous results to know that form does not suffice where substance is lacking.

What then, is necessary for an effective program? We can first look back at Chapter 3 on compliance programs—as noted, compliance and ethics leaders and their programs often are combined, for good reasons, as many of the same success factors are relevant to both. So, as with compliance programs, we see ethics built into the business, a culture based on integrity and strong ethical values, effective use of technology, and a strong and effective ethics office.

Looking at the elements of effective ethics programs more directly, here's what we find is essential.

## Code of Conduct

Historically too many companies' codes of conduct are written in legalese; a skeptic might think they were written by lawyers for lawyers to be technically comprehensive. Recently a number of companies have revamped their codes, presenting them in plain language to make them readily understandable to the company's people. And translations from a parent company's home country language into local language similarly are done in a way readily understood by personnel wherever they reside.

We've also seen a move from companies leaving codes untouched, gathering dust on shelves, to putting them on internal (and sometimes externally available) web sites to be readily accessible at the click of a button. Organization is improved, so an employee who needs to determine how to handle a particular issue can go directly to relevant material.

Importantly, codes are kept current, with personnel comfortable that they represent the latest requirements and guidance. Each section or topic has a specified owner charged with responsibility for periodically reviewing and revising as necessary. These owners also track instances of noncompliance or concerns raised by employees to learn where more guidance may be needed.

## Recruiting the Right People

Perhaps this is self-evident, but how often have we seen new hires brought in with only superficial screening? It's increasingly important that recruiting and hiring processes include meaningful background checks and other due diligence to ensure that new hires have personal characteristics consistent with the company's policies and culture.

For people brought into the higher managerial ranks, even more care needs to be taken. And not to be overlooked is the need to review the ethical behavior and track record of people considered for movement into more senior roles.

## Education and Training

Because every person in an organization must understand what's required, it's crucial to have an effective program to ensure that people understand what is expected of them. We know too well that many companies' training programs are less than effective. To achieve desired objectives, training needs to be conducted such that people come away with good knowledge of what the ethics program is about, what behavior is required, why the rules are in place, when to ask for help, and where to go when needed. And people need not only to understand but to embrace and act on what they've learned.

Again, no one size fits all. Some ethics training is conducted locally in small groups, with meaningful questions and answers and give and take on what's needed and why. A number of large organizations have gone to computer-based training, which when designed well can be effective. Feedback from participants determines the success of knowledge transfer and can be facilitated with use of the right technology.

But it's not enough to hold even an effective training course and believe you have finished the job. Rather, the educational effort needs to be ongoing, providing reinforcement and updates based on new events, activities, and circumstances, as well as refreshing memories and acceptance.

## Job Responsibilities

The most effective way an individual in an organization can get help usually is to go to the person to whom he or she directly reports. Especially where there's a close working relationship, people feel comfortable raising ethical issues with their boss. But that process works only where managers have the knowledge and experience to deal effectively with the issues and to know when they need to raise a matter further upstream in the organization.

Managers need to recognize that dealing with ethical issues in making business decisions and monitoring behavior is an essential part of reinforcing formal training with on-the-job training and is a fundamental part of their job responsibilities. And as with compliance responsibilities, managers should recognize the need for monitoring as part of their normal management responsibilities.

Directly related is the need to enhance HR programs to ensure these job responsibilities are fully understood and incorporated into objective setting and performance assessment processes. We know that "we get what we measure," qualitatively as well as quantitatively, and managers need to know that these responsibilities must be taken seriously—which we find is the case where they're built into the appraisal, promotion, and salary adjustment process.

## Whistleblower Channel

The reality is that some employees simply don't feel comfortable going to their boss to discuss ethics issues—either because of the topic or relationship, or worse still, because of possible involvement of their boss or someone further upstream in the organization. So, many companies have put in place some form of alternative communication channel, commonly called a whistleblower channel, where anyone in a company can provide information on illegal, unethical, or other transactions or behavior prohibited by the company's code of conduct and cultural base.

Public companies that didn't already have an alternative channel established one pursuant to requirements of the Sarbanes-Oxley Act. And while the act called for a relatively narrow focus—providing information around improper financial reporting—many companies broadened their whistleblower channel beyond those narrow parameters to include a broad range of misconduct, ranging from illegal to unethical behavior. A number of companies provide the channel for use by outside parties with which the company does business, permitting communication of concerns or instances of employee misconduct or other matters that may be relevant to the company's activities or reputation. If the channel is to be effective, its availability must be made known widely and its use encouraged, and matters reported must be carefully considered and followed to appropriate conclusion.

Management at a number of companies I've worked with established the channel in good faith, believing it was working well. That there were few complaints or issues raised supported that notion. Management of one company in particular was pleased that since inception of the internally managed program there was only one reported incident! The company now knows better and plans to move to a third-party managed system.

The reality of what's working, of course, often is very different from the perception. A recent survey found that 74 percent of employees witnessed wrongdoing at work in the previous year, but few reported it, and experience points to a number of reasons. One is that people have seen that previous efforts to report misconduct through the whistleblower channels did not see corrective action taken—that is, such reporting is seen as not doing any good. Even more significant is fear of retaliation, which unfortunately too often is well founded. Individuals reporting illegal or improper activities can find themselves ostracized or out of a job. So keeping one's mouth shut is seen as a reasonable and pragmatic course to take.

Another reason is employees' misunderstanding of misconduct's effect on the company. Employees mistakenly believe doing something that may be against the rules or even the law actually *helps* the company achieve its business objectives. So they see speaking out not only as being a tattletale, but also as damaging the company—never mind that we know from study and experience that the opposite is the case.

How can companies change that mentality? First they can ensure that the corporate culture makes integrity and ethical values a must—dictated not only by words in ethics policies, but also by management's actions up and down the line. It's necessary to ensure that company personnel, as well as those with whom the company does business, understand the mandate for ethical behavior and why that mandate exists.

The *why* is absolutely critical, including how acting properly is in both the company's and individual's best interests. And there must be absolute assurance that information provided will be treated confidentially and there will be no reprisals—indeed, stressing that a positive reward for speaking out will happen where warranted. There also needs to be ongoing communication, including feedback mechanisms, to make sure the message is understood and embraced. The whistleblower process needs to be front and center in the code of conduct, education and training, and on-the-job responsibilities discussed previously.

As for thinking that only a few reported matters indicates the process is working, that simply is not the case, but rather is evidence that the system is not working well. At the same time, if a whistleblower channel is flooded with minor complaints that turn out to be nothing more than unnecessary grumbling, there needs to be better education on how to use the channel—as well as getting to the source of the unhappiness or unease among the company's personnel.

## Cause for Concern Going Forward

The Dodd-Frank Act has a section that may further prove the theory of unintended consequences—the provision providing incentives to company employees who report suspected fraud to the SEC. By giving the SEC original information about a securities law violation, the individual is positioned to receive up to 30 percent of total penalties, quite possibly an award of tens of millions of dollars. And Dodd-Frank provides protections from retaliation such as demotion, dismissal, suspension, threats, or other harassment.

A concern among corporate compliance, ethics, legal, and other officers is well founded—that employees will bypass the internal reporting mechanisms in order to take a shot at a huge payday. Perhaps not surprisingly, only two months after Dodd-Frank became law, law firms began advertising to secure new clients willing to blow the whistle, with New York City moviegoers looking at the silver screen and seeing these ads, reportedly aimed at Wall Street employees! So, despite ethics and compliance programs that may be well designed, implemented, and reinforced, with outside legal support available, employees will be tempted and some will find a potential financial bonanza too hard to resist.

Whether this will actually happen is thus far an unanswered question. We can, however, get a glimpse of what might ensue by looking at what happened at pharmaceutical company GlaxoSmithKline, which recently agreed to pay $750 million to settle criminal and civil charges that it knowingly manufactured and sold tainted products to consumers. The whistleblower is set to receive a huge $96 million payday, and that's from the federal portion alone, with more to come from the states!

A fair question to ask is: If one of your company's employees has knowledge of serious problems, do you think he or she would take a shot at what amounts to hitting a huge lottery payoff? Actually, in the Glaxo-SmithKline case, the employee who later turned whistleblower had been sent to the company's troubled plant to straighten out quality control problems identified and reported to the company by the FDA. Reports say this team leader found use of broken equipment, tainted water used to make medication, required sterilization not maintained, packages of medications mixed with other medications—and after she repeatedly informed upper managers of these and other massive ongoing problems, and recommended changes including shipment stoppage and product recalls, reportedly little if anything was done. The individual went so far as to tell senior management that unless action was taken, she would contact the FDA. Well, not much was done, other than her job being terminated as a "redundancy." It seems the only thing that got management's attention was when federal marshals arrived at the plant with badges flashing and guns ready, seizing a reported $2 billion of products. So here's an individual who reportedly went to great lengths to work within the company's management structure before going to the outside. It remains to be seen what will happen going forward when opportunities for such huge paydays appear to be readily available by going directly to outside sources. By the way, federal agencies have vowed in these kinds of cases—of which hundreds are in the pipeline—also to go after the executives personally.

Several ideas have been put forth to help deal with the potential of employees immediately circumventing internal processes. One that should be considered is for companies to include in codes of conduct and related policies a requirement for employees to use internal communication channels first, before going to the SEC. Whether such a mandate would pass legal muster, however, is open to question but worth considering.

More impactful is the idea of a lawyer formerly with the SEC who references a section of the Securities Exchange Act that states auditors who believe they've discovered an illegal act must first report it to company management and the audit committee. Only if the company fails to act is the auditor required to report to the SEC. A similar requirement could be put in place for employees under Dodd-Frank. We can hope for meaningful action by the SEC—its director of enforcement said the agency will be "mindful of competing interests" as it shapes regulations around the new law.

It seems the SEC is taking a somewhat different tack. It has proposed rules designed "not to discourage whistleblowers who work for companies that have robust compliance programs" to first report internally, while also "preserving the whistleblower's status as an original source of the information and eligibility for an award." One element of the proposals would allow the SEC to pay higher awards to individuals who first report internally within their companies. The rules also would allow an employee in a company's compliance function to report information to the Commission when the company didn't itself report within a reasonable time or acted in bad faith.

Late in 2010, the Association of Corporate Counsel sent a letter to the SEC signed by top lawyers from 266 leading companies—including Delta Airlines, FedEx, Gap, Intel, McDonalds, Nike, Oracle, and Pfizer, to name a few—saying the proposed rules "disincent employees from looking for ways to improve or correct corporate behaviors, and incent them to find ways to profit from corporate wrongdoing. . . . Fraudulent misconduct, the bane of good compliance systems, then becomes the gold mine." The letter says employees will be encouraged to turn a blind eye to early signs of fraud, maximizing SEC penalties and their own payouts. An Association officer adds, "The proposals cut to the very core of what it is that every responsible U.S. company has been trying to do for the last couple of decades, which is to create effective, robust compliance reporting systems. . . . This just pulls the legs off the stool." We all look forward to seeing the SEC's final rule.

In any event, one company has already taken action, reportedly paying $55,000 to one employee and $135,000 to another group of employees for reporting suspected Foreign Corrupt Practices Act violations. A media report adds that while SEC whistleblowers might be awarded much larger awards under Dodd-Frank, "the prospect of a $55,000 bonus [from their company], without the hassle or retribution attendant to whistle blowing, might give them pause."

Well, it appears a lot of employees are not pausing. In February 2011 an SEC official reported that the number of high-value tips the Agency received before Dodd-Frank was about two dozen a year—roughly 24 tips. Since then, the number has skyrocketed to what he says is one or two per day, which by my calculation translates to about 550 per year. And we can only wonder what the trend line looks like.

Interestingly, just as the plaintiff's bar is advertising for whistleblowers, defense attorneys are looking to generate business as well. At least one major law firm formed what it calls a "multidisciplinary whistleblower team" offering "experienced, comprehensive counsel on the full range of issues that arise under the new statute." The firm says it will draw on its experts in labor and employment, securities enforcement, corporate governance and securities regulation, white collar defense and investigations, and litigation. It sounds to me like they're anticipating lots of chargeable hours.

## Ethics Office

Whether separate or combined with compliance or legal, a chief ethics officer provides a central point for helping design, implement, monitor, and adjust as necessary a company's ethics program. As with compliance, this officer and any needed staff should be responsible not for ensuring ethical actions and behavior, but rather for seeing that the program is working well—with primary responsibility for conduct resting with managers throughout the line and staff units.

Sometimes overlooked is the benefit of an ombudsman, who can be a highly effective resource for employees benefiting the workings of the ethics program. The reality is that employees often have information they believe might be important to report upstream, but they don't know for sure. An independent, objective person with relevant training and background can be invaluable to such employees, serving as a sounding board and advisor regarding whether a matter should be reported, as well as how best to present the information and to whom.

## Communication from Senior Management

We know that first and foremost the CEO is directly responsible for and sets the ethical tone of the organization, through words, deeds, and behavior. And while the CEO's actions are most significant, words are important as well.

The CEO and senior management team need to reinforce the mandates of the code of conduct on an ongoing basis—with internal meetings, video conferences, written words, and other forms of communication. It's not a once-and-done approach, but rather continual reinforcing of what's needed for the best interests of the company.

## Monitoring

The ethics program must be monitored to ensure ongoing effectiveness. This can be done by the ethics office as well as by including the program within the scope of the internal audit function. Also, managers throughout the organization are positioned and should be charged with responsibility to be aware of activities within their spheres of responsibility.

A number of techniques exist for monitoring the program. One technique several companies I've worked with found particularly effective is conducting a direct survey of employees. All levels of personnel are surveyed electronically on an anonymous basis about the messages they receive from their business unit leaders and senior management. The surveys address usefulness of the code of conduct and support systems, ethical values exhibited by management, employees' comfort with whistleblower channels, and other relevant factors. These survey results have proven valuable in understanding what the ethical behavior really is at the company and whether there are widespread or localized issues that need to be addressed.

##  SETTING THE TONE AT THE TOP: HEWLETT-PACKARD

We sometimes read in governance literature that responsibility for the tone at the top of an organization rests with the board of directors. Well, ultimately everything in an organization can be said to rest with the board, but that's neither realistic nor accurate. The board has the authority to delegate the everyday management of the company to the CEO, and invariably that's the case. So, it's the CEO, supported by his or her senior management team and cascading through the management ranks, that sets the tone of the company through his or her words and actions.

With that said, there's no doubt that a board of directors itself must provide effective oversight to the culture, including tone at the top, and to the ethical behavior of the company and its people. The board must receive relevant information, question and challenge it as necessary, and ultimately decide whether modification might be needed. More about that in Chapter 15.

Also relevant here is the fact that a board's own actions can and often do directly affect the culture and tone of an organization. And in some instances, the effect is profound.

A good example of a board's impact on a company's culture and ethical values is what occurred recently at Hewlett-Packard and the actions taken by its board. To refresh memories: Mark Hurd, the hard-charging chief of HP—who through acquisitions, layoffs, and cost cutting raised the company's fortunes—was fired by the board. The surrounding circumstances are the stuff of tabloids, including allegations by a female consultant of sexual harassment. We may never know exactly what transpired, and we probably don't need to. But there are some lessons here worth examining.

## Why the HP Board Did What It Did

Media reports say that the lawyer for Jodie Fisher, the woman at the center of the scandal, contacted the company in June 2010 with the sexual harassment charge. Fisher was a contractor hired as a marketing consultant by the office of the chief executive, and she attended events for HP in various locales; "knowledgeable sources" said Hurd often dined alone with her after HP events. Her lawyer said there was "no affair and no intimate sexual relationship between our client and Mr. Hurd," and Hurd made a similar statement. The board investigated the incident and allegations, concluding that while the harassment charge was unsubstantiated, Hurd filed "inaccurate expense reports that covered payments made to the woman" and "failed to disclose his use of company funds." General Counsel Michael Holston said Hurd's actions "showed a profound lack of judgment."

What reasons did the board put forth for its conclusion? As noted, one was Hurd's lack of judgment, though it's not entirely clear which judgmental element is at issue here. Directors pointed to the falsified expense reports and, importantly, the associated breaking of trust with the board in Hurd's attempt to hide his relationship with Ms. Fisher. Also, it's been said that some directors couldn't understand how Hurd could justify a "close personal relationship" with a former actress in "sexually charged films." Another seemingly important factor behind the board's conclusion was the advice of a consulting firm brought in by the board, which reportedly told the company it would likely suffer "a devastating public relations hit" with "months of humiliation" and a "media nightmare" if the sexual harassment allegations against Hurd were not disclosed and later became public.

But the plot thickens. HP Director Marc Andreessen provided interesting insights, saying Hurd "concedes" to "facts and circumstances" leading to "violations of the company's standards of business conduct." And it is not the "sort of behavior and . . . conduct that we certainly expect of all employees, certainly the CEO." Andreessen adds there was a "fundamental conflict of interest" and "issues with expenses that had the effect of essentially obscuring the personal relationship and the pattern and behavior," making the board's decision very clear, adding our CEO must "be able to stand in front of employees and live up to the values and the standards of the organization."

There's some opaqueness around these statements, but the fog is partly lifted by another report. It says Hurd settled with Fisher the evening before a scheduled mediation session with the two principals and their lawyers. Evidently, the HP board felt this resulted in "short-circuiting of the board's investigation and increased mistrust among directors who already were complaining that Hurd had not been fully cooperative with the internal investigation." Based on this, one might presume that despite "not finding evidence" of sexual harassment, the board never concluded it didn't happen.

Despite the above, one media columnist says the board's claims are merely a "smoke screen," and calls the HP directors cowards. The columnist says one reason Hurd was fired was because he was despised by the company's employees, from senior executives to the rank and file. This, he says, was a "consensus in Silicon Valley," knowing that employees resented Hurd's high compensation—$72 million in the last two years—while rank-and-file jobs were being cut. He notes that the R&D budget was slashed from 9 percent of revenue to 2 percent, destroying "what had always made HP great," and that recent internal surveys at HP showed nearly two-thirds of the company's employees would leave if offered a job elsewhere.

## But Why Did He Do It?

Of course, we don't know why Hurd did what he did. We can't (and might not want to) get inside his head. But the impact to his wallet is huge. Negotiations were taking place around a new contract under which Hurd would be paid $100 million over three years—this against a backdrop of the misreported expenses of less than $20,000. Presumably the expense reports were prepared in a way to disguise whatever behavior was taking place, so the dollar amounts aren't really the issue, but the difference in amounts involved nonetheless is staggering.

Hurd's formal statement includes the admission: "I believe it would be difficult for me to continue as an effective leader at HP, and I believe this is the only decision the board and I could make at this time. As the investigation progressed, I realized there were instances in which I did not live up to the standards and principles of trust, respect, and integrity that I have espoused at HP."

For what it's worth, Fisher said, "I was surprised and saddened that Mark lost his job over this. That was never my intent." If she's referring to her charge of sexual harassment, then her statement indicates incredible ignorance regarding corporate America in the twenty-first century.

## HP's Troubled Past

You may recall the recent troubled history of the HP board. In 2006, an HP director leaked sensitive information to the media. What followed was Chairwoman Patricia Dunn's engagement of third-party investigators, resulting in the now-famous pretexting scandal. I wrote then: "Thus far there is little if any indication that Hurd was directly involved in the investigation or had knowledge of any illegal activity." Interestingly, a recent book on the subject accuses Hurd of "hijacking" the internal investigation by requiring an outside law firm he hired to report directly to him rather than to the board. The author says, "There was a residue of mistrust because of the pretexting scandal," perhaps pointing to one more reason the board fired Hurd. More on that episode in Chapter 15.

## Reaction to the Firing

A number of corporate governance experts have applauded the board's actions. University of Delaware's Director of the Center for Corporate Governance, Charles Elson, says, "They handled it exactly as they should. Once trust is broken between a CEO and a board, it makes it harder to have confidence in anything he says in future. He had to go." And Jeffrey Sonnenfeld, a professor at Yale's School of Management, notes the board showed "the perfect balance of due process to investigate . . . and acting with speed and decisiveness."

One outlier is Oracle CEO Lawrence Ellison, reportedly a close friend of Hurd's, who said, "The HP board just made the worst personnel decision since the idiots on the Apple board fired Steve Jobs many years ago." He added that the HP board "fully investigated the sexual harassment claims . . . and found them to be utterly false." That statement is subject to debate, and it doesn't get to the crux of why the HP board says it acted. Regardless, soon afterwards Ellison hired Hurd as President of Oracle, reporting directly to Ellison.

But most pundits are praising the board for making a courageous decision. With HP's stock price doubling while Hurd was at the helm, the board had to know firing him would cause the stock to take a hit. And it did, falling by almost 10 percent following the firing announcement.

## Why the HP Board Should Have Fired Hurd

Based on the many reports, I'm convinced the directors did absolutely the right thing. With Hurd's track record, it may have caused major soul searching—though as noted, reports are mixed on what the board thought of Hurd. Whether it might have guessed that Oracle would have hired Hurd to a senior management position, taking with him intimate knowledge of HP that for a short time became the subject of a lawsuit, is unknown outside the boardroom.

But the board evidently had many good reasons to do what it did, including those publicly stated, such as inaccurate expense reports. Some have used the term "fudging," suggesting a corporate misdemeanor. But if indeed Hurd didn't simply omit information or make an honest mistake, then it's lying. And lying involves intent to deceive—a corporate felony. And the loss of trust with the board also is a deal breaker.

But there's another reason Hurd should have been fired that hasn't been put forth by the board, or, for that matter, anyone else that I've heard. While passing reference was made to living up to the values of the organization, there's a significant missing piece. What's ignored is the critical relevance of the tone at the top of the organization, which must be based on integrity and ethical values, and how actions of senior executives, particularly a CEO, drive the tone and corporate culture. We know well that the actions of top management send clear messages throughout an organization of what actions and behavior will be embraced and what will not be tolerated. A CEO's actions get into the fabric of an organization, establishing the environment and context for how the company and its people deal with everyday tough decisions affecting the current and future fortunes of the company. If a CEO lies on expense reports, is disingenuous with the board, or takes actions that prevent the board from completing a full investigation of alleged improper behavior, then a board must act decisively. If the board does not, then the board is not doing its job in ensuring the desired corporate culture.

Based on all that's been reported, the board had good reason to fire Hurd. For me, this last reason is a critical one. Whether the board should have given Hurd a reported $40 million to $50 million "going-away present" is another issue entirely.

## The Aftermath

Subsequently, the HP board hired Léo Apotheker as the company's new CEO, raising a whole new set of theories and accusations. One media columnist asserts that Apotheker, formerly CEO of software company SAP and a fierce competitor of Oracle, was hired by HP to get back at Ellison, a charge denied by the then soon-to-be board chair of HP. The columnist notes that Oracle and SAP were involved in a court case where SAP already acknowledged stealing intellectual property, adding that "as a member of SAP's executive board, Mr. Apotheker clearly knew about the theft." And, "more important, for a company that professes to be concerned with ethics . . . it is astonishing that it would find Mr. Apotheker's lapses acceptable. He may not have been directly involved in this brazen theft of intellectual property, but it defies belief to say he didn't know about it. And he did nothing to stop it until it was far too late. Apparently, the H.P. directors adhere to the highest ethical standards—but only when it's convenient." Hmm.

Yet incoming HP board chair Ray Lane defends the actions, saying Oracle never offered any evidence of Apotheker's involvement, and the copyright infringement occurred before Apotheker became CEO. Lane then said Mark Hurd repeatedly lied to the board during the ethics investigation, adding, "No board can retain a CEO who violates the trust and integrity needed to lead a public company."

Since then a shareholder lawsuit requesting further investigation prompted HP to initiate a new probe, led by directors coming on board after Hurd's resignation—which points to Lane and Apotheker. Reports also surfaced that the SEC is investigating Hurd related to insider trading issues, focusing at least in part on whether Hurd passed information on to Ms. Fisher on HP's planned acquisition of Electronic Data Systems, and possible destruction of documents.

Subsequently HP announced four board members are leaving, including some of the most outspoken for and against Hurd's departure, and are being replaced by five new directors. A media report says the new directors are expected to be supportive of the agenda of Apotheker and Lane and help to put Hurd's departure in the rearview mirror. This, however, has raised further questions. Institutional Shareholder Services recommended that shareholders withhold votes from three nominating and governance committee members, saying Apotheker was too active in identifying the new board members. ISS pointed out that the committee's charter says the committee has responsibility for identifying new directors, and each board member must be independent, adding, "A CEO's participation in the appointment of directors, especially if the director has a significant relationship with the CEO, can make it difficult for such directors to be objective."

Chairman Lane shot back, reportedly saying the new board members "aren't buddies of Apotheker . . . I knew these people better than Leo. But because Leo and I know the industry it would be hard to pick any name we don't know." HP's shareholders seemed to agree, ratifying the director slate that was put forth.

With all that's gone on, we can wonder whether there's more to come on the HP scene.

5

# Risk Management and the Financial System's Near Meltdown

N OW FOR THE R in GRC—risk management. Before we get into what makes risk management processes really work effectively, let's look at what transpired in the near meltdown of the global financial system. It wasn't that long ago that we were on the brink of real disaster. And there's no doubt about the failure of risk management—by financial institutions, regulators, and others. We can learn important lessons from what transpired—here are the highlights.

 ## WHAT WENT SO TERRIBLY WRONG

At the risk of oversimplification, it began with financial institutions seeing an opportunity to do some good things by:

- Writing or otherwise generating mortgages to less than normally qualified home buyers, anticipating returns sufficient to cover the expected higher default rates.
- Packaging the debt obligations in ways that spread the risk, thereby presumably lowering the risk, and then selling the paper to a range of investors.

- Allowing those who otherwise would not be able to achieve the American dream of home ownership to do so and to build equity for their families.

And, of course, they would make some very good money in the process.

On the surface, it all sounds pretty good. One can readily see why so many of the U.S.-based and international financial institutions got into the act. Some were initiators, some jumped on the bandwagon as it was rolling along, and some eagerly invested on the other side of the equation.

## Cutting to the Core

Some government officials following the happenings warned of a coming crisis, and astute investors did indeed see the true risks and stayed on the sidelines.

What did they see? That the players in this process were making several fundamentally flawed and related assumptions: that spreading the risk would lower the risk, that the returns would be sufficient to cover the higher default rates, and—most significantly—that the housing market would continue to rise in value forever.

That last point is the key. As long as the price of houses continued to go up, the borrower-homeowners could, when the low teaser rates expired, refinance the mortgages, make the new mortgage payments, and maintain home ownership. If not, foreclosures would happen, but because of higher home values, the mortgagee, while inconvenienced, would nonetheless likely recover its full investment.

## Where It Went Wrong

A root cause of the subprime mess is that housing prices did not continue to rise. In many markets values began to decline, and because some borrowers never had the wherewithal to continue making mortgage payments, the defaults started. And when other mortgagors saw the much higher interest rates on the horizon, they found (surprise!) that they were forbidden by the mortgage terms to refinance without a steep penalty. The downward spiral began. You know the rest of the story. With mounting defaults and threat of more, the value of the mortgage-backed paper dropped to the point where the markets for this paper dried up.

My former partner and FASB Chairman Bob Herz offers further insight into what went wrong. As he put it, at the crux of the problem were non-traditional loans, based on questionable mortgages and structured into "an increasingly complex array" of securities sold and resold to other investors. These institutions and investors "apparently saw little need to conduct their own due diligence, risk management, modeling, and valuation processes. And as the music grew ever louder, the dance, premised on an apparent belief that U.S. home prices would continue to rise or at least not decline, became ever more frenzied." And "unfortunately, balkanized regulatory systems, both in the United States and across international financial markets, may have made it difficult, if not impossible, to rein in the exuberance driving the markets. And just as in the savings and loan crisis, regulators apparently failed to fully understand the risks their regulatees were taking on, and apparently thus saw little reason to try to curb what turned out to be mounting problems."

The pain was extensive and widespread. Some of the most highly respected financial firms and their shareholders paid a dear price, with the likes of Citigroup, Merrill Lynch, Bear Stearns, and Morgan Stanley all suffering tremendous losses. Some of these esteemed institutions reported the first quarterly losses in their history, fired their CEOs, and found themselves selling off chunks of their firms to foreign investors. And the announced losses got bigger all the time.

Others suffering serious losses included state pension funds and other investors holding the debt obligation paper, employees who lost their jobs, and of course, the families losing their homes who were suffering their own nightmares—not to mention the broader economy.

## Let's Point Some Fingers

It's easy to point out who's to blame for this horrible mess, and there are plenty of fingers to go around. (By the way, hopefully without being unduly immodest, I'd like to note that I first put forth this analysis some years ago—in late 2007, before it became rather obvious to many commentators.) Here's where responsibility rests:

- *Management.* Executives of the loan generators and sellers should have known better. If these organizations had truly effective risk-management processes, they would have been apprised of the tremendous risks involved. Regardless of the fact that the institutions involved supposedly had some of the most sophisticated risk-management systems in place, something went terribly wrong. Some say incentives for short-term upside potential caused CEOs to ignore the risks, placing huge bets with corporate resources so they could line their pockets. While there may be an element of reality in those assertions, my experience with large organizations suggests circumstances where, although certain managers in these organizations knew what the risks were, they either didn't sufficiently communicate upstream or their communications fell on deaf ears. Yes, quantitative models were deficient and there was inadequate stress testing, but another fundamental of risk management—effective communication and response to known information—failed terribly.

■ *Mortgage generators.* Those banks, mortgage companies, and others directly involved in making the loans seemed not to care. Making loans to potential home buyers hoping to get a piece of the American dream (let's put the speculators aside), with terms that locked families into debt they had little chance of keeping current or didn't understand, is unethical at best—and subsequent lawsuits and settlements suggest possible crossing of legal lines. It seems to be another case of "I'll make my money up front, and whatever happens to the other guy is just too bad." Part of this is the result of institutional processes that rewarded employees for putting loans on the books with little concern about whether those loans would ever be repaid.

■ *Borrowers.* Borrowers must share some of the blame. People signing on the dotted line without fully knowing what they were agreeing to later asked themselves why they didn't take the time and effort to find out. On the other hand, those speculating on new condos with ocean, golf-course, or desert views with the intent to flip them for a tidy profit can only, like the mortgage generators, take a long look in the mirror.

■ *Rating agencies.* It's evident that something is terribly wrong with major rating agencies that gave and kept superior ratings on this stuff until the problem not only surfaced, but the damage had already been done. Didn't these organizations see what was happening? One of the credit raters had been looking at financial services companies' risk-management processes during this period, making us ask whether the rater knew what effective risk management is all about. The answer apparently lies in the massive failures of highly rated companies and securities.

■ *Insurance companies.* At least two insurance companies guaranteeing the mortgage paper were forced to raise new capital. One looked to be bailed out by some of the same financial institutions mentioned earlier, who now fear the insurance company's loss of its AAA rating could force the banks to suffer billions more in losses. The fault here seems to rest in basic fundamentals. No less than Warren Buffett, who knows something about insurance, reportedly described these insurance contracts as financial time bombs, because traders mispriced the risk of default without setting aside sufficient reserves to cover related claims.

- *Others.* No doubt there are other culprits, such as realtors who should have known better, intermediaries in the collateralized debt obligations pipeline, and certainly institutional and other investors who bought into the concept that this paper presented a reasonable risk/return ratio. And of course, there was a widespread shortcoming of boards of directors. More on that in a moment.

- *Regulators.* At least one Federal Reserve governor, a senior Treasury official, and other regulators warned years before of forthcoming problems and lobbied for action. Unfortunately, they were ignored. The regulatory system failed us, and how it did that is worth looking at in a bit more depth.

 ## THE REGULATORY SYSTEM

While we're concerned here principally with the microeconomic level, it's true that the regulatory system does, or should, play a key role in maintaining healthy flow of capital, fair markets, and an economy supportive of corporate growth, providing a sound basis and protections for all parties. As such, regulators have a direct effect not only on macroeconomics, but also on individual industries and companies. But a number of things went terribly wrong in the subprime debacle.

### Securities and Exchange Commission

The SEC has long been considered one of the most effective government institutions, held in high esteem on both sides of the Congressional aisle. Well, its reputation has been tarnished. There was a brief and little-noticed meeting of the Commission way back in the spring of 2004 with major investment banks. News later came out that the banks asked for and received an exemption regarding the amount of debt their brokerage units could take on. Billions of dollars held as a cushion against losses were freed up and invested in mortgage-backed securities and exotic derivative instruments, while the SEC relied on the bank's own computer models to determine the risks inherent in those investments.

We now know what transpired. The bank's leverage ratios skyrocketed, with Bear Stearns's ratio, for example, going as high as 33 to 1. Reportedly the SEC did little to monitor the situation. Reports at the time indicate that the office originally identified as having responsibility to oversee the situation had no director for significant periods of time, and had conducted no inspections for 18 months. How could this have happened? Some say it was due in part to the broader deregulatory culture of the administration then in office. Regardless of the reason, the lack of effective regulation clearly played a significant part in the near meltdown.

## Federal Reserve

Talk about being held in high esteem. Who in government in recent times had a better reputation than Alan Greenspan? Well, in some quarters the judgment of the former Fed chairman has been questioned. News reports point to his fierce objection whenever derivatives came under scrutiny. In 2003, for example, he told the Senate Banking Committee, "We think it would be a mistake" to regulate derivative contracts more closely. Had Greenspan acted differently, some economists say, the crisis might have been averted or muted. Actually, by 2008 the derivatives market rose to $531 trillion, up from $106 trillion in 2002, and from a relative pittance just two decades earlier. Note that we're no longer talking about billions, but now *trillions* of dollars!

Of course, it's easy to make assertions based on hindsight. But there were smart people who seemed to know back then what was coming down the pike. Reports note that well-known and highly regarded investment banker Felix Rohatyn described derivatives as "potential hydrogen bombs," and Warren Buffett said five years ago that derivatives were "financial weapons of mass destruction, carrying dangers that, while now latent, are potentially lethal." Chairman Greenspan took the opposite view, believing the risks could be managed by the markets themselves.

Way back in 1994, Charles Bowsher, head of the U.S. General Accounting Office, told a House subcommittee: "The sudden failure or abrupt withdrawal from trading of any of these large U.S. dealers could cause liquidity problems in the markets and could also pose risks to others, including federally insured banks and the financial system as a whole." At the time Greenspan testified that "risks to financial markets, including derivatives markets, are being regulated by private parties. . . . There is nothing involved in federal regulation per se which makes it superior to market regulation."

We know that Fed Chairman Greenspan provided our country with tremendous service, and he has long been viewed as the oracle who helped steer the economy through years of prosperity. But we now wonder whether more regulation of the risks financial services firms were taking would have been better than less. Interestingly, the former Fed Chairman has since called for tighter regulation and, according to a Bloomberg report, is "distancing himself from the free market culture that he helped to create."

## Insurance Company Regulators

We know that insurance companies are regulated at the state level, which seemed to have worked reasonably well—until the problems hit. But how well regulators tracked activities of the since bailed-out American International Group is perhaps now all too clear. We've learned that a small London-based AIG unit began writing credit default swaps on collateralized debt obligations, on the basis that if an issuer of CDOs defaulted, AIG would make good.

Where was the regulation of this insurance and the related risks? A media report noted that this AIG Financial Products unit was not deemed to be an insurance company and thus didn't have to report to state regulators, adding that there was an element of review by the Office of Thrift Supervision, but the extent and quality of its involvement was suspect at best.

How this small unit could bring this huge and highly regarded company to its knees, and threaten the entire worldwide financial system, will serve for years to come as a textbook case study in the failure of regulatory risk management.

## Going Forward

With Dodd-Frank in place, the Fed, SEC, and other regulators now are putting in place rules to curb some of the most egregious lending practices, but it's really closing the proverbial barn door after the horse has left. This may help prevent such abuses from occurring in the future—though many experts question that notion—but in any event regulators should be looking for seeds of where the next debacle might come from.

 ## MERRILL LYNCH

Let's look a bit more closely at one of the failed companies. As an aside, I occasionally dabble in the stock market, with my few trades going through a broker I admire at Merrill Lynch.[1] I remember that some years ago I asked him about the potential implications should Merrill someday go under.

After he stopped laughing, he said there was no possibility of that happening. We now know that it almost did, with bankruptcy averted only by a shotgun wedding.

What happened at this well respected brand-name firm? Let's begin with senior management. Media reports describe Merrill's then-CEO, Stanley O'Neal, as an autocratic leader overseeing a group of trusted lieutenants who led Merrill's profitable but "belated push" into the market for collateralized debt obligations. One executive, the overseer of the firm's mortgage operations, often played the "tough guy . . . silencing critics who warned about the risks the firm was taking." Another, who oversaw risk management, contributed by "loosening internal controls."

What immediately comes to mind is a tone at the top that not only allows a firm to move toward the edge of a cliff, but actually drives it there. We know how a chief executive and loyal team can have a take-no-prisoners approach, mandating action while stifling dissent.

The phrase *belated push* is telling. More than a few financial firms in the last few years saw competitors reaping bushels full, or more likely warehouses full, of profit. Merrill reportedly was one of the late arrivals, envying Lehman Brothers and other early birds for the cash they were hauling in. Disaster awaits those late to the party, playing catch-up and struggling to gain on competitors, because that's when rules get broken and common sense ignored. (One can view this as the "keeping up with the Joneses" syndrome, which I come back to in Chapter 15.)

## Looking Deeper into the Abyss

Particularly telling are the observations of John Kanas, then CEO of North Fork Bancorp, which had been considering a merger with Merrill several years earlier. After spending time getting acquainted with Merrill's management team, Kanas said, "In the end, we were put off by the fact that we couldn't get comfortable with their risk profile, and we couldn't get past the fact that we thought there was a distinct possibility that they didn't understand fully their own risk profile."

It gets more interesting, with reports saying:

▪ The vice chairman responsible for credit and market risk management, corporate governance, and internal control allegedly "weakened Merrill's risk-management unit by removing longstanding employees who 'walked the floor,' talking with traders and other workers to figure out what kinds of risks the firm was taking on"—this according to former Merrill executives.

- Replacements of those employees were loyal to the chairman and his lieutenants, pushed to be "more concerned about achieving their superiors' profit goals than about monitoring the firm's risks."
- Another senior executive, known to carry a notebook with daily profit and loss information, "would chastise traders and other moneymakers who told risk-management officials exactly what they were doing."
- The toxic environment was reported to be such that "there was no dissent . . . so information never really traveled."

Against this backdrop, and unlike Goldman Sachs and JPMorgan Chase, which seemed to better understand the dangers of the CDO and synthetic CDO markets and to have more success in managing the risks, Merrill "seemed unafraid to stockpile CDOs to reap more [and more] fees." Within four years, Merrill went from a bit player to reportedly the world's biggest underwriter of these products.

And it only gets more interesting. The reports point to a scenario where American International Group, which had been insuring Merrill's CDO exposure, decided to pull out. But did this stop or even slow the firm? When Merrill "couldn't find an adequate replacement to insure itself [and] rather than slow down, Merrill's CDO factory continued to hum and the firm's unhedged mortgage bets grew, its filings show."

## The Lessons Become Obvious

You may well be asking, where was the logic, the risk management, the common sense? Who allowed controls to be ignored? Weren't there established risk tolerances and a portfolio view of risk in relation to the firm's risk appetite? Where was the infrastructure?

Unfortunately, what happened at Merrill has happened before—and, regrettably, I'm comfortable predicting that it will happen again. When a senior management team decides to drive at breakneck speed toward the edge of a cliff, only a few things might be able to save the company and its shareholders:

- Senior line or staff personnel—such as knowledgeable operations executives, a chief risk officer, chief compliance officer, or chief audit executive— with sufficient understanding of what's happening and ability and courage to go straight to the board. Such action is fraught with personal danger, and may well cost the individual his or her career, especially when the communication falls on the board's deaf ears.

- Communications channels that allow personnel who see a company heading for danger to provide warnings outside normal reporting channels, up to the board level, with enough strength to gain attention.
- A board of directors that truly understands the company's culture and tone at the top, strategy, operations, and risks, and knows where the company is going, and is willing to confront a strong CEO and top management team.
- A regulatory system that has a similar understanding, and is positioned and willing to take action to provide protections. Clearly this has not been the case heretofore, and we need to wait to see what the coming regulatory changes will bring—and to what extent a future regulatory structure will focus on individual firms versus systemic risk.

As we consider what can help save a company from the blindness that ruined Merrill, a few fundamental necessities emerge. The board of directors must ensure that the company's strategy makes sense, that the internal environment is healthy, that an effective control infrastructure is in place and operating well, and that risks are well understood and communication channels open.

So, we come back to the board of directors. Directors have an incredibly difficult job, with significant risks inherent therein. They work part time, outside the mainstream of a company, and with tremendous responsibility. But there is no role more important to corporate America, and boards must have the right participants, protocols, and skills to do the job well.

## WHERE WERE THE BOARDS?

Jim Kristie, editor and associate publisher of *Directors & Boards*, whom I respect as highly knowledgeable about governance matters, made up his mind to this question, saying: "Frankly, boards have let down the nation and its capital markets. Boards have not had the right leaders in place; they have not adequately analyzed risk; they have not had the depth of knowledge of their company's operations that they should have had; they have not done a sufficient job of helping management see the big picture in front of them and in seeing around corners as to what lies ahead; and they have not acted smartly and speedily as conditions deteriorated and management faltered."

Some may view that as a harsh assessment, but based on what transpired, challenging it is difficult. With that said, we can't know with certainty what happened in these firms' boardrooms unless we were sitting there as deliberations unfolded, and I wasn't. Still, we can readily speculate on what did or didn't occur, and several viable scenarios emerge. First, let's briefly review what responsibilities boards have pertaining to these and any other sort of risks. In brief, oversight involves a board that:

- Determines whether management is appropriately identifying, assessing, and managing significant risks the company faces
- Receives sufficient information that appropriate, disciplined processes are in place for this purpose
- Is confident that management is bringing the more significant ongoing and newly emerging risks to the boardroom, and that it receives relevant and timely analysis of those risks and management's actions and planned actions
- Reviews the risks and risk responses, as well as the company's risk appetite and portfolio view of risks, and considers whether modifications are needed.

So, we return to the question: Where were the boards of these companies? Logic tells us possible scenarios for each company are as follows.

- The company did not have an effective risk-management process in place, and senior management was not appropriately apprised of the risks. Under this scenario, the boards couldn't have been informed of the risks, because management wasn't aware of them.
- An effective risk-management process was in place and management was aware of the risks, but didn't communicate them to the board. That is, management withheld important information from the board.
- Management knew the risks and communicated them to the board, and the board was comfortable with the company's risk appetite and didn't object to continuing down the established path.

No, we don't know with certainty whether or not the boards of these firms appropriately carried out their responsibilities because we weren't in the boardrooms. And the extent of blame depends on what the boards did to gain comfort that an effective risk-management process was in place, that they were receiving relevant information on risks and related actions to manage the risks, and that they were comfortable with the company's risk appetite and that appetite wasn't being exceeded. Important here is that a board operates in an *oversight* and not a *management* capacity, and to a large extent depends on information that management brings to the boardroom.

My sense is that some of these organizations lacked an effective risk-management system, and senior management at these companies wasn't sufficiently informed of what the risks really were. But I also suspect some of the boards did not delve as deeply as they should have to ensure that the appropriate risk-management processes, including the communication of key risks and actions to the board level, were in place and fully functional. If those processes and channels were operating effectively, then it comes down to the boards' agreeing to what seems to be an extraordinarily high risk appetite and thus subjecting shareholders to serious loss of share value. I'd like to think that the kind of individuals who serve on those boards wouldn't allow that to happen had they known.

##  DID CEOS SEE IT COMING?

So we come back to management and, ultimately, the CEO. As noted, we look first to management to effectively manage risk to the organization, and in the near meltdown the CEOs have paid a high price. In the end, in a number of the world's largest and most prestigious financial institutions—including Citigroup and Merrill Lynch, to name just two— the boards of directors, regulators, and investors ultimately, after the fact, held the CEOs accountable for the major fiascos. Losing tens of billions of dollars and consequently requiring huge capital injections at fire-sale prices certainly qualifies as a major fiasco. At Bear Stearns, not only is the CEO gone, but the once-prestigious firm collapsed into the hands of JP Morgan and no longer exists.

But the reality is that in many such cases, the CEO never saw it coming, for a number of reasons. Let me say first that large company CEOs are among the smartest, most capable people on the planet. But from years of experience working with CEOs of some of the largest companies, I believe perhaps the most relevant underlying cause is that these business leaders truly didn't know the nature or extent of risk their companies were taking on. Worse, they didn't know what they didn't know.

How is that possible? Aren't these companies supposed to have some of the most sophisticated risk-management systems anywhere? We know they deal with ongoing market risk, counterparty risk, liquidity risk, credit risk, operational risk, and so forth and so on. Yet, the losses these institutions suffered stagger the imagination, and have cost chief executives their jobs and possibly their reputations.

## How Good Is Risk Management?

We know that every company is in business to take risk. How well the C-suite manages that risk directly drives the company's success or failure. Yes, a sound strategy is critical, as are the people and processes for effective implementation. But identifying and managing risks inherent in achieving the company's business objectives plays a crucial role in whether the company will succeed, and indeed whether it will survive.

All too often, the problem is that the chief executive truly believes his or her senior management team understands what the risks are, has analyzed them, and is effectively managing them—when, in fact, the team doesn't know the risks as well as they should. I've seen this first-hand in major companies when advising how to enhance risk-management processes. Corollary realities are:

■ The board of directors often is not apprised of the risks, because the chief executive isn't positioned to provide relevant information to the board.
■ Managers at lower levels in the organization usually do know what the risks are, but are not reacting to them nor communicating them up to more senior levels.

While there are many companies where this is not the case, in too many businesses it is, and it's worth taking a moment to look at why.

## Going for the Gusto

Of course no single management style or personality profile fits all CEOs. Nevertheless, in many instances there are commonalities that influence how they focus on risk. First, chief executives typically have a laser-like focus on major growth and return objectives and the strategic and tactical plans needed to achieve them. They look at the positive, identifying opportunities to open new markets, bring new products to the marketplace, and recognize and satisfy customer needs and wants. On top of that, they're deal-doers, looking to develop new alliances or partners or to build further growth through acquisition. And of course, they spend significant amounts of time with the company's board of directors on an array of governance issues.

The point is, the chief executive's mind-set is forward-moving, seizing opportunities and motivating direct reports and other senior managers to climb aboard a ship that's going as fast as possible to the identified goal.

Yes, chief executives are well aware that risks exist. They or their companies might have been previously burned, and they may well spend some time on the discussion of risk factors in their annual reports' section on Management Discussion and Analysis. But what we've seen time and again is that many CEOs presume other senior managers are dealing with the possibility that things can go wrong and are well positioned and equipped to manage those risks. That presumption, made unconsciously or otherwise, has resulted in disaster for too many CEOs and the businesses they were running.

## The Reality

What we've seen is that other managers indeed do recognize that risks are inherent in what they're doing, more so as we move away from the C-suite. These managers deal with day-to-day implementation, working toward their individual and business unit goals. They usually recognize the pitfalls that exist and, depending on the risk-management process in place, may or may not take the necessary actions to counteract those risks.

But even where appropriate risk-management activities occur at some levels in an organization, a problem that happens too often—and which seems to be the culprit of major breakdowns in the large financial institutions—is that the communication simply isn't there. If the risks are known within an organization, which often is the case, but aren't known at the top, then communication is lacking. And if the CEO doesn't recognize the nature and magnitude of risk the company faces, then it's highly unlikely that the board is appropriately apprised.[2]

The words of Warren Buffett are worth a listen:

In my view a board of directors of a huge financial institution is derelict if it does not insist that its CEO bear full responsibility for risk control. If he's incapable of handling that job, he should look for other employment. And if he fails at it—with the government thereupon required to step in with funds or guarantees—the financial consequences for him and his board should be severe.

**NOTES**

1. For full disclosure, I have an indirect financial interest in several companies mentioned in this book, although my expressed observations about those companies are generally negative.
2. For more details on the financial system's near meltdown, readers might want to look through "Wall Street and the Financial Crisis: Anatomy of a Financial Collapse," the 650-page report issued by the Senate Permanent Subcommittee on Investigations. It's chock full of details on those who played a role in the crisis. With the report's issuance, Co-chairman Carl Levin pointed to "shoddy, risky, deceptive practices on the part of a lot of major financial institutions," and notes "the overwhelming evidence is that those institutions deceived their clients and deceived the public, and they were aided and abetted by deferential regulators and credit ratings agencies who had conflicts of interest."

# CHAPTER SIX

# What Is Risk Management About?

E KNOW THAT FINANCIAL institutions' risk management processes failed miserably in the near meltdown. Certainly effective risk management is critical to financial firms, but it's also important more broadly, as every company must deal with risk. It's well known that being in business is about accepting risk—what's essential is to know what the risks are and how to manage them to achieve business goals.

While many executives and directors have some knowledge of risk management and what's called enterprise risk management, I've seen first-hand that many continue to struggle in understanding exactly what they are, why they're needed, and how they work. In this chapter, we seek to provide clarity and insight into the whats, whys, and hows, with a particular focus on enterprise risk management.

Why bother with enterprise risk management? Well, among other things, ERM can help companies—at both the strategic and tactical levels—enhance risk-response decisions, reduce operational surprises (and related losses), identify and seize opportunities, and enhance deployment of capital. It's used by companies in deciding, for example, whether to invest in new product development, exploit new markets, or open new sales channels. It helps executives make strategic decisions, like whether to expand brick-and-mortar retail outlets or enhance Internet capabilities, or whether to migrate to enhance legacy systems or advance to a new technology platform. And ERM helps companies ascertain whether exposure to political, socioeconomic, or complex financial risks—like foreign-currency, commodity-price, or interest-rate movements—or risks at the process level, should be better managed to achieve operational goals. And it can help companies determine whether financial reporting or compliance processes need strengthening.

You may have noticed we jumped right over what risk is. We will deal with risk next, from both a conceptual and pragmatic perspective, then touch on risk management, and then focus on ERM.

##  RISK

Colloquially, we may talk of "taking a risk" when referring to such actions as starting a new business line or acquiring another company. But in context of risk management, risk means uncertainty surrounding a potential event. It is the possibility that something will happen—that is, an event will occur—with a negative outcome. The key here is possibility, meaning that an event might occur, not that something bad has already happened.

A while back I came across the writings of Peter Bernstein, editor of an economics and portfolio strategy newsletter, who brought forth an insightful perspective and simplicity to the topic of risk.

### The Four-Letter Word *Risk*

Given all the mismanagement we've seen, Bernstein refers to risk as a "four-letter word," and draws from Elroy Dimson of the London Business School in defining risk in the context of forecasts to mean that more things *can* happen than *will* happen.

Bernstein explains that we don't know what will happen, although we can devise probabilities of possible outcomes. But importantly, we will never know in advance the true range of outcomes we may face. In life, questions are posed: How will we deal with outcomes different from what we expect? What are the consequences of being wrong in our expectations? Risk means the chance of being wrong, of seeing outcomes different from what we expected. And key to that are the consequences of being wrong.

I would add that almost anything forecasted in a business context is going to be wrong. We don't know by how much the forecast will be wrong, or in which direction. What's critical to risk management, then, is recognizing the consequences of being wrong by a little or a lot, and making decisions to reduce those consequences to an acceptable level. The term *consequence* is analogous to *impact*, the commonly used word when talking about an adverse event's or circumstance's effect on a business.

## Making a Bet on God

For those of us who may still have difficulty grasping Bernstein's notion of risk management, we can look at another analogy he provides, drawn from an example put forth by a seventeenth century French mathematician. The illustration centers on the idea of betting on whether or not God exists.

It goes like this. If we presume God does exist and we lead a good life, we might find in the end that we were wrong. In that case we may have sacrificed a little along the way, perhaps forgoing some so-called fun. We also probably gained comfort from our belief, and felt good about and gained respect for our behavior. On the other hand, if we presume God does not exist and we lead a life of sin, then we may discover in the end that God indeed does exist—and we learn too late that the downside can be huge.

In other words, betting that the consequence is there, and planning accordingly, is wiser than betting that the consequence isn't there and plunging ahead recklessly.

The simplicity here contrasts with value-at-risk models and their *fat tails* or *black swans*, which refer to what might happen a relatively small percent of the time, based on past data fed into a model. Bernstein again brings the concept back to readily understood terms such as encountering rain after leaving home without an umbrella, where the consequences are minimal. On the other hand, betting the ranch on home prices only going up has huge consequences, as we've sadly seen in our financial system and economic plight.

When one ignores the black swans as being unrealistic, especially when depending only on recent years' data, or believes that forces are moving in only one direction—housing prices only going up—we court disaster. Risk management recognizes and considers the range of possibilities and consequences. As such, Bernstein says, we need to concentrate "either on limiting the size of the bet, or on finding ways to hedge the bet so you are not wiped out if you take the wrong side—if home prices do start to go down, or even stop rising."

## Ignore Risk at Your Peril

A fundamental reality is that things with seemingly little chance of occurring do in fact happen. And they happen more often than we expect them to. How many times in the last few decades have we seen a 100-year storm—either the weather kind or the business kind? Clearly an event occurring several times in a few decades happens more than once in 100 years. When we consider the savings-and-loan fiasco, the junk bond debacle, the dot-com bubble, several economic recessions, and the recent near meltdown of the financial system and credit markets seizure, we know this so-called perfect storm happens with relative frequency. Former SEC Chairman Harvey Pitt said it well: "Rare events aren't all that rare. Lightning does strike twice, and the unimaginable occurs more frequently than most of us believe. It's important to expect the unexpected—while that may seem as if it's an oxymoron, it's actually a good prescription for avoiding cautionary tales." Quite simply, just because something is unlikely to happen doesn't mean it won't happen.

We're also talking here about bringing old-fashioned common sense to the table. A producer of a public radio show tells how he asked an experienced business reporter: "Why are they lending money to people who can't afford to pay it back?" The reporter patiently explained about collateralized debt obligations, yield and risk curves, and increasing amounts of international capital in need of investment. But the producer still "couldn't understand how they could expect to be paid off when everyone I know was maxed out on their credit cards."

The producer then found a man whose house was in foreclosure, did not have a full-time job or any assets to speak of, and yet had received a loan of $450,000. The producer asked this man whether he would have loaned a guy like himself the money. His response is telling: "I wouldn't have loaned me the money. And nobody I know would have loaned me the money. I know guys who are criminals who wouldn't loan me that, and they break kneecaps."

A key lesson to be learned from these past failures is that risk management is not rocket science, and those who make it more complicated than it is are asking for trouble.

So, what are some of the types of risk businesses face? Examples range almost as wide as one's imagination, and we've seen them all rear their ugly heads: a hurricane destroying a crop, production machinery failing, in-appropriately disclosing customers' personal financial information, losing key personnel, overstating revenue in financial statements, customers ignoring a new product launch, and commodity-price fluctuations. Certainly, there even are risks inherent in these risks, such as a new product launch being ignored because incorrect market research data is being used. Risks exist at many levels and need to be considered at a level that's pragmatic and manageable.

 ## RISK MANAGEMENT

What then is risk management? Myriad definitions exist but suffice it to say it involves identifying a risk, understanding it and its implications, and doing something about it—either to lessen the likelihood of the event occurring or its impact, or making it go away altogether.

Importantly, it's not about reacting to a problem after it occurs. There's a good example of how one organization is moving from a reactionary mode to instituting risk management—perhaps surprisingly, it comes from the federal government.

In December 2010 the U.S. House of Representatives passed a bill, expected to be signed by the President, to make the nation's food supply safer. It was in reaction to illness and deaths among the American public from such foodborne diseases as salmonella from eggs and peanuts and *E. coli* from spinach. According to surrounding media reports, here's what the law will change:

- Rather than reacting after the fact to outbreaks of such diseases, with warnings and recalls, the focus will be on disease prevention.
- Food manufacturers must assess their systems to identify ways food could be contaminated, and come up with detailed plans to prevent contamination.
- Companies are required to provide plans to the Food and Drug Administration, along with results of product tests showing how effectively they're being carried out.
- The FDA will conduct frequent inspections.
- The FDA's inspections will extend to other countries where food is processed for export to the United States.
- The FDA will have expanded authority, going from its current ability of requesting a food recall to being able to order recalls.

What we have here is a basic risk management process, designed and implemented by those directly responsible for dealing with the risk. The system extends to what is analogous to outsourcers. There's monitoring by an independent function, and there's oversight with the power to effect action where necessary. There also are implicit cost-benefit considerations, as the system will apply to only 80 percent of the regulated food supply, and high-risk plants will be inspected more frequently than low-risk ones. And budget realities may come into play, as Congress still has to appropriate the funds to make it work.

Another example from the government involves NASA, where failure to manage risk resulted in disaster. Around 1990 a researcher identified a risk that heat-resistant tiles protecting space shuttles during reentry into Earth's atmosphere could be damaged by debris from the shuttles' insulating foam. Well, as we know, years later, in 2003, the Columbia disintegrated, with the foam identified as the cause. Of course, only then was corrective action taken, including a reportedly thorough process to assess and better manage risks going forward.

Both of these government actions are a result of events that caused damage, and indeed loss of life. Establishing or enhancing processes to managing risks related to events that have already occurred in the past is extremely important. But just as relevant is identifying potential events that have not yet happened but could in the future. It's about looking around the corner, seeing what could go wrong and taking action to manage those risks before they wreak havoc. Because there's a good likelihood the next big problem will be something that has not happened before.

In a business environment, risk management is a process that involves looking at events that could occur to derail a strategic plan, a marketing program, production processes, reliable financial reporting, adherence to laws and regulations, and myriad other company objectives—and understanding the implications and taking action to mitigate the risks. But as we'll see, it's not only about avoiding the downside. Importantly, the process also includes identifying opportunities that can help the company better achieve its business goals.

 **ENTERPRISE RISK MANAGEMENT**

Okay, on to enterprise risk management. At the risk of putting the cart before the horse, let's look at common misconceptions of ERM. The reality is that many people use the term to mean very different things.

Unfortunately, the term *ERM* has been used in connection with buying insurance to cover specified risks, dealing in financial instruments, and deciding what new corporate initiatives should be approved. Indeed, managers in every company navigate a wide range of business risks on a daily basis in seeking to achieve corporate objectives. But often this is done ad hoc with dramatically varying scopes, results, and consequences. All of this involves some aspect of risk management, but it isn't ERM.

In many companies, internal auditors assess risks to determine where to devote limited audit resources in the audit process and to provide relevant information to management. Sometimes management teams conduct broad-based risk assessments. In these exercises risks may be categorized and rated or ranked, sometimes using heat maps or other graphic depictions, providing important analyses to management and to the board. It's important to recognize, however, that by definition risk assessments are simply snapshots at a point in time and do not represent an ongoing process for identification and analysis of continuing and newly emerging risks and decision-making on how they need to be managed.

What, then, is ERM? One can look to any number of sources for a definition, but the one many if not most knowledgeable users use is the COSO report *Enterprise Risk Management—Integrated Framework.*[1] It defines enterprise risk management; sets out its principles, objectives, and components; and highlights effective application techniques.

ERM is a company's holistic process to identify, assess, and manage risk that could interfere with achieving any of its corporate objectives. In simpler terms, it is a systematic approach to dealing with all risks with reasonable likelihood of significantly affecting a business. Once those potentialities are identified, management analyzes the risks and determines what to do to manage them. This may involve taking action to reduce or eliminate the risk or doing nothing if the risk is already within the company's risk tolerances.

ERM encompasses eight components, beginning with the control environment and objective setting; centering on risk identification, assessment, and responses; and including control activities, information and communication, and monitoring. These components are outlined in Exhibit 6.1, though to fully grasp what's involved it's useful to spend some time with the source. The COSO ERM report describes what effective ERM entails and provides underlying principles and pragmatic application techniques.

**EXHIBIT 6.1**   Categories of Objectives and Components of Enterprise Risk Management

---

ERM is designed to achieve a company's business objectives, set forth in four categories:

1. Strategic: high-level goals, aligned with and supporting its mission
2. Operations: effective and efficient use of its resources
3. Reporting: reliability of reporting
4. Compliance: compliance with applicable laws and regulations

**Components of Enterprise Risk Management**

ERM consists of eight interrelated components derived from the way management runs the company, and integrated with the management process.

1. **Internal Environment.** The internal environment encompasses the tone of an organization, and sets the basis for how risk is viewed and addressed by an entity's people, including risk management philosophy and risk appetite, integrity and ethical values, and the environment in which they operate.
2. **Objective Setting.** Objectives must exist before management can identify potential events affecting their achievement. Enterprise risk management ensures that management has in place a process to set objectives and that the chosen objectives support and align with the entity's mission and are consistent with its risk appetite.
3. **Event Identification.** Internal and external events affecting achievement of an entity's objectives must be identified, distinguishing between risks and opportunities. Opportunities are channeled back to management's strategy or objective-setting processes.
4. **Risk Assessment.** Risks are analyzed, considering likelihood and impact, as a basis for determining how they should be managed. Risks are assessed on an inherent and a residual basis.
5. **Risk Response.** Management selects risk responses—avoiding, accepting, reducing, or sharing risk—developing a set of actions to align risks with the entity's risk tolerances and risk appetite.
6. **Control Activities.** Policies and procedures are established and implemented to help ensure the risk responses are effectively carried out.
7. **Information and Communication.** Relevant information is identified, captured, and communicated in a form and time frame that enable people to carry out their responsibilities. Effective communication also occurs in a broader sense, flowing down, across, and up the entity.
8. **Monitoring.** The entirety of enterprise risk management is monitored and modifications are made as necessary. Monitoring is accomplished through ongoing management activities, separate evaluations, or both.

To get a better sense of what ERM involves, we can look at some of the key characteristics of an effective ERM process:

- Risks are understood in context of business strategy and linked objectives.
- Managing risk is ongoing, baked into the business processes and fabric of the organization with real-time identification, assessment, and management.
- The organization has a shared view of risk and a common language.
- There's a disciplined approach aligning objectives, processes, people, and technology.
- Risks are openly acknowledged and discussed with clear responsibilities for managing.
- Managers receive information to identify and manage risks.
- Risk information is communicated up, across, and down the organization.
- Risks are brought within established risk tolerances.
- Opportunities are identified and seized.
- Risks are managed not only individually, but also on an aggregate basis.
- Management and the board attain a portfolio view of risk.
- Risk is managed within the company's risk appetite.
- Capital is allocated based on growth, risk, and return.

To be effective, ERM must encompass all eight components as described in the COSO report, but ERM will never be exactly the same in any two companies. To be useful, it must fit the company's strategic direction, organization, and culture. ERM can fit a company with little formality in management style or one with highly structured management processes. Inherent in all ERM processes, however, is the discipline in the process and that it operates *throughout* the organization. ERM initially was called enterprise-wide risk management; the "-wide" was dropped for convenience, but the concept remains. If it doesn't have the requisite discipline, scope, and function throughout an organization, we call it risk management, not enterprise risk management.

Another way of looking at ERM that has proved useful is put forth by a colleague of mine who is a corporate chief risk officer:

> Fundamentally, ERM is about building a healthy organizational immune system. ERM is simply business management with a more systematic and deliberate focus on risk. It builds risk thinking into the fabric of an organization, institutionalizing a company's ability to identify risks, assess their impact and respond within the context of

business objectives. It breaks down silos and connects the dots across an organization to enable the best decisions about allocating capital and solving systemic problems.[2]

ERM enables a sharp focus not only on the downside, but also on upside potential. By identifying potential events with ability to affect achievement of business objectives, an organization is positioned to look at what might open doors as well as close them. Shifting customer needs and preferences, new logistics capabilities, upheaval in sourcing availability, advances in technology, and new domestic and foreign laws and regulations all can harm businesses or benefit those with sufficient foresight, creativity, and agility.

As noted, ERM must be pervasive in scope and built into an organization's management processes. While it's not possible in this space to describe any one company's ERM process, we can get a sense of how several companies have incorporated enterprise risk management into their organizations. A key point is it doesn't have to be overly complex, and can and should fit a company's individual circumstances and management style:

- *Mid-size financial services company.* To fit with its face-to-face management approach and to avoid unnecessary administrative activity, one company's management decided to deal with risk in its monthly management meetings. A limited portion of each meeting is devoted to identifying new, emerging risks and related opportunities, with qualitative analysis and actions decided then and there to manage the risks or to seize the opportunities, except for those requiring further analysis, where assignments are made for subsequent follow-up. This process is in place at all management levels, and risks and related actions are reported upstream through normal in-person communications. One manager is tasked with tracking significant risks and actions, and providing a portfolio view of risk to the CEO and the board.
- *Large consumer products company.* Another company's management decided that somewhat more structure was needed, and began the ERM process in the annual strategic planning and budgeting process. The process was brought to the entire organization, where identified risks and opportunities are considered as part of the ongoing management process, and recorded on a simple, one-page template. Most risks are analyzed qualitatively, although quantitative techniques are used where needed. The template serves as a focal point for managers at every level as

well as an upstream communications mechanism to track risk and action plans on an ongoing basis.

■ *Large financial institution.* This organization uses sophisticated methodology to identify and assess risk. The corporate center takes the lead in risk analysis, quantitatively assessing credit, market, interest rate, liquidity, and other risk categories. Operational risks are considered by managers throughout the organization, and software is used to communicate risk-related information, including summarization where appropriate, establishing accountabilities for agreed-upon actions to manage the risks, and developing portfolio information for senior management and the board for making capital allocation decisions.

This, of course, is a high-level overview of elements of how these companies approached ERM.

 ## IS IT REALLY WORTH THE EFFORT?

While simple in concept, implementing an ERM process does take time and effort and carries associated costs. But not knowing what risks a company faces is dangerous, and engaging in limited risk-management activities in an undefined or ad hoc manner can lead to unwanted surprises at best, and the kinds of disasters outlined earlier at worst. Imagine driving a car on an unfamiliar back road at night with parking lights only and part of the windshield covered with mud. You know where you want to go, and with all the best intentions you think you know how to get there, but you don't know what's out there that could keep you from arriving timely and safely. The result could be as minor as hitting a pothole and popping a tire or as disastrous as going too fast around a sharp curve and tumbling off a cliff.

Management needs to know what could keep the company from achieving its business objectives, as well as what opportunities can help it get there. On that back road there could be a sign to a new highway that would cut the travel time in half, which the driver could take if only he saw the sign. Another oft-used auto analogy for opportunity goes like this: A key reason a racing car has great brakes is to allow it to go faster. Analogies aside, suffice it to say here that in order to manage risks and seize opportunities, companies need to know what's coming and to act proactively.

Companies continually deal with factors that create uncertainty: globalization, technology, restructurings, changing markets, competition, and regulation, to name a few. Uncertainty also is inherent in a company's strategic choices. For example, a company that has a growth strategy based on expanding foreign operations faces risks and opportunities related to stability of the overseas country's political environment, resources, markets, channels, workforce capabilities, and cost structure. ERM enables management to deal effectively with uncertainty by:[3]

- *Aligning risk appetite and strategy.* Management considers the company's risk appetite in evaluating strategic alternatives, setting objectives, and developing mechanisms to manage the related risks. To protect its brand value, a pharmaceutical company with a low-risk appetite relative to its brand value maintains extensive protocols to ensure product safety and regularly invests in early-stage research and development to support its brand-value creation.
- *Enhancing risk-response decisions.* ERM provides the rigor to identify and select among alternative risk responses. Management of a company that uses company-owned and -operated vehicles recognizes risks inherent in its delivery process, including vehicle damage and personal injury costs. Alternatives considered with ERM techniques include reducing the risk through effective driver recruiting and training, avoiding the risk by outsourcing delivery, sharing the risk via insurance, or simply accepting the risk.
- *Reducing operational surprises and losses.* By providing the enhanced capability to identify potential events, assess risk, and establish responses, ERM reduces surprises and related costs or losses. A manufacturing company tracks production parts and equipment failure rates and deviation around averages, and assesses the effect of such factors as time to repair, ability to meet customer demand, employee safety, and the cost of scheduled versus unscheduled repairs, and responds by setting maintenance schedules accordingly.
- *Identifying and managing cross-enterprise risks.* Effective management involves not only managing individual risks, but also understanding interrelated impacts. A bank faces a variety of risks in trading activities across the enterprise, and management developed an information system that analyzes transaction and market data from internal systems. Together with relevant externally generated information, this system provides an aggregate view of risks across trading activities. It provides drill-down capability to department, customer or counterparty, trader, and transaction levels and quantifies the risks relative to tolerances in established

categories, bringing together previously disparate data to respond effectively to risks.

- *Providing integrated responses to multiple risks.* Business processes carry many inherent risks, and ERM enables integrated solutions. A wholesale distributor faces risks of over- and undersupply positions, tenuous supply sources, and unnecessarily high purchase prices. Management identified and assessed the risks in context of the company's strategy, objectives, and alternative responses, and developed a far-reaching inventory control system. The system integrates with suppliers, sharing sales and inventory information and enabling strategic partnering, and avoiding stock-outs and unneeded carrying costs, with longer-term sourcing contracts, enhanced pricing, and suppliers taking responsibility for replenishing stock.

- *Seizing opportunities.* By considering a full range of potential events, rather than just risks, management identifies opportunities. Years ago a large money-center bank learned customers could no longer readily get to branches during normal banking hours, confronting a need to extend hours with the associated costs or loss of business. Turning risk into opportunity, it devised a machine that gave customers the figurative keys to the bank, and the resulting ATM changed retail banking dynamics. More recently, a food company considered the potential events likely to affect its sustainable revenue-growth objective. Management determined that the company's primary consumers are increasingly health-conscious and changing their dietary preferences, indicating a decline in the future demand for the company's current products. Management identified ways to apply its existing capabilities to developing new products, enabling the company not only to preserve revenue from existing customers but also to create additional revenue by appealing to a broader consumer base.

- *Improving the deployment of capital.* Obtaining robust information on risk allows management to assess overall capital needs effectively and enhance capital allocation. A financial institution became subject to new regulatory rules that would increase capital requirements unless management calculated credit- and operational-risk levels and related capital needs with greater precision. The company assessed the risk in terms of system development cost versus additional capital costs and made an informed decision: With existing, readily modifiable software, the institution developed the more precise calculations, avoiding a need for additional capital sourcing.

These capabilities of ERM are real, enabling management to create value for companies' shareholders. And ERM provides boards of directors comfort not only that management is positioned to protect the company's reputation and achieve growth and return objectives, but also that the board knows that it is receiving the information necessary for it to properly carry out its oversight responsibilities.

## ERM APPLICATION TECHNIQUES

There's an almost infinite number of techniques businesses use in applying ERM, of which some of more effective ones are described in the *Application Techniques* volume of the COSO ERM report. They're organized around the *Framework*'s eight components, with descriptions and illustrations of how the techniques are used. If you're looking for more in-depth guidance in applying ERM, I recommend spending time with that material. In the space available here, let's look at a few of those techniques.

### Internal Environment

The internal environment is similar to the control environment in internal control, and is the foundation on which an effective ERM process rests. Among the techniques available to ensure a strong internal environment is use of what's called a *risk-related culture survey*, which enables management to gain insight directly from its people into how well the company's risk-management philosophy is integrated into the organization's culture.

Well-constructed surveys allow management to keep its finger on the pulse of the organization, which is especially helpful during times of change. The results—which can be in numerical or heat-map form—provide directional indicators of areas of strength and weakness in the organization's risk culture and a basis for management to zero in on where attention is needed. As with many surveys, while raw scores are telling, more relevant are directions and rates of change over time. An example of how survey questions can be presented and interpreted is presented on page 8 of the *Application Techniques* volume.

### Objective Setting

ERM involves establishing how much risk a company is prepared to take, stated in qualitative or quantitative terms as its *risk appetite*. One technique enables management, in setting the company's business objectives, to view capital at risk versus return in relation to its risk appetite. The relationship can be presented in graphical form with return on the vertical axis and capital at risk on the horizontal, with linear depiction of its target risk-return profile. Within the profile are business units or strategic initiatives showing the current state of risk return, and the target state.

As illustrated in the *Application Techniques* volume (page 18), a company seeks to diversify its business initiatives to earn a return in sync with its target profile. The graphic shows where the company is currently and where it wants to go, reflecting how much risk it's prepared to take on. This also facilitates aligning corporate objectives with the risk appetite, providing a basis for establishing risk tolerances.

## Event Identification

With ERM, management identifies potential events that could affect the company and determines whether they represent risks or opportunities affecting its ability to implement strategy successfully and achieve its objectives. In addition to considering individual potential events, management needs to consider the effect of multiple related events. To gain insight into interrelationships, some companies use event-tree diagrams, also known as fishbone diagrams. These provide a means by which to identify and graphically represent uncertainty, generally focusing on one objective and how multiple events affect its achievement.

An example in the *Application Techniques* volume (page 31) focuses on a company's objective of achieving a 30 percent gross margin on sales. The fishbone diagram identifies internal and external factors that drive factors and events affecting product demand and cost of production, which in turn affect achievement of the 30 percent margin objective. With this depiction of the relationships, management is positioned to better understand and deal with those primary drivers and related factors and events.

Among other event identification techniques are use of event inventories, facilitated workshops, interviews, questionnaires, surveys, process flow analysis, leading event indicators, escalation triggers, and loss event data tracking.

## Risk Assessment

Risk assessment allows management to consider what effect identified potential events may have on achieving the company's objectives. Management assesses events from two perspectives—likelihood of occurrence and impact—and normally uses a combination of qualitative and quantitative methods to measure the effect and any of a number of different methods to portray the assessment. Risk maps, for example, may take the form of heat maps or process charts that plot quantitative or qualitative estimates of risk likelihood and impact.

One example depicts assessment of risks relating to the objective of retaining high-performing employees. Likelihood of the event occurring is shown on the horizontal axis, its potential impact on the vertical, with risk factors presented on the grid in the form of bubbles representing estimated ranges. You can see the graphic on page 49 of the *Application Techniques* volume. This portrayal facilitates management's development of responses to those risks that are most significant, in turn enhancing its ability to achieve the stated objective.

Risk-assessment techniques can be used to focus on either inherent risk, residual risk, or both, and allow management to assess the effect of a single event on multiple business objectives. Among techniques available are such qualitative techniques as ranking and questionnaires, and quantitative approaches such as probabilistic techniques (value at risk, market value at risk, loss distributions, and back-testing) and nonprobabilistic techniques including sensitivity analysis, scenario analysis, stress testing, and benchmarking. Also available are techniques for risk and capital attribution used to estimate the amount of capital required for accepted risks, portraying risks with heat maps or numerical presentations, and techniques for entity-level views of risk.

## Risk Response

ERM involves management's determination of how it plans to respond to risk, either by avoiding it altogether, reducing it, sharing it, or accepting the risk with a response that brings residual risk within desired risk tolerances. Management also identifies opportunities that might be available.

Responses to risk management could involve any of a broad range of actions. Risk avoidance, for example, might involve disposing of a business unit, product line, or geographical segment, or deciding not to engage in new initiatives or activities that would give rise to the risks. Risk reduction might involve diversifying product offerings, establishing operational limits, enhancing business processes, strengthening management's decision making and monitoring, rebalancing asset portfolios to reduce exposure to specified types of losses, and reallocating capital among operating units.

Sharing risks might involve such actions as obtaining insurance coverage for significant unexpected loss; entering into joint ventures, partnerships, or syndication agreements; hedging risks through capital market instruments; outsourcing business processes; or sharing risk through contractual agreements with customers, vendors, or other business partners.

And then there's making an informed decision to accept the risks, which might involve "self-insuring" against loss (that is, simply not purchasing insurance coverage), relying on natural offsets within a portfolio, or determining that the associated risk already conforms to risk tolerances.

Ultimately, management takes an entity-wide, or portfolio, view of risk, determining whether overall residual risk is within the company's risk appetite. This is an integral part of ERM and can be depicted in one of several ways. One example illustrated in the *Application Techniques* volume (page 62) shows, by major risk, the inherent risk, related risk responses, and the residual risk in terms of effect on the company's earnings per share. Another example (page 61) presents a graphic with frequency of occurrence on the horizontal axis, impact on operating earnings on the vertical, and major event categories in quantitative form via arrows within the grid. These techniques present valuable information to senior management and the board in readily understandable terms.

\* \* \*

The *Application Techniques* volume also presents techniques related to the other COSO ERM components—control activities, information and communication, and monitoring—which also are worth a look.

When giving presentations on ERM, I sometimes say tongue-in-cheek that the COSO ERM report is a sure cure for any attendees with a case of insomnia. Well, while that may be true, the report indeed does have a great deal of important information on how companies are successfully using ERM techniques. So readers are well advised to also find some daylight hours to take a good look at what's there.

 ## KEY RISK INDICATORS

The COSO *Application Techniques* volume touches on the topic of key risk indicators (KRIs), but use of KRIs has continued to evolve. In recent years, along with key performance indicators (KPIs), which focus primarily on past performance, more organizations have incorporated forward looking key risk indicators into their ERM processes, further enhancing effectiveness. To provide additional guidance, COSO recently issued *Developing Key Risk Indicators to Strengthen Enterprise Risk Management—How Key Risk Indicators Can Sharpen Focus on Emerging Risk,* which explains KRIs and how they can be of benefit. A couple of simple examples are illustrative:

- One deals with customer credit, where a common KPI includes data about customer delinquencies and write-offs. KRIs are developed to help anticipate future collection issues, focusing on analysis of reported financial results of a company's 25 largest customers or general collection challenges throughout the industry to see what trends might be emerging among customers that could potentially signal challenges related to collection efforts going forward.
- Another involves a chain of family-style restaurants where management sought to avoid a negative earnings event that could arise with unexpected market conditions. Recognizing that restaurant traffic is directly affected by customers' discretionary income—where as discretionary income levels fall off, customers are less likely to dine out—management establishes as a KRI average gasoline prices people pay at the pump. This is based on the premise that when gasoline prices rise, discretionary income for individuals and families representing their core customer base decreases, and customer traffic begins to drop.

KRIs enable management to take quicker action in dealing with the risks. In the later example, management is positioned to adjust marketing and promotion events to reduce the impact of the risk.

Importantly, KRIs are most effective when closest to the ultimate root cause of the risk event, providing more time for management to act proactively. Multiple KRIs can provide still more relevant information, keeping in mind that a close relationship between a KRI and the risk, and accuracy of information used, are both critical. Another benefit is the ability to readily track trend lines with dashboards or exception reports, quickly and easily communicating where action may be needed. With KRIs gaining recognition as important elements of enterprise risk management, this COSO guidance provides readily usable information and is worth the read.

 **BP**

To better grasp what needs to go right in risk identification, assessment, and management, let's look at something that went terribly wrong at one major company: BP. In looking over these highlights, you might want to consider what likely would have been very different if the company had an effective risk management process founded on a culture based on integrity and ethical values with the desired tone at the top.

When the *Deepwater Horizon* offshore oil rig exploded on April 20, 2010, it killed 11 workers and wreaked economic ruin across the Gulf Coast states and environmental ruin along the coastal shoreline. For months, efforts failed to stop the continuing undersea oil spill. What went wrong? We're not inside BP, but media reports provide a good indication of what happened and what can be learned from this horrible disaster.

Context here is important. Until the *Deepwater Horizon* went down in flames, we might have forgotten other disasters that had befallen BP. Its Texas City, Texas, refinery exploded in 2005, killing 15 workers. Its pipeline on Alaska's North Slope ruptured in 2006, spilling 200,000 gallons of crude oil. Going back to 2003, a BP platform in the North Sea endured a violent release of pressured gas; the station avoided an explosion only by sheer luck, and BP later admitted to breaking safety laws by failing to guard against corrosion of the ruptured pipe.

Safety violations are numerous, including more than 700 at the Texas City refinery alone. Many relate to critical temperature and pressure valves, and BP's Toledo, Ohio, refinery has been cited for willful safety violations. Regulators cited the company for "serious safety and production incidents" in recent years in Prudhoe Bay, the nation's largest oil field, and they are now investigating allegations of safety violations at the *Atlantis PQ*, one of BP's newest offshore drilling platforms in the Gulf of Mexico.

When CEO Tony Hayward took over in 2007, he admitted, "Our operations failed to meet our own standards and the requirements of the law," and pledged to improve its risk management. On the whole, Hayward's words seem not to have had much effect. Federal officials and industry experts say BP continued to lag other oil companies on safety. As one official from the Occupational Safety and Health Administration put it: "BP has systemic safety and health problems . . . They need to take their intentions and apply them much more effectively on the ground, where the hazards actually lie."

## Managing the Risks

Companies engaged in offshore drilling know full well they face significant risks, so we can safely presume BP management was aware of what might go wrong. The real challenge is analyzing those risks and deciding how to bring them to an acceptable level. Looking at just a few of the decisions BP made in the *Deepwater Horizon* well, we find:

- For the well itself, BP used a *long string* design, rather than a *liner tieback*. In layman's terms, the long string is easier and cheaper to build and doesn't have the safety features of the liner tieback.
- BP ignored "deviations from normal industry practices," including such danger signals as evidence of a torn gasket and other problems in the blowout preventer.
- In attempting to seal the "nightmare well," to save time and money BP decided to remove heavy drilling mud and replace it with much lighter sea water. The pressure bearing down on the well no longer exceeded the upward pressure of the buildup of gas, directly resulting in the blowout.

The national commission that investigated the disaster reportedly said, among other things, that BP management had known of problems evidenced by negative pressure and other test results, and decided to avoid the cost of installing a lockdown sleeve safely device—and the commission concluded that, overall, the "explosive loss" could have been prevented. While we don't know all the details surrounding how and why these fateful decisions were made, fingers point back to the overriding issue discussed in Chapter 2—the company's culture.

## Embedded in the Culture

Hayward's promise to improve safety may have been comforting. And we know actions begin with what a CEO says. But we also know that words without actions provide unfounded comfort at best, and are counterproductive and dangerous at worst.

At least two people with intimate knowledge of BP's attitude toward safety provide damning evidence that BP's culture was toxic. Going back some years, Oberon Houston was a rising star in BP's engineering management group who saw firsthand BP's approach to safety. Reports say Houston was distressed with the following:

- Layoffs "seemed to target the best and most seasoned engineers, [and BP] had slashed the maintenance budget for the vast and aged Forties Alpha platform [which suffered the near blowout] to a dangerous, even reckless extent."

- BP "was taking on increasingly ambitious exploration and production challenges, while demonstrating an increasingly indifferent or cavalier attitude toward engineering discipline and excellence. On top of all that, senior management seemed less than fully engaged in the difficult task of extracting and producing petroleum."
- "Senior BP management focused so heavily on the easy part of safety— holding the hand rails, spending hours discussing the merits of reverse parking, and the dangers of not having a lid on a coffee cup—but were less enthusiastic about the hard stuff, investing in and maintaining their complex facilities."[4]

To his credit, Houston walked the talk and left the company.

## Failures in Managing Risk

An engineering professor and expert on offshore platform disasters brought in by the company to study its approach to catastrophic risk management says: "BP worried a lot about personal safety—slips, trips, and falls—high frequency, low consequence accidents. They did not worry as much (at all) about the low frequency, high consequence accidents—the real disasters."

The picture we see is a company that talks a good game but puts short-term profit before potential environmental disaster, and indeed potential destruction of the company itself.

We can contrast the workings of BP against some of the basics of what a successful company should do to manage its major risks:

- *Communication.* Critical information must flow up, down, and across an organization, and be heard and acted upon. Management must hear concerns of their direct reports, cascading up and through the organization, filtering out the unimportant and focusing intently on what matters. This takes communication processes and protocols, but also judgment to know what's truly relevant. Part of an effective communication process involves a whistleblower process, where employees can bypass the deaf ears of superiors. It's been reported that at BP this system did not work. Regarding *Deepwater Horizon* specifically, "The rig survivors . . . said it was always understood that you could get fired if you raised safety concerns that might delay drilling. Some co-workers had been fired for speaking out."

- *Respond to high-impact risks.* Most executives know the importance of identifying risks based on the likelihood of an event occurring and on the related effect if the risk were to happen. High-probability, high-impact risks therefore get much attention. But too often a low-probability event that could destroy a company doesn't get the attention deserved. This certainly was the case with BP, which found itself struggling for its very survival. And with the company's history of disastrous events, one could say that the *Deepwater Horizon* tragedy didn't carry such a low likelihood at all.
- *Preventive and corrective.* Companies must act to prevent risks from ever happening, yes, and there are a number of ways to do that. But for something like offshore drilling, they must also be ready to fix a problem immediately and effectively if it ever does occur. What should *not* happen is after-the-fact trial and error, hoping to find some solution to a spill after a well is already gushing oil. It's been reported that in some parts of the world, for example, offshore drilling requires simultaneous drilling of relief wells—so that when a spill on the main well happens, the relief wells are already in place to stem the damage. That seems much wiser than spending months to drill relief wells after the fact.[5]
- *Board-management interface.* A board of directors must know what management is doing to identify, analyze, and manage the company's risks. Indications are that the BP board did not get sufficiently involved in ensuring management was doing its job in managing risk. One alternative possibility is that the board was comfortable with an extraordinarily high corporate risk appetite, where it was willing for management to put the entire company at risk, although that would seem unlikely.

Well, BP is paying a heavy price, with some cost estimates reaching US$40 billion. Hundreds of lawsuits reportedly have been filed, with a recent one taking an interesting tack: charging securities fraud. Reports say institutional investors—two large state pension funds—accused the company and senior officials, including the former and current CEOs, of lying about how committed they were to safety. The plaintiffs say past disasters and internal communications were ignored amid claims of safety consciousness while cutting health, safety, security, environment and compliance staff and budgets—and breaking U.S. securities laws by misleading investors.

The U.S. Department of Justice has filed civil charges, and is looking at the Clean Water, Oil Pollution, and Endangered Species Acts. It reportedly also is investigating whether CEO Hayward's and other BP executives' testimony in

Congressional hearings was consistent with what they actually knew at the time. And the Justice Department is considering criminal manslaughter charges against BP managers in connection with decisions they made leading up to the *Deepwater Horizon* explosion. The U.S. Attorney General has vowed to "prosecute to the full extent any violations of the law."

In observing what happened at BP, I'm reminded of what Citigroup's CEO said in 2007 before the financial system's near meltdown: "When the music stops, in terms of liquidity, things will be complicated, but as long as the music is playing, you've got to get up and dance. We're still dancing." This statement smacks of several incredible assertions, also applicable to BP: first, that it's just fine to reap short-term profits regardless of a disaster waiting to happen, and second, that until a major disaster strikes, there's no need to focus on risk!

Maybe BP management has learned something from this disaster. Under CEO Robert Dudley the company reportedly has instituted new safety standards and has turned down drilling rigs that didn't meet BP's standards. He also said BP halted operations where problems were noted: "We have shut . . . one production platform to repair the fire water pumps, and a producing field was shut down to enable pipeline integrity work to be carried out." Dudley adds, "When we see a problem we want to be able to stop operations—we are rewarding people for doing that. This is part of the cultural change." Well, that's a good thing, though it seems BP still is talking about taking action after a problem has already reared its ugly head.

It appears still more learning is needed. With a joint venture with Russian partner TKN-BP in place, Dudley entered a multi–billion dollar deal with Russian oil company Rosneft, causing the joint venture shareholders to become outraged and take legal action to kill the new deal. This episode raises an entirely new set of questions about how well Dudley and BP are managing major risks, accused by some of having badly misread Russia's legal and power systems. But wait—how is this possible, with Dudley having worked in Russia as TKN-BP's CEO until he was, well, thrown out of the country? Some analysts are now questioning whether the company will have any future in Russia, which is said to be the world's largest oil producer and is where TKN-BP has one quarter of BP's total gas reserves.

There's one point I'd like to leave you with here, and I apologize for being repetitive, but it's a point that's often overlooked. It's that risk is not about what has happened—rather, it's about what could happen. And even risks that may appear unlikely to occur that could destroy a company need to be dealt with. What's happened at BP indeed provides lessons for us all.

**NOTES**

1. COSO is the Committee of Sponsoring Organizations of the Treadway Commission. For full disclosure, I led the PricewaterhouseCoopers team that developed this framework. The ERM framework is built on the Internal Control—Integrated Framework, used in conjunction with reporting under SOX 404, and is discussed in Chapter 8. Among other reports on risk management some find useful are ISO 31000, issued by the International Organization for Standardization, and AS/NZS 4360, issued by a joint committee established by Standards Australia and Standards New Zealand.
2. Rick Machold, Head of Enterprise Risk at Invesco, Ltd.
3. Based on the COSO ERM report.
4. CBS News.com, June 22, 2010.
5. Reported on MSNBC, May 24, 2010. An industry executive says, however, that simultaneous drilling of relief wells is not required, but rather drillers must have proven access to another drilling unit in the event a relief well is required.

# 7

# Implementing ERM

F AT THIS POINT you're sufficiently interested in enterprise risk management, you probably want to know what's involved in implementation. In this chapter, we look first at where the impetus for implementation usually comes from, and then at what experience shows does and doesn't work in successfully establishing an effective ERM process.

 **DRIVERS FOR ERM**

What drives ERM implementation? In some cases senior management realizes it doesn't really have a good handle on what risks out there could jump up and bite the company. Executives may be aware that they don't know what dangers are lurking and want to be proactive in avoiding unpleasant if not disastrous surprises. They may have heard a good deal about enterprise risk management and decided to gain the associated advantages.

While that scenario sometimes plays out, quite frankly it's rarely what happens, especially when we're talking about a company's chief executive. CEOs typically are focusing primarily on future goals and working hard to carry out strategic plans to profitably grow the business. The vast majority of

CEOs I've worked with are optimists, seeing the potential of the business and motivating their people in the organization to stay on course to get the company where they want it to go.

So where does the impetus for ERM normally come from, if not from the CEO? Typically it comes from one of two sources—the board of directors or senior management staff.

## Directors

To properly carry out its oversight responsibilities, the board must be comfortable that management is doing a good job in identifying and managing risk. And it's difficult for a board to gain such comfort unless it knows that management has an organized process for risk management.

Boards' focus springs from other sources as well. A primary driver is the New York Stock Exchange listing requirement that a board's audit committee focus on the company's risk assessment and risk management. And boards of many companies not listed on the NYSE look to those standards as best practice. Beyond the NYSE rules, boards are mindful of the Securities and Exchange Commission and Justice Department enforcement programs that weigh a company's compliance initiatives to prevent and detect misconduct and the U.S. Federal Sentencing Guidelines, which explicitly speak to how a company addresses the risk of criminal conduct. Directors are well aware that regulators are looking for the companies they oversee, especially those in the financial services industries, to maintain effective programs for disclosing and managing risk. And directors can't and don't ignore decisions handed down by the Delaware Chancery and Supreme and other state courts dealing with director responsibilities for obtaining relevant risk-based information and associated potential liability.

Also significant is seeing what's happened to the major banks and other companies where risks overlooked resulted in massive failures. Directors don't want surprises—they want to go to sleep at night feeling comfortable that any potential icebergs are on management's radar screens, and that the corporate ship is being navigated effectively.

Directors may also have come to realize that with an effective company-wide risk-management process they will be better positioned to add value by allowing the company to take on appropriate risks. ERM can help boards become less risk-averse. Excessive aversion to risk, which can frustrate management and stifle innovation and growth, brings with it high opportunity cost. Unfortunately, we've seen the boards of some companies becoming more risk averse as the spotlight shines brighter and brighter on technicalities of corporate governance. But at companies that have implemented effective enterprise risk management processes, boards tend to avoid a risk-averse mind-set. Rather, directors are comfortable that management is making informed decisions in taking on the right risks and is bringing relevant information to the boardroom.

These directors understand that ERM is not a panacea, and that they need to demonstrate ongoing diligence in their attention to risk. But with effective ERM they believe their companies are better positioned to seize opportunities, avoid major pitfalls, and grow share value.

## Senior Managers

The other main source of attention to ERM is senior managers, such as a company's chief financial officer, chief legal counsel, chief compliance officer, or chief audit executive. In many organizations these professionals have become knowledgeable in enterprise risk management, where through readings, conferences, professional associations, or discussions with colleagues, they've come to understand ERM and what it can do for an organization. Importantly, they tend to have clear insight into what form risk management may take in the company and what failures have occurred or what opportunities have been lost because the organization lacked a cohesive program.

In one of the companies I've worked with it was the general counsel who had intimate knowledge of what was and wasn't being done to identify, assess, and manage risks, and he recognized the shortcomings. It's not insignificant that this individual also held the title of executive vice president and his influence went far beyond legal matters, extending to a broad range of the company's strategic and operational issues. In this case the general counsel/EVP engaged the company's CEO and they with other senior managers moved forward to implement an effective ERM process.

Similarly, I've worked with CFOs, chief internal auditors, and other corporate executives, sometimes with added impetus from the board or its audit committee, who successfully made the case to a CEO in recognizing the benefits of ERM and thereby resulting in the organization embarking on an ERM initiative.

## The Business Case

Beyond impetus from the board and their direct reports, CEOs want to be presented with a rationale for moving forward with any major initiative, and more often than not they want to see the business case. Inherent in this request is the need to demonstrate a return on investment or associated cost-benefit relationship.

The business case can be constructed in any of a number of ways. Frankly, one of the most effective is to reflect on past risks that resulted in unmet business objectives or missed opportunities that were subsequently seized by the company's competitors. Yes, it's relatively easy to make a convincing business case where a company has suffered a major setback. While one might think the same holds true when one or more of a company's peers suffered from failing to recognize a risk, unfortunately a common reaction is, "That couldn't happen here."

An important element of a business case is demonstrating the type and value of information that will be available to managers to make better business decisions and allocate capital where the best risk-return ratios exist. When practical, it's useful to quantify these benefits to supplement a qualitatively based rationale, which must be provided in context of the up-front and ongoing costs of an ERM process.

Why is making the business case to the CEO so important? An obvious reason is that in most organizations, for an enterprise-wide initiative to begin, the CEO must endorse it. But another reality is that without the CEO's support, it's unlikely the initiative will succeed. There have been numerous instances where, with the best of intentions, senior staff have attempted to bring ERM to their company without first gaining the full support of the chief executive officer, only to find insurmountable obstacles, often in the form of lack of acceptance in the managerial ranks.

 **PITFALLS**

Before getting into what works well in ERM implementation, it's useful to highlight where an initiative can get derailed. Managements have often fallen into any number of traps while seeking effective ERM. Having been fortunate enough to work with many companies that have avoided the pitfalls, here I will share those experiences to help those of you looking to embrace ERM in order to avoid similar traps.

### Wavering Support from the Top

As noted, the initial impetus for ERM usually does not come from the chief executive. Rather, discussion of ERM often is initiated at the board level, with the full board or audit committee seeking to ensure it is apprised of all significant risks. The immediate question is: "How does senior management know that it has identified the key risks, to be positioned to take appropriate action to manage the risks and to communicate that information to the board?" Typically after a CEO gets past the initial "My direct reports and I run this business, so of course we know what's going on and where the risks are!" the dialogue moves to how to establish the necessary discipline around whatever risk identification and management processes might already be in place.

Why is this so relevant here? Because when a CEO is not the initial driver, and especially when the board initiates a call for an ERM program, senior management may agree to move forward but their hearts might not be in it. That's not always the case—in one large company the impetus for ERM came from the audit committee chair, but the CEO fully embraced the idea and enthusiastically provided the needed support. But where top management is not truly committed, the likelihood of successful implementation drops like a rock.

And this is the point: To have a reasonable chance of gaining the full benefit of an effective ERM program, the CEO and other senior managers must have bought into the proposal. Where the impetus comes from can be an indicator, but is not always critical to success. The all-important issue is whether the needed support at the top exists.

## An Administrative Burden

Another major pitfall is drifting away from a main purpose of implementing ERM in the first place—to support managers' ability to make better business decisions in accomplishing corporate objectives—and instead turning the program into an administrative nightmare. This trap looms large, especially when too much emphasis is placed on reporting information upstream to more senior levels of management and ultimately to the board.

What sometimes happens is that staff supporting ERM development think in terms of forms and procedures, and they get immersed in excessive detail and formality. The process becomes one of form over substance, unfortunately resulting in the company's people seeing ERM as an administrative exercise, serving no purpose for themselves or the company.

Yes, providing information to the board is an important benefit, but one really best viewed as a normal outgrowth of effective ERM. The real focus should be on how ERM integrates into the culture and processes of the business, to provide managers with meaningful information enabling them to better manage risks and seize opportunities. Indeed, clear communication channels upstream to higher levels of management must exist, to facilitate agreement on what risks need to be addressed and how, and what opportunities should be pursued with additional investment. But that is best done in the context of existing management processes, not as an administrative overlay or, even worse, an entirely separate process.

## Misplaced Responsibility for Risk Management

Senior management tends to want to fix responsibility for risk management in one individual, usually an existing or newly designated chief risk officer. They want to look to that individual for information on identified risks, their relative seriousness, and how they are being managed.

While going this route might initially seem appealing, it seldom works well in practice. Yes, a chief risk officer, however named, is extremely helpful if not critical to effective ERM. This person or office can and should act to support line and staff managers in understanding how best to implement ERM in their spheres of responsibility. But operating managers must be responsible and held accountable for effective risk management. The reasons are manifold, but in summary ERM works well when and because it's built into the fabric of the organization and executed by those with the requisite authority and responsibility for running the business.

So while the risk officer is positioned to be in the reporting loop as information flows upstream, and can be a focal point for top management inquiries, information is best communicated upstream by managers through normal reporting channels in the normal course of managing the business. Managers communicate emerging risk information upstream in regular meetings or written reports or electronic entries, or they may pick up the phone or send an e-mail with time-sensitive information. Actions to be taken to manage risks are discussed through routine dialogue. The chief risk officer should be aware of important risks and ensure they are being reported though normal channels. If not, then the risk officer should urge that dialogue take place, and in the event of continued inaction should communicate the information directly to senior management. In that way, the risk officer continues as a staff function, providing support and summary information where desired, and acting as a fail-safe in providing information on specific risks.

## Losing Momentum

Perhaps the most common pitfall to successful ERM implementation is failure to maintain momentum. My age is showing when I think back to the early days of ABC's *Monday Night Football*, with Frank Gifford, Howard Cosell, and Don Meredith in the announcers' booth. If memory serves, it was "Dandy Don" who, after a turnover, harped on the terrible price of losing momentum, coining the term "old Mo."

Forgive my walk down memory lane. Still, the same point applies to the topic at hand. ERM implementation often begins with the best of intentions, sometimes with great internal fanfare and resources and a great project plan to design, build, and install ERM throughout the organization. People are excited—as even those fearing change decide they can't or won't try to wait out this initiative, and climb aboard—and the initiative moves forward.

But then bad stuff gets in the way. The project leader is moved to a new role, project team members get caught up in other ongoing responsibilities, the business hits a snag and budgets are cut. Or other initiatives are begun, dealing with business process improvement, data analytics, key performance indicators, or other matters seeking to enhance performance. (By the way, ERM has proven to be a solid platform and enabler for these types of initiatives.) Whatever the cause, momentum for ERM implementation can be disrupted, and when it is, it can be difficult to regain.

Success occurs when project team members have enough time allocated to their participation in ERM, with some or perhaps all other responsibilities reassigned for the duration of the project. Senior management can't knowingly or unwittingly lose interest, even in favor of other pressing needs. And time must be committed to see the project through—typically 18 months from start to finish for a company of, say, $5 billion to $10 billion in revenue, or one or two major units of a larger company.

A company I worked with was headed into this trap. About a year into the 18-month plan to design, build, and implement the ERM process, events began to obstruct the project, jeopardizing the entire investment. Recognizing the pitfall, management took the necessary actions to focus attention where needed, with momentum regained and the project brought to successful completion.

## Viewing Training as a Panacea

Another danger is thinking that all implementation issues somehow can be dealt with through training. The idea is simple: Bring people to a half-day ERM training session and presto! All works perfectly.

Yes, clarifying what people need to know about ERM is a must—including how ERM is designed in the company to fit the way the business is managed. But long before training can begin, decisions need to be made on whether

ERM will be built into all business processes and departmental units during the project's design and build stages, or whether for some processes/units that will be done by the process/unit leaders after initial implementation. It's important that ERM be incorporated into the more significant processes, such as objective setting, budgeting, performance assessment, and at least several key line processes, to provide a sufficient foundation for ERM in the company to serve as a model for other processes/units. If some design/build work is to be done later by process/unit leaders, then training must provide that knowledge and technique as well.

The key is that training must be developed and conducted only after effective design and implementation of the ERM process. The heavy lifting must be completed before looking to teach people how to use the system.

Further, a one-time session generally is not sufficient. Implementing an effective ERM program requires cultural and behavioral change, calling for well-orchestrated use of change management techniques, of which ongoing training is a part.

## Getting to the Promised Land

With all these pitfalls, one might ask whether moving forward with ERM implementation is worth the effort. In my experience, the answer is a definite *yes*! It takes commitment, planning, and execution, and those companies that have done it right have gained the tremendous expected benefit.

 ## EFFECTIVE IMPLEMENTATION

Having highlighted the pitfalls, let's look at what needs to go right—focusing on what methodologies are most effective for successfully implementing an ERM system.

## A Proven Method

Let's proceed on the basis that a company's CEO is fully supportive of moving forward with the ERM initiative. Whatever the impetus—perhaps urging from the board of directors or the audit committee, or learning a hard lesson from failure to see some critical risk, or simply recognizing the many benefits of ERM—the CEO and senior management team are committed to developing an effective ERM process.

For guidance on how to proceed, we can look to COSO's ERM report, which is based on significant experience with companies that have implemented

ERM in their organizations. Drawing from that guidance we can outline the basic steps to ERM success.

- *Core team preparedness.* A core team is established with representation from business units and key support functions, with a common understanding and language providing a foundation for the ERM program's design.
- *Implementation plan development.* An initial plan is created setting out key project phases, including defined work streams, milestones, resources, and timing. Responsibilities are identified, and a project management system put in place.
- *Current state assessment.* The core team considers how and the extent to which the company currently identifies and manages risk across the company, and assesses existing risk-management capabilities within the organization.
- *Enterprise risk-management vision.* The core team develops a vision that sets out how ERM will be designed and integrated within the organization to achieve its objectives.
- *Capability development.* The current-state assessment and ERM vision provide insights needed to determine the people, technology, and process capabilities already in place and functioning, and what new capabilities need to be developed. This includes defining roles and responsibilities, processes, methodologies, tools, techniques, information flows, and technologies.
- *Implementation plan.* The initial plan is updated and enhanced, adding depth and breadth to cover further design issues and deployment.
- *Change management development and deployment.* Actions are developed to implement and sustain the enterprise risk management vision and desired capabilities—including deployment plans, training sessions, reward reinforcement mechanisms, and monitoring of the remainder of the implementation process.
- *Monitoring.* Management reviews and strengthens risk-management capabilities as part of its ongoing management process.

## Other Factors

It's important to recognize several additional factors that can be critical to success. One involves a fundamental truism that while some people are excited about and embrace change that they see as enhancing their personal and their unit and company performance, many other employees simply neither like nor want change. So, it's necessary to understand the kinds of roadblocks that can be put up, and anticipate and proactively address them. Here are some of the more common ones that, if not proactively dealt with, can undermine ERM implementation:

■ Risk management interferes with our real work.
■ It's a negative thought process, not relevant to us action-oriented can-do people.
■ Managing risk is someone else's (staff's) role.
■ We know what went wrong elsewhere, and it won't happen to us.
■ Risk management exists simply so management can report to the board.
■ Of course we already manage risk—so go away!

Other critical actions needed for effective deployment include taking positive actions to ensure personnel recognize how ERM will enhance their business decision-making and help them achieve their units and personal business objectives, demonstrate how ERM is being built into existing business processes, and make clear how and why it is being built into performance assessment and related HR processes. Finally, as an overriding consideration, it has proven highly useful to establish a steering committee to oversee the core project team and the implementation process. A committee comprised of senior leadership, including selected line managers along with key staff leaders, provides needed credibility and support through high-level direction, sponsoring change, enabling senior managers to learn through the process, and reinforcing the commitment of senior managers.

## Where to Begin

The described methodology provides an effective way to get the job done. But a typical question arises: Where in the company do we begin? That is, do we look to implement ERM throughout the organization in one fell swoop, or do we do it in bits and pieces?

The answer, not surprisingly, is, "It depends." Experience shows that for a mid-size company, it makes sense to implement ERM across the organization. With the core team in place and senior management support, it's often most efficient and effective to move the entire organization forward together.

But for larger companies it's difficult to install ERM all at once, and doing it in stages provides significant benefits. This is especially the case for multinationals or other large organizations with multiple locations, or ones with many business units whose leaders have reasonable autonomy in how they run their businesses. A particularly successful approach is to initiate ERM first in the central strategic planning and budgeting process. This brings important advantages, with senior management directly involved with and becoming comfortable with identifying and dealing with risk in developing strategy and related implementation and plans. And usually senior management's direct reports are involved as well, further spreading direct knowledge in the upper management ranks.

Additionally, it's often useful to implement ERM first in one or two significant business units, especially those that are highly visible within the company and have solid reputations of successfully achieving business objectives. With appropriate care to ensure success, those units serve as models for other business units. Experience shows that once other business unit leaders see those success stories, they'll want to emulate them.

## Additional Guidance

About the same time as COSO released guidance on key risk indicators, as discussed in Chapter 6, it issued *Embracing Enterprise Risk Management— Practical Approaches for Getting Started*, which suggests ways in which companies, especially smaller ones, can begin a risk management initiative, with the objective of ultimately moving to an ERM process. It puts forth *keys to success* in terms of a number of themes, beginning with being sure to have support from the top. Theme 2 is building on incremental steps, which includes implementing key practices to gain immediate and tangible results. Theme 3 continues with focusing first on a small number of top risks, and theme 4 is leveraging existing resources by utilizing the capabilities of the chief audit executive, chief financial officer, or other executive as a catalyst to begin the initiative. The guidance continues with theme 5, building on existing risk management activities already being performed, for example, by internal audit, insurance or compliance functions, fraud protection/detection measures, or credit or treasury functions. Theme 6 involves embedding risk management into the fabric of the business, and concludes with theme 7's continuing to update and educate senior management and the board on evolving ERM practices.

The guidance also provides seven action steps to support development of an ERM initiative:

1. Seek board and top management leadership, involvement, and oversight.
2. Select a strong leader for the ERM initiative.

3. Establish a risk committee or working group.
4. Conduct an enterprise-wide risk assessment and develop a related action plan.
5. Inventory existing risk management practices.
6. Develop a communication and reporting process.
7. Develop the next phase of action plans and communication.

As stated in the report, the suggested step-by-step approach may be particularly useful to smaller companies and, importantly, is only a starting point for moving to an enterprise risk-management process. I believe the report is well meant, looking to break down barriers and resistance to embarking on building an ERM process, and as such may be useful to companies considering taking a first step. But that's all it is. It doesn't provide guidance on how to design an ERM process or how it can be effectively implemented throughout an organization. Yes, some of the steps are a start, but my concern is that, despite the warnings, companies going down this path will somehow believe they will have installed ERM in their organizations.

Worth considering in this guidance is discussion of two factors in risk analysis supplementing the focus on the likelihood of a risk event occurring and its related impact. One such factor is velocity—the speed at which a risk event can come at a company, or more precisely, the time between occurrence of a risk event and its impact—and the other being the company's readiness in dealing with it. Velocity in particular has gained attention in recent years and can be a particularly useful addition.

All in all, in looking at the two recently issued reports, in Olympic Games terms, with these as the sole entrants, this report gets the bronze. The one on key risk indicators definitely wins the gold.

## Relating ERM to SOX 404 and Other Compliance

Years ago, when companies were establishing and refining processes to deal with internal control over financial reporting under Sarbanes-Oxley Section 404, some decided at the same time to expand their 404 focus to include ERM principles. In the same way processes were being developed to identify, assess, and manage financial reporting risks, those companies broadened their scope to address strategic, operations, and compliance objectives as well, with a sharp focus on risk and opportunity. Because they already used the COSO internal control framework for 404 purposes, they were readily able to build on those efforts using the COSO ERM report. Because the COSO ERM report is built directly on the internal control report, those companies found the underlying fundamentals already are in place.

Senior managements of several companies took that approach. A major electronics manufacturer and a large financial services company, for instance, each decided early on in dealing with Sarbanes-Oxley that they wanted to gain a real business benefit from the 404 exercise.

In these two cases, management looked not only at their company's financial reporting controls, but also at the other categories under COSO—compliance and operations controls and extended the focus on risk management. By taking a disciplined, integrated approach, these companies leveraged the 404 work to enhance their processes, which helped them ensure compliance with laws and regulations, and make their business operations more effective, efficient, and risk-based, focusing on bottom-line enhancement.

These successes are in contrast to a number of other companies that waited a year or more after establishing their approach to dealing with financial reporting controls under SOX 404 and then attempted to build on what had been put in place to establish an ERM process. Conceptually this made eminent sense—building on the risk identification, analysis, and management process for financial reporting to better achieve the company's operations and compliance objectives as well. In many instances, however, these initiatives did not work for a number of reasons. The organizations simply were burned out with their 404 implementation, and were not accepting of embarking on anything further having to do with risk management. Also, the cost of 404 compliance had become a major issue. And project teams taken from other assignments to lead the 404 efforts had been disbanded, with personnel having returned to their normal responsibilities. So, unless a company embraced a broad risk management initiative from the outset, attempts to build on 404 generally didn't work well.

There were, however, some exceptions worth noting. Management at a large consumer products company, as with most companies, decided initially to focus on getting the 404 work done, with the sole objective of getting its financial reporting controls right in order to justify a clean management report and auditor's opinion. But as this process was moving toward completion, the company's executives were looking at a number of converging factors. These included:

■ *Ongoing Sarbanes-Oxley requirements.* Having gone through what amounted to a more than year-long fire drill to ensure effectiveness of internal control over financial reporting, these executives began to focus on the fact that this was not going away. Unlike the earlier Y2K exercise, when January 2000 arrived and companies' IT systems didn't crash, 404 wouldn't go away. With 404, reporting goes on indefinitely, year after year.

- *Sentencing guidelines.* The U.S. Sentencing Commission had amended its federal sentencing guidelines, expanding the scope with emphasis on corporate culture around ethical conduct, clear responsibility and accountability, risk reduction and assessment, personnel incentives, and board oversight.
- *OCEG.* Then a relatively new organization, the Open Compliance and Ethics Group, issued guidance, then in draft form. Involving corporate general counsels and law firms, as well as a number of business leaders, OCEG provided a benchmark for companies to measure their ethics, integrity, and compliance programs.
- *COSO ERM.* About that time COSO issued its ERM framework, which as noted builds on the COSO internal control framework used for 404 reporting, with a broader and more robust focus on risk management and the related benefits.
- *Legal and regulatory precedent.* Clear messages were sent by the SEC, Justice Department, and a number of court cases emphasizing the critical importance for companies to maintain effective compliance processes.

This company's management decided that it made sense not to look at these rules and guidelines one-off, but rather to consider the commonalities and deal with them in integrated fashion. The goal was threefold: to ensure that the company's environment, culture, and processes were in line with the above mandates; to do so as efficiently as possible; and to gain real bottom-line benefit.

With the support of the audit committee and full board, management generally followed the implementation approach outlined earlier, first assessing its current status, then designing an end state where it aimed to be and developing a clear-cut plan for getting there. The company created an eight-month start-to-completion project plan.

The company leveraged its 404 work in several respects. It decided to use some of the same team leaders of 404 in building the desired processes for broad-based legal and regulatory compliance and operational effectiveness and efficiency. It used the COSO ERM framework as a foundation, thereby facilitating integration of other compliance mandates in an efficient, coordinated manner, enabling managers throughout the organization to make more informed risk-based decisions, establish greater alignment with the company's business objectives and strategies, and effect better results while avoiding operational and compliance surprises.

Attempting to build on 404 to establish a broad-based ERM process in today's environment is challenging. Certainly the matter of being burned out on 404 generally is no longer an issue. But in many quarters 404 is seen as an unnecessary compliance exercise and waste of resources. So, while depending on attitudes and existing 404 processes it may be possible to successfully build on prior 404 efforts, today success is more likely to proceed on the basis of a new initiative without overt reference to financial reporting controls under 404.

## Technology

In Chapter 3 we discussed critical issues around the need to build the compliance process into existing business processes, being founded on a basis of integrity and ethical values, and sound use of technology. The same is true for ERM processes. Importantly, because an effective ERM process encompasses all of a company's objectives—strategic financial reporting, effective and efficient business operations, and compliance with laws and regulations—conceptually and practically there should best be one process, with use of one powerful piece of technology.

Vendors' technology solutions have been greatly enhanced since the early software of initial 404 days, with some serving as a sound basis supporting ERM processes. This enables not only documentation of risks and risk responses, but also establishes accountabilities and supports communication and effective ongoing management of the ERM process.

You might bear with me on a personal note regarding ERM technology. Some years ago I believed that while it was challenging to implement enterprise risk management effectively, it could be done without use of advanced technology. Well, my thinking has evolved as to the need for effective software. It's true that in mid-size companies (I generally don't work with smaller organizations) that were centralized with few levels of management, I saw opportunities for enterprise risk management to work successfully with protocols that didn't necessarily require use of specialized software. Effectively addressing risk factors in each operating and staff unit at every management level, with highly effective information sharing and communication, made ERM workable.

But over time I came to recognize that the above scenario is rare or nonexistent in larger companies. With increasingly challenging economic, regulatory, and competitive environments, fewer personnel stretched thin and channels and markets rapidly changing, the need for effective software becomes essential. Otherwise, capturing all significant risks related to business objectives and related mitigating actions and control activities becomes difficult if not impossible. And coupled with a need to track assignment of responsibility to specific personnel and manage accountability—along with effective communication throughout the organization—specialized technology becomes that much more important. It not only strengthens communication upstream to senior management, but also *across* an organization's layers and business units, so information useful in other business units is readily available for decision making. The last thing a company wants is a significant risk or compliance problem that's known in the organization, but not communicated to those with the perspective and ability to fix it. And when we superimpose a need for senior managers to readily obtain relevant risk-related analyses with dashboards with drill-down capability, then it's a no-brainer that the right software solution is essential.

## Don't Underestimate the Required Effort

What I knew then and know now is that while the benefits of ERM are great, so too is the effort to implement it in any organization. Every company has its own unique way of doing business, with organization, culture, and management style to match. Implementing ERM involves not only change in process and procedure, but also a shift in attitude—that is, how managers think about decisions they make on a day-to-day basis. As such, it's necessary to use change management techniques to make this happen quickly and efficiently.

As noted, typically, the time required to implement ERM is about 18 months. This is for a mid-size company, or for one or two large business units of a large one. While this average time frame has been reduced in some instances, it's difficult to do so in the context of ongoing business issues and other initiatives that a company is likely to be pursuing at the same time. Trying to cut the time significantly can be counterproductive, causing initial enthusiasm to wane and attention to divert elsewhere.

Designing and implementing an effective ERM process is not a cakewalk. It takes support, commitment, time, and money. But there's no doubt that when done well, the benefits are more than commensurate and well worth the effort.

 ## ROLES AND RESPONSIBILITIES

As noted, experience shows that a company starting down the ERM path often does so because of impetus from the board of directors. The board or audit committee wants to be sure the company is appropriately identifying and managing risk, and that the board itself is apprised of the most significant risks and how management is dealing with them.

Accordingly, senior management tends to focus initially on the upstream reporting, seeing to it that managers at various levels provide the risk-based information that ultimately is processed and synthesized for presentation to the board. An associated natural inclination is to assign to one individual, perhaps a chief risk officer, responsibility for accumulating the information and developing presentations to the board. And a related tendency is to look to that individual to ensure that risks remain within desired risk tolerances and that the totality of risk is within the company's risk appetite. That is, this chief risk officer is responsible for risk management in the company.

While this approach is appealing in its simplicity and focused accountability, it seldom works, for at least two critical reasons. First, reporting risks upstream through a centralized function adds administrative burden and actually gets in the way of enabling managers to interface in normal reporting relationships to deal effectively with risk in their spheres of responsibility. And second, it's not possible for any one staff individual to be responsible for managing a company's risk—it simply doesn't work.

## What Works

Responsibility for identifying, assessing, and responding to risk is best placed in the line and staff unit leaders—from senior management cascading down through the organization. That is, risk management needs to be owned by managers closest to the action. For example, an insurance company instituting ERM clearly showed that sales managers are best positioned to deal with the risk of using obsolete (and inaccurate) sales materials, ensuring that sales materials remain current and target-appropriate. At a construction equipment manufacturer, line executives in foreign locations are best positioned to identify risks related to changing local economic conditions and customer demand. Another example is a consumer products company, where managers running production processes know best where breakdowns could occur. In each of those companies, responsibility along with requisite techniques and training enable those process owners to effectively identify, assess, and manage the relevant risks.

As such, business unit and staff function leaders are charged with responsibility for effectively managing risk and identifying opportunities in their spheres of responsibility. In cascading fashion, these leaders are responsible for ensuring their direct reports identify relevant risks, assess them, and make informed decisions on how best to manage the risks. They are charged with building these responsibilities into existing business processes to promote efficiency and embed risk management and compliance into the fabric of the organization. They also must communicate relevant risk-based information upstream. Experience shows that this is best done through normal reporting channels, to facilitate information flows and allow discussion as needed through existing management processes, without adding new protocols and administrative costs.

Within this context, responsibilities for effective enterprise risk management are as follows:

- *Chief risk officer.* The CRO is a senior-level staff person responsible for educating managers at all organizational levels in risk management; providing the necessary enabling methodologies, tools, and techniques; and otherwise supporting and facilitating effective risk management throughout the organization. The CRO also should have responsibility for monitoring the upstream reporting process, and be positioned—if communication through normal reporting channels should break down—to provide relevant information to the chief executive. That is, the CRO needs to monitor risks that the line and staff managers are dealing with and ensure relevant information is communicated as needed throughout the organization, preferably through normal management reporting channels, but where necessary, communicated nonetheless.
- *General counsel.* In some companies the general counsel is charged with responsibility for risk management. That is, the CEO looks to this individual to keep the company out of trouble. But for the same reasons outlined with respect to a chief risk officer, that approach simply does not work. The general counsel's office does, however, have important responsibilities in making ERM work. It must identify new legislation and regulation on the horizon and provide relevant information to the line and staff leaders whose units are or will be affected. New rules need to be analyzed and communicated in straightforward language and manner to enable busy unit leaders to grasp what's needed and determine how most efficiently to build any needed protocols into their business and management processes. And inside counsel, sometimes in conjunction with a chief compliance officer, needs to be a strong support function to others in the company as needed, providing advice and counsel in dealing with existing or new requirements.
- *Chief audit executive.* Increasingly CAEs are building into internal audit's ongoing audit processes an expanded focus on risk management. This

includes, usually in coordination with the CRO, determining the extent to which business unit and staff functions have established appropriate risk-management processes and are executing them, and relevant risk information is being reported upstream.

■ *Chief executive and senior management team.* With the responsibility of running the company, the CEO reviews risk decisions of direct reports and uses risk-based information in strategy development, determining whether the risk portfolio is within established risk appetite and reflected in capital-allocation decisions. The CEO is responsible for bringing the more significant risks and risk-management decisions to the board of directors or board committee with oversight responsibility.

■ *Board of directors.* The board is responsible for determining whether management is appropriately identifying, assessing, and managing all facets of risks the company faces. The board needs to have sufficient information that appropriate, disciplined processes are in place for this purpose. It must feel comfortable that management is bringing the more significant ongoing and newly emerging risks to the boardroom and that it receives relevant and timely analysis of those risks and management's actions and planned actions. The board will review the risks and risk responses, as well as the company's risk appetite and portfolio view of risk, and consider whether modifications might be needed.

## An Integrated Approach

We find that ERM is most effective when primary ownership lies with line and staff function leaders. They're closest to the action and best positioned to identify and deal with risks as they emerge. This includes all management levels, up to and including the CEO, and works most effectively and efficiently when built into existing business and management processes. Legal counsel keeps those managers properly informed of new legal and regulatory requirements, so the line can factor them into their risk protocols, and internal audit takes a risk-based approach and factors risk into its testing plans. The CRO provides methodologies, tools, techniques, education, support, and a safety net on upstream reporting. And the board or designated board committee provides appropriate oversight.

# CHAPTER EIGHT

# Does Internal Control Really Matter?

I F YOU'VE BEEN DEALING with Sarbanes-Oxley Section 404 as an audit committee member, CEO, CFO, or auditor, or otherwise dealing with financial reporting, you probably have heard more about and spent more time with internal control than you ever imagined. And you undoubtedly have come to know about COSO's *Internal Control—Integrated Framework*, which serves as the standard against which your company's internal control system is evaluated.

Let's get one important fact out of the way. When we talk about internal control under SOX 404, we mean internal control over financial reporting—that is, the process to produce reliable public financial statements. But internal control has as much—actually more—to do with two other major categories of corporate objectives. Some controls are directed at helping ensure compliance with laws and regulations affecting a company, and others are in place to see that the company's business operations objectives are achieved. These latter controls, called *operations controls*, deal with everything from implementation of a new marketing plan to efficient inventory control to effectively carrying out profitable research and development activities to recruiting and training employees. One might think those three categories of objectives would include everything a company seeks to accomplish, and one would be correct. What doesn't fall under financial reporting or compliance by definition falls under operations.

I won't bore you with more on what internal control is, because you can read (and may already have read) the COSO report or at least its executive summary. If you'd like a memory refresher, the summary of internal control components is set forth in Exhibit 8.1.

**EXHIBIT 8.1** Components of Internal Control

---

**Control Environment**

The control environment sets the tone of an organization, influencing the control consciousness of its people. It is the foundation for all other components of internal control, providing discipline and structure. Control environment factors include the integrity, ethical values, and competence of the entity's people; management's philosophy and operating style; the way management assigns authority and responsibility and organizes and develops its people; and the attention and direction provided by the board of directors.

**Risk Assessment**

Every entity faces a variety of risks from external and internal sources that must be assessed. A precondition to risk assessment is establishment of objectives, linked at different levels and internally consistent. Risk assessment is the identification and analysis of relevant risks to achievement of the objectives, forming a basis for determining how the risks should be managed. Because economic, industry, regulatory and operating conditions will continue to change, mechanisms are needed to identify and deal with the special risks associated with change.

**Control Activities**

Control activities are the policies and procedures that help ensure management directives are carried out. They help ensure that necessary actions are taken to address risks to achievement of the entity's objectives. Control activities occur throughout the organization, at all levels and in all functions. They include a range of activities as diverse as approvals, authorizations, verifications, reconciliations, reviews of operating performance, security of assets and segregation of duties.

**Information and Communication**

Pertinent information must be identified, captured, and communicated in a form and time frame that enable people to carry out their responsibilities. Information systems produce reports, containing operational, financial, and

**EXHIBIT 8.1** (Continued)

compliance-related information, that make it possible to run and control the business. They deal with not only internally generated data, but also information about external events, activities, and conditions necessary to informed business decision-making and external reporting. Effective communication also must occur in a broader sense, flowing down, across, and up the organization. All personnel must receive a clear message from top management that control responsibilities must be taken seriously. They must understand their own roles in the internal control system, as well as how individual activities relate to the work of others. They must have a means of communicating significant information upstream. There also needs to be effective communication with external parties, such as customers, suppliers, regulators, and shareholders.

**Monitoring**

Internal control systems need to be monitored—a process that assesses the quality of the system's performance over time. This is accomplished through ongoing monitoring activities, separate evaluations, or a combination of the two. Ongoing monitoring occurs in the course of operations. It includes regular management and supervisory activities, and other actions personnel take in performing their duties. The scope and frequency of separate evaluations will depend primarily on an assessment of risks and the effectiveness of ongoing monitoring procedures. Internal control deficiencies should be reported upstream, with serious matters reported to top management and the board.

\* \* \*

There is synergy and linkage among these components, forming an integrated system that reacts dynamically to changing conditions. The internal control system is intertwined with the entity's operating activities and exists for fundamental business reasons. Internal control is most effective when controls are built into the entity's infrastructure and are a part of the essence of the enterprise. "Built in" controls support quality and empowerment initiatives, avoid unnecessary costs, and enable quick response to changing conditions.

There is a direct relationship between the three categories of objectives, which are what an entity strives to achieve, and components, which represent what is needed to achieve the objectives. All components are relevant to each objectives category. When looking at any one category—the effectiveness and efficiency of operations, for instance—all five components must be present and functioning effectively to conclude that internal control over operations is effective.

What you may find particularly useful is a sense of why some major companies have suffered due to poor internal controls, especially the controls over companies' operational activities. We get to some of those in the next chapter. Here, we focus attention on why something as mundane as internal control over financial reporting is truly relevant.

##  IMPACT OF SOX 404 ON FINANCIAL REPORTING

We know that the costs of SOX 404 are significant, far exceeding what legislators and regulators expected. But with the impetus of what happened with Enron and then WorldCom, SOX became the law of the land. The result was senior management and staff having to deal with the assessment and reporting requirements, as well as boards and their audit committees spending more time on monitoring, and thereby being diverted from activities viewed as adding more value. Here's what we saw.

- *Reviews and certifications.* Certainly the associated costs far surpassed what anyone expected. Initially corporate management and auditors, both internal and external, had to absorb what the law entailed and what they had to do. Some thought that in light of the internal control provisions of the Foreign Corrupt Practices Act of 1977 there would be little additional effort. But others knew well that there's a major difference between what companies did pursuant to the FCPA—which calls for companies to maintain an effective system of internal control over financial reporting (the FCPA's wording is slightly different, but the thrust is the same)—and being required to state publicly and certify that the system indeed is effective. Of course, the difference is multiplied by the SOX requirement that the external auditor opine on management's statement.
- *Distracted, risk-averse boards.* Some boards of directors provided less advice to management and became more risk-averse. This stemmed from SOX's requirements beyond Section 404, but 404 was a factor. Although unintended by lawmakers, a number of boards and audit committees focused a majority of their attention on their role as a monitor of management, while their value-added advisory role took a back seat. And fear of personal liability and reputational damage caused some directors to want the companies they served to be more cautious in general, fearing an Enron-esque meltdown.

- *Time sink for management.* CEOs, CFOs, and other C-suite corporate officers spent inordinate amounts of time addressing compliance, taking time away from other pressing business. With only so many hours in a day, these already hard-pressed executives struggled to deal with strategy implementation, leadership responsibilities, major deals, opening or expanding business operations and markets, and tending to myriad business matters requiring their attention.
- *Exiting the public markets.* Some smaller public companies decided to go private, some other domestic companies decided not to go public in the first place, and some foreign companies decided not to use our capital markets, with a potentially adverse effect on capital formation and resulting economic implications.

But what about the benefits? There's limited empirical data, but after SOX 404 became effective we saw evidence of a number of positives.

- *Confidence in reports.* Senior managers and boards of directors became more confident in the reliability of the financial reports on which they sign off, and investors gained increased comfort with information available to the capital markets.
- *Streamlined processes and enhanced information.* Armed with new information about how business processes actually work—often different from the ways those processes were originally designed—management teams identified ways to reduce labor and effort while enhancing process effectiveness. And processes were enhanced to provide not just data but valuable information to make better business decisions. Companies discovered, for example, that within their vast and disparate databases they own information valuable for enhancing marketing, customer service, and other business objectives. A number of companies found that some data they had been using for decision making was, well, less than reliable. As a result of the 404 process, they enhanced the accuracy, completeness, and relevance of critical data assets for use in making smarter decisions.
- *Seeds of ERM.* Some companies used the internal control assessment and enhancement process as a foundation for initiating an enterprise risk management process, though with limited success, as discussed in Chapter 7.
- *Benefits to smaller companies.* While smaller companies—those with less than $75 million market capitalization—are required to comply with the management reporting requirements of SOX 404, Dodd-Frank put to rest

the SEC's plans to also require auditor attestation. Many of these companies' managements applauded the ability to avoid incurring additional costs and taking focus away from running and growing their businesses. There's a different perspective, however, with observers outlining benefits lost for a number of reasons. These include:

- Smaller companies traditionally have less sophisticated systems and less experienced individuals in management positions, with statistics showing greater incidences of fraud and restatement of financial results.
- The auditor attestation costs have come down with the advent of the PCAOB's Auditing Standard No. 5 and guidance for smaller businesses issued by COSO.
- Studies indicate that companies that are not SOX compliant or have material weaknesses in their internal controls receive a lower valuation, whereas those that are compliant receive higher multiples when sold.
- These companies are less likely to take advantage of IT solutions that provide enhanced efficiency and management capabilities well beyond better controlled financial reporting.
- CEOs and CFOs who already must certify to the effectiveness of financial reporting controls don't receive the comfort provided by auditor attestation.

As required by the Dodd-Frank Act, the SEC staff conducted a study on reducing the burden of complying with the audit requirements of SOX 404(b) for companies with a market capitalization between $75 million and $250 million. The recently issued report recommended to the commission that those companies not be exempted from the requirements, as potential savings would not justify the loss of investor protections.

 **RESPONSIBILITY FOR SOX 404**

We know that management is responsible for implementing and executing internal control over financial reporting, but who should have responsibility for carrying out the assessment process required for reporting under SOX 404?

In the early days of 404 compliance, the job typically fell to companies' chief audit executives and their staffs, who stepped up to the plate big time. Studies show that internal audit functions spent one-half or more of their resources dealing with this new role. Because of its knowledge, skills, and experience, there's typically no better group than internal audit to compre-hend, document, and test the enterprise's internal control over financial reporting, or to monitor remediation efforts.

Chief audit executives with whom I've worked have found that their groups' performance with 404 received high marks. Their ability to quickly grasp the scope of the 404 initiative, mobilize staff, coordinate with others internally, and provide expert guidance in documenting and testing controls enabled many companies to meet deadlines with positive results. Even in companies at which senior management and audit committee members already held internal audit in high esteem, there was a newfound appreciation of the chief audit executive's ability to provide critical leadership under intense pressure.

Another result has been greater attention from audit committees on internal audit's resources, positioning the function to better carry out its mission. Audit committees look more closely at the level and depth of internal audit's staff, with budgets analyzed with a sharper focus—not to cut, but rather to ensure sufficient credentialed and experienced resources are in place. Attention is given to specialized IT and other expertise—along with sufficiently sophisticated audit-based technology and methodology—and appropriate levels of managerial capability needed to ensure requisite high audit quality and efficiency, as well as closer consideration of internal audit plans, coverage, and reports.

All of this indeed is positive, as who wouldn't want their team and efforts to receive applause from the highest levels of corporate leadership? However, these accolades come with associated pitfalls.

- *Diminished objectivity.* For those chief audit executives asked to continue the role of chief internal control officer, with lead responsibility for 404 compli-ance, there's a double-edged sword. Gaining additional responsibility typically is a good thing for any executive. And, indeed, the job might be doable, where a chief audit executive wearing both hats has one key lieutenant heading the internal audit function and another heading internal control, preferably with separate staffs. I've seen this work well in one large company. But even with such a configuration there can be difficulties—where internal audit has responsibility for leading the 404 effort there can be diminished objectivity when it comes to auditing the controls.
- *Neglected responsibilities.* Attention normally given to other important cor-porate activities can be diverted. Even when high-risk, priority operations are covered, less immediate but still important areas might be neglected, especially those addressed on a cyclical basis. We've seen cases where

activities related to a company's strategic and operational objectives, business processes, foreign operations, and legal and regulatory compliance were put on the back burner. As more responsibility is accepted, unless there is a commensurate increase in resources, something has to give.

- *Disappearing staff.* The more visibility and recognition are achieved, the greater is the likelihood that senior management or business unit leaders will request internal audit to perform strategically focused special projects. Their investigative and analytical skills can be used to achieve many business needs, and—if not careful to control those requests—staff needed for critical audit work can quickly dissipate. Similarly, as internal audit staff works with line and staff executives, and their capabilities become more widely known, there may be requests for internal transfers to work full time in other units—although this can be a positive in recruitment and retention efforts.

Anecdotal evidence shows that many companies' management and audit committees recognized these pitfalls and put ongoing responsibility for SOX 404 compliance with a project team separate from the internal audit function. Internal audit, however, can continue to play an important role by providing guidance and selected resources where necessary.

In any event, a chief audit executive must have regular communication with top management and the audit committee to ensure clear understanding and concurrence regarding any long-term role in SOX 404 and to define how the breadth and depth of normal audit coverage will be achieved. Where expectations exceed available resources, there must be agreement on whether and how to enhance resources or modify audit scope. There may be opportunity to add staff, or to co-source where that makes business sense. As for deploying staff, decisions should be risk-based and consistent with internal audit's charter and, as noted, with the demands and expectations of top management and the audit committee. Alignment is essential or something will blow up—in all likelihood sooner than expected.

##  OTHER RELEVANT SOX PROVISIONS

Other SOX provisions, of course, have had significant implications on the reliability of financial reporting. Companies previously lacking codes of conduct developed them, and many others strengthened codes previously in place. A significant number of companies went beyond the letter of the SOX requirements, with broad-based codes applicable to all employees, and many used the impetus to establish broader ethics programs going beyond the code to ensure messages would be heard and embraced throughout the organization. Also, companies previously without a means to report allegations of misdeeds developed SOX-mandated whistleblower channels. Many companies, however, found they needed to do more work to make employees feel confident that action would be taken without reprisals. This issue continues today in many organizations.

Another impact was that audit committees became better positioned to fulfill their mandate, with their independence, enhanced capabilities, and sharper focus on financial reports and related internal controls strengthening the integrity of the reporting process.

Benefits in many cases were real, but did they outweigh the costs? The marketplace has sent mixed messages when companies have reported material internal control weaknesses. Depending on such factors as company size and industry, whether or not the weakness was pervasive, and whether it had already been or was being remediated, the markets reacted in varying degrees—for the most part the market's reaction has been mild. This is in contrast to news of misstated financial statements, where investors have hammered a company's stock price. One message can be gleaned: There's less concern about a control weakness indicating a higher potential for misstatement than exists about the occurrence of an actual misstatement in financial reporting.

According to surveys, as well as many individuals with whom I've discussed 404—from C-level executives to board directors, auditors, and regulators—viewpoints are mixed, although sentiment leans toward the notion of SOX 404 bringing more value than cost. Yes, initial costs were too high. But as the Public Company Accounting Oversight Board provided better guidance, financial reporting managers and internal and external auditors gained knowledge and experience and became more comfortable with what was truly needed, and as technology improved and was embraced, costs became more manageable. With the associated benefits of SOX 404, it is viewed by many in a positive light.

## DO EFFECTIVE FINANCIAL REPORTING CONTROLS REALLY PREVENT FRAUDULENT FINANCIAL REPORTING?

This is the big question, usually put forth in the context of the SOX 404 requirements. In answering, let's make one thing clear. Neither SOX nor any other legislation on the books or being considered—or for that matter, that can be conceived—will stop all fraud. There's no doubt in my mind that there will continue to be instances of major fraudulent financial reporting. The issue is not whether it will be stopped, but whether the likelihood has been reduced. To this I say, "Absolutely yes."

With studies showing somewhat mixed results, let's look at the major features of SOX that really matter in dealing with reporting.

- *The audit committee.* A well-qualified, capable, serious, and diligent audit committee undoubtedly is among the most important elements of preventing fraudulent financial reporting—or, for that matter, erroneous reports. Audit committees became more empowered, feeling the spotlight emanating from the major reporting failures, Sarbanes-Oxley, tighter stock exchange listing standards, and the like. With an audit committee armed with good knowledge of the business and carrying out its expanded oversight responsibilities with due care and focusing on the financial reporting process, there's less likelihood that improprieties in financial reporting will occur in the first place and greater likelihood that if they do occur they'll be noticed. While no guarantee exists, by taking their role seriously and working diligently, the deterrent factor is greater and there's a better chance indicators of wrongdoing will be identified. Although the audit committee is an oversight body and doesn't conduct audits itself, by executing its responsibilities effectively it serves as a vital line of defense.
- *Code of conduct.* Whether restricted to those in the financial reporting process as required by law or (as in many companies) expanded to cover all company personnel, the code is a cornerstone in preventing fraudulent reporting. Many organizations recognized that a code by itself won't do the job, but must be complemented by the right messages and actions from all levels of management, effective training, and two-way communication to determine the extent to which the code is understood and embraced throughout the organization.
- *Whistleblower channel.* With this long-standing best practice mandated, companies established mechanisms by which employees who know of fraudulent reporting can blow the whistle. This, too, justifiably is seen as important to preventing bad reporting, especially of the type where senior officials mask reality by overriding established controls, concocting transactions, or manipulating reports at the highest levels. In most instances a fraud designed at the top requires, or results in, others in the organization knowing about it.

A few years ago when I said in a published commentary that these three are the most significant features of the Sarbanes-Oxley Act, one reader wrote back saying:

> I agreed totally with your statement when you concluded that independent and qualified audit committees, codes of conduct and whistleblower channels 'are the most significant results of Sarbanes.' However, [you] might have [said] they [are] the only significant results. Let's remember who actually perpetrated [the] heinous acts of fraud and deception. It was [not] the A/P clerk or the cash management specialist. It was the C-level executives . . . [and] very little of what was implemented as a result of Section 404 will prevent Ken Lay or Andrew Fastow from colluding to commit fraud.

On the surface, these sentiments may seem valid. But first let's look at other factors aiding in such prevention of fraudulent reporting:

- *Integrity and ethical values.* Obviously, managers and all personnel with high levels of integrity and sound ethical values form a basis for doing the right thing in all respects, including financial reporting. As elements of the right kind of corporate culture, these attributes drive behavior at all levels. While they can't be legislated, integrity and ethics nonetheless are key drivers of reliable reporting.
- *Incentives and temptations.* Avoiding the wrong kind of incentives and unhealthy temptations is critical to helping prevent improper financial reporting. Appropriate motivations for achievement are part of sound business practices, but pressure to meet unrealistic performance targets, extreme rewards based on reported financial results, and poor or nonexistent segregation of duties all contribute to an unhealthy environment.
- *Management's philosophy and operating style.* Management's attitude toward financial reporting, conservative or aggressive selection from available alternative accounting principles, conscientious development of accounting estimates, and attitudes toward data processing and accounting functions and personnel all help determine the reliability of financial reporting.
- *Internal audit.* A well-qualified and effective internal audit function can both be a deterrent to fraudulent financial reporting and detect it when it does occur. Certainly Cynthia Cooper, the internal auditor who some years ago blew the whistle at WorldCom and subsequently graced the cover of *Time* magazine, is a good example of how important internal audit can be.

▪ *External Audit.* Audits of financial statement audits and internal control can detect, and have detected, fraudulent financial reporting, and also serve as a deterrent to prevent improprieties by those concerned about discovery.

Well, guess what? Other than external audit, each and every one of these factors, including the big three—an effective audit committee, code of conduct, and whistleblower channel—indeed *are part of a company's system of internal control over financial reporting.* So, while some individuals have decried the lack of internal control's relevance and even depicted it as meaningless low-level activity, actually internal control has many components that work together to, among other things, help prevent fraudulent financial reporting.

The external audit, while it can deter or detect fraudulent financial reporting, is not part of a company's internal control system. But certainly it is an important element in the overarching system to ensure that reliable information is provided to investors in the capital markets.

 ## REAL LIFE IN THE C-SUITE

As noted, integrity and ethical values, management's philosophy and operating style, and related factors play a significant role in the reliability of financial reporting. The reality is that chief financial and other officers can and often have played a key role in avoiding fraudulent reporting, including in situations where a dominant CEO insists on making the numbers at any cost.

Over the years I've worked with many CEOs, mostly of large companies but some mid-size ones as well, and a significant number would be viewed as dominant, if not domineering, by anyone's measure. And we've seen unfortunate instances where a company's CEO orchestrated major and devastating financial reporting fraud. In some of those instances the CEO was the driver with the CFO going along for the ride; in others the CFO played a critical role in initiating and devising schemes to make it happen.

What might not be readily visible from the outside are the many chief executive officers who never have and never would suggest financial reporting fraud, and the many CFOs who would stand up to such a suggestion or order by refusing to participate and taking the consequences. Yes, in past years there might have been some shading at the edges, even so-called earnings management, for which regulators' and the investing public's appetite has been all but eliminated.

In any event, there's no doubt that even in past years the great majority of CEOs would never consider fraudulent financial reporting, and in the relatively few instances where it was proposed, the great majority of CFOs had the backbone to say no. Yes, they might have entered into discussions, out of courtesy and respect for the reporting relationship, about going to the edge of acceptable behavior—but at the end of the day most CFOs would not be browbeaten into submission, despite the threat of being fired and the potentially devastating effect on the CFO's life in terms of career, income, and possibly personal life.

Rather, what we've seen are CFOs under such pressure convincing overreaching CEOs that stretching financial reporting to the breaking point is in the interest of neither the company nor the CEO himself, for several reasons. One is that, quite simply, the facts ultimately will come out, pointing to those senior executives who manipulated the books by borrowing from the future on the basis that the current problems would turn around in the next period, only to face the reality that this seldom happens. Another argument is that not only is fraud fundamentally and unequivocally wrong, but on a purely pragmatic basis the risks are too great—for the company, its shareholders, and the executives. They may get away with a temporary, short-term advantage, but in all likelihood the end result will be reality crashing down around their professional and personal lives.

I believe the great majority of CFOs have long operated in this vein. Certainly, in the post-SOX environment, those few that might have succumbed to the pressure now think more than twice before agreeing to any such illegal activities. And the marketplace now tends to reward companies whose financial reporting provides more reliable and understandable information and stays far away from the fringes of legality.

Beyond the chief financial officer, experience shows that other senior personnel—including general counsels, controllers, chief accounting officers, and chief audit executives—would and do act similarly. Here, too, most of these individuals have high levels of integrity and ethical values, with the emotional fortitude to push back at the thought of breaking the law, even in the pre-SOX environment.

Prime examples of not accepting wrongdoing—and indeed taking action to do the right thing—are provided by Sherron Watkins of Enron and Cynthia Cooper of WorldCom, who along with FBI Agent Coleen Rowley were pictured on the cover of *Time* magazine. They found themselves in the limelight, but they really are representative of the many honest and committed executives in American business.

With that said, there are still people out there who would do bad things, and no system is foolproof. So we need to continue to ensure the integrity, ethical values, and capabilities of our business leaders, and the necessary systems of oversight, checks and balances, to have a reasonable likelihood of preventing or quickly identifying those outliers whenever they might surface.

* * *

So, yes, internal controls, including those related to reliability of financial reporting, do indeed matter. In Chapter 9 we move on to operational controls, and the effects they, or their absence, can have on a company's reputation, prospects, and even survival.

CHAPTER NINE

# Control over Operational Performance

W E'VE SAID INTERNAL CONTROL over financial reporting addresses only one of a company's major categories of objectives, the others being compliance with laws and regulations and effectiveness and efficiency of operations. The distinction is critical but sometimes overlooked, even by smart and capable people. More fascinating is that some accomplished businesspeople believe that because their companies comply with SOX 404, they have what's needed with respect to the entirety of internal control and even extending to risk management.

Working recently with a large multinational company, I spent time with each of the directors, one of whom is a nationally known and highly regarded educator and business advisor. His explicit message to me was that since the company already complies with SOX 404, including auditor attestation, risk management is well addressed in the organization—and there's no need, therefore, for the board to look into that area. Using all the tact I could muster, I asked whether he had considered that the SOX 404 rule focuses only on internal control over financial reporting—and does not address internal control over either operations or compliance objectives—and while there is a risk-identification/analysis element therein, 404 does not extend to a company's broader risk management processes. After much discussion he better understood that the company's and auditor's compliance with 404 doesn't provide comfort regarding operational or compliance objectives and their related risks and controls.

In this chapter, we look at the broadest category of objectives, effective and efficient operations. To get a sense of what internal control over operations is about, we can point to a wide range of a company's business activities—sourcing, inventory control, production processes, distribution, marketing, selling, customer service, brand management, treasury, human resources, and information technology, and others. If it doesn't address risks related to financial reporting or compliance with laws and regulations, the internal controls are directed at a company's operations.

As to why operations controls are so important, we can look at companies that have suffered from lacking adequate controls. While there are numerous examples, we focus here on a few recent serious control lapses: first oil companies that didn't have adequate controls to protect some of their most valuable assets, and then the financial services industry—namely Société Générale, Washington Mutual, and Countrywide Financial—as well as banks suffering in the foreclosure process. Each illustrates a failure to consider and institute basic internal controls relative to the effectiveness of business operations.

 ## IT CONTROLS

Serious problems with information technology controls recently surfaced at five major oil companies. No, we're not talking about obvious problems with deepwater drilling, oil spills and related damage, discussed in Chapter 6, but rather about protecting critically sensitive corporate information. You may have seen the media coverage; a recent *New York Times* headline announced, "Hackers Breach Tech Systems of Multinational Oil Companies."

Now, we've long known the importance of identifying and analyzing risks related to corporate information and establishing relevant controls to keep that information secure. IT managers and security executives, internal auditors, and others in many companies have worked diligently to provide assurance that specified sensitive information is available internally on a need-to-know basis, and that valued trade secrets remain as such. And we've known the risks of hackers getting inside the secret vault of information, with the potential to wreak havoc. Certainly we would like to think the largest corporations have well-designed and up-to-date control systems to achieve these important operational objectives.

Back to the oil industry: Cyber attacks apparently emanating from somewhere in China hit what might be viewed as a corporate jackpot. According to media reports, experts at IT security firm McAfee said systems at the five (unnamed) multinational oil companies were breached, with the intrusions aimed at corporate espionage. What did the hackers get? Apparently a mother lode: a haul no less than "oil and gas field production systems and financial documents related to field exploration and bidding for new oil and gas leases," as well as information related to industrial control systems. Talk about high-value information!

How did the hackers do it? Information is sketchy, but it points to hackers operating out of Beijing who set up servers in the United States and the Netherlands to break into computers in a number of countries, including the United States. According to the McAfee report, "The intruders used widely available attack methods known as SQL injection and spear phishing to compromise their targets. Once they gained access to computers on internal company networks, they installed remote administration software that gave them complete control of those systems. That enabled the intruders to search for documents as well as stage attacks on other computers connected to corporate networks."

Now, we recognize that hackers are becoming ever more sophisticated (although the report says these attacks were less sophisticated than successful ones against Google a little more than a year ago) and staying ahead of evolving methods to break into corporate computers is challenging. With that said, however, one wonders how large oil companies wouldn't do everything necessary to prevent cyber attacks, knowing they're occurring with increasing frequency.

Unfortunately, it appears these controls don't seem to be highlighted on radar screens. A Carnegie Mellon CyLab report survey of executives and board members of companies with $1 billion to $10 billion revenue found that while 56 percent considered improving risk management a top priority, none viewed improving computer and data security to be a priority. A distinguished CyLab said: "They don't understand that IT risk is part of enterprise risk."[1] We can add that related internal control over those operational activities also appears not to be a priority.

 ## SOCIÉTÉ GÉNÉRALE

You know the story, how "rogue trader" Jerome Kerviel was at the center of what's been called the largest bank fraud in history. In brief, this mid-level employee, supposedly unbeknownst to anyone else at one of the most venerated banks in France, bet $73 billion of the bank's money, costing it $7.2 billion. The newspapers covering the story promptly dusted off all the familiar names in the annals of bank fraud, including Joseph Jett of Kidder Peabody and Nick Leeson of Barings Bank, among others. But this one tops them all by far.

Having been involved in a number of the most high-profile frauds—let me rephrase that: having been involved in investigating and cleaning up after a number of such frauds—I'd like to share some thoughts on what went wrong. And clearly a lot did go wrong. Let's refresh memories.

## What Happened

Basically, Kerviel made unauthorized trades and hid them from others at Société Générale. He was authorized to trade in the European stock indexes, so long as he hedged much of the risk. But he didn't complete the hedge transactions, in effect placing what became bad bets that European markets would continue to rise. To cover his tracks he fed false transaction data into Soc Gen's computer system to make it appear that he had indeed carried out the hedges. When bank executives finally found out, they moved to unwind the $73 billion of Kerviel's bad bets, resulting in the loss.

The accompanying news reports show the bank's responses to be fascinating. Here are some of the more telling quotes coming from the top:

- Société Générale has been victim of a serious internal fraud committed by an imprudent employee.
- Kerviel was mentally weak. I have no idea why he did that.
- Kerviel is a terrorist.
- Kerviel was a very junior trader, not a star, starting to work on a small portfolio. He's more of a shy person than an extrovert.
- Research has not shown any link with anyone else at Société Générale.
- Kerviel breached five levels of controls [and was] a computer genius.
- Hiding it was a full-time job, because you needed to know exactly what to do.
- We have no explanation for why he took these positions, and we have no reason to believe he benefited from a financial point of view. We don't understand why he took such a massive position.

The last point is underscored by reports that the bank's management was at a loss to describe Kerviel's motivations, with chairman-CEO Daniel Bouton saying that *the trader didn't earn a dime on his actions.*

## Motivations

Risk management experts, especially those knowledgeable in fraudulent activities, have long known that identifying the motivations behind fraud is critical to understanding the risks and establishing controls needed to reduce the risk of fraud to manageable levels. The key is that major frauds of this type often have nothing to do with employees stealing money. They have everything to do with other motivating factors.

The statement by the bank's executives that they're at a loss to describe Kerviel's motivations is hard to fathom. Anyone who's been in the business world for more than five minutes should know there are two kinds of frauds: one to put money in somebody's pocket, the other to make the performance of the individual, unit, or business look better than it is.

It's rather clear that Kerviel wasn't looking to steal money for himself. After an initial interrogation, he said he did what he did to be respected in an organization where, because of his background, he had relatively little respect, and to earn a big bonus. This is not atypical of bank frauds, where the perpetrator wants to show he's capable of doing great things for the institution and hopes to receive recognition, promotions, and bigger compensation.

When you probe a bit deeper into these sorts of frauds, history shows that usually the individual doesn't believe he (I can't remember any women ever involved in major bank frauds) will get caught. And even if he does, the fraudster doesn't understand all the fuss about his actions—after all, he was trying to make money for his employer, not himself. When his trades start to go bad, he sees it as only a temporary situation, fully believing that more such trades will solve the problem; ultimately, he thinks, the trades will work out and demonstrate that he really is a smart, capable person.

And for some it seems there's not much to lose. With difficulties in other areas of their lives, it seems to them to be a case of heads we win, tails you lose. After all, they're playing with someone else's money, and of course they don't intend to lose in the first place.

While it's doubtful that this next point is at the forefront of a fraudster's mind, the reality is that a number of them, after a stint in prison—Kerviel was sentenced to three years behind bars—become sought-after consultants and stars on the lecture circuit, reaping more glory and money than they ever hoped to make when working for a living!

## Where Was the Internal Control?

Let's begin with how the fraud ultimately was found out. Reports say that Kerviel changed a tactic he had been using to conceal his trades. He took a position that prompted a possible margin call, which raised a red flag in the computer system and caught the attention of the bank's risk control specialists. An investigation of trading records the next day uncovered the extent of the fraudulent trading, and after about a week to unwind the open positions, Société Générale disclosed the fraud publicly.

It's also been reported that:

- While the bank initially believed Kerviel engaged in his scheme "only" for less than a year, he apparently had been doing so for three years.
- He knew that other traders at the bank engaged in similar (though smaller levels of) unauthorized trades, but were never questioned about them.
- He knew and used access codes and passwords of colleagues in the trading unit and IT department.
- He was not required to take vacations, instead taking off only four days in his last year.
- Several times his actions accidentally signaled problems to the bank's risk-management personnel, but they never investigated further than asking Kerviel about what happened and accepting his explanations.

As internal control goes, this is pretty basic stuff. Where was security over access codes and passwords, including procedures for maintaining privacy and frequent automated changes? Where were the mandatory vacations and thorough follow-up on signals of impropriety? And we can only wonder about other basic controls, such as automated application controls over trading patterns, supervisory controls—four supervisory executives at the bank have since been fired—and monitoring controls, including appropriate procedures performed by risk-management and internal-audit functions.

More specifically, we can ask whether the bank had satisfactory identification and management of the risks of unauthorized trades. Certainly other banks have been brought to their knees or brought down entirely by a so-called rogue trader. Clearly, these risks have long been well known. So, either these risks weren't taken seriously at Soc Gen, or the right procedures and controls weren't put in place to manage the risks to a reasonable level.

Two additional factors proved critical. One is that even though Eurex's surveillance office had noted irregularities in Kerviel's trades, the bank's risk control experts simply explained the irregularities away. And amazingly, it's reported that the bank has a culture not only of allowing traders at Kerviel's level to regularly exceed authorized limits; it seems there was an expectation that they conduct "proprietary trades to make money for the bank" and the results were explicitly considered in performance evaluations! Major issues of culture were behind what brought the bank to its knees.

## Further Response from the Chairman

Société Générale's chairman-CEO Bouton wrote clients saying that "control procedures have been revised and reinforced to avoid any recurrence of further similar risk." On this note, three thoughts immediately come to mind. First, why weren't those controls in place previously? Second, how is it possible, in the space of one week, to know the details of exactly what transpired and what specific controls need to exist to manage such risks? Third, what was being done to deal with similar risks that could cost the bank billions of dollars?

It's interesting how one can put a positive light on almost anything. The chairman also reportedly said: "Had we not acted swiftly, the loss could have been 10 times worse." That's an interesting position to take, considering the fraud had evidently been going on for years; the bank was brought to its knees and needed a massive influx of new capital; it's being blamed as exacerbating a precipitous downturn in the capital markets; and the bank has had to deal with numerous lawsuits. It's hard to imagine what "10 times worse" might have been.

With the billions in losses incurred, calls for Bouton's ouster started almost immediately, and soon afterward he stepped down as CEO. He was at the helm when the Soc Gen ship hit an iceberg that should have been seen and avoided. Management knew the company was in dangerous waters—regulators and others apprised them that damage appeared to have already been done—but did nothing to investigate and steer clear of disaster. He did stay on as board chairman, at least temporarily.

 ## WASHINGTON MUTUAL

At hearings of the U.S. Senate Permanent Subcommittee on Investigations looking into causes of the financial crisis, Kerry Killinger, CEO of the now-defunct bank Washington Mutual, contended that his company hadn't been treated fairly. Documents were released that disclosed how he compared liquidity—which, he complained, was provided to other banks in distress but not to WaMu— to oxygen.

Well, according to reports of the hearings, it looks more like WaMu created such a toxic, oxygen-starved control environment for itself, one so bad that you have to wonder how anyone within the organization could survive, and whether any amount of help—oxygen, liquidity, or otherwise— could have saved the company.

It's well known that years ago Washington Mutual drilled a mantra into its managers' heads: "The Power of Yes." I say mantra because Senate testimony depicts how in at least one meeting, WaMu managers actually had to chant those words. Well, that might have been a catchy and effective marketing line, but it also seems to have been one of the root causes of a culture at WaMu that strived to generate as many mortgages as possible, quality be damned.

Senator Carl Levin, the committee chairman, put it succinctly: "Using a toxic mix of high-risk lending, lax controls, and compensation policies that rewarded quantity over quality, Washington Mutual flooded the market with shoddy loans that went bad."

You might think that a lending institution would carefully consider the quality of pending loans—that is, the ability of a borrower to repay the debt, promptly and with the stated interest. All this evokes the old notion of selling product below cost, and then trying to make up the shortage with volume. How could this happen at such a well-recognized financial institution?

Here's how it's done:

- First, develop an incentive system where those involved in loan origination are compensated on the basis of volume—the more mortgages processed, the higher the paycheck.
- Second, focus on higher risk loans, which would presumably bring higher rates and, of course, more compensation.
- Third, pay staff even more for overcharging borrowers with higher points or interest rates, and include some harsh prepayment penalties as icing on the cake.
- Fourth, focus heavily on interest-only or adjustable-rate mortgages and similar terms, where borrowers face higher, crushing payments down the road.
- And fifth, give borrowers help in overstating their income or assets—that is, lying—to meet the bank's already low minimum standards.

For good measure, you can also add to this mix (all the above are alleged to have happened at WaMu) having at least one employee take under-the-table payments to process substandard and even fraudulent loans—yet another allegation against the formerly reputable WaMu.

## More Systemic Problems

The Senate investigations do portray some within the organization as trying to curb the rush to the bottom. WaMu's risk officer from that period reportedly said he tried to change the culture of always making the loan, making repeated efforts to cap the portion of high-risk and subprime loans in the portfolio and to cut down on new loans made with no income or other verification—but all to no avail. His successor as chief risk officer paints a similar but broader picture, saying the firm's failure was caused not only by lax underwriting and a shift away from loan performance and quality toward production and speed, but also by poor regulation, complacent credit rating agencies, and the appetites of Fannie Mae and Freddie Mac. Well, that sounds like a burglar blaming a homeowner for not having a better security system.

The Senate investigations also suggest that WaMu's management wasn't interested or concerned over the state of affairs even after serious problems surfaced. In one instance, an internal investigation found high rates of confirmed fraud in two of WaMu's highest loan-producing units, but according to the Senate subcommittee, "no steps were taken to address the problems, and no investors who purchased the loans originated by these offices were notified."

Well, now the FDIC has sued Killinger, along with two others—the bank's president of home lending and its chief operations officer—for taking "extreme and historically unprecedented risks." The complaint says they "focused on short-term gains to increase their own compensation, with reckless disregard for WaMu's long term safety and soundness," and alleges failure to institute proper risk management systems and internal controls. At the risk of piling on, I only wonder whether and how often the defense will use the term "oxygen deprived."

## The Broader Picture

This brings us to the other side of the equation: the selling of these tainted mortgages.

We've heard many descriptions of what WaMu and other major banks did in the securitization and selling of mortgage products. But I've yet to see what transpired described as succinctly as by Senator Levin, who said: "They built a conveyor belt that dumped toxic mortgage assets into the markets like a polluter dumping poison into a river. Down river, there was Wall Street, with its huge appetite for these mortgage-backed securities. They bottled that polluted water, slapped a label on it from the credit rating agencies that said it was safe drinking water, and sold it to investors." Levin's assessment becomes even more damning, saying that WaMu packaged and sold loans *precisely because* they were likely to go bad or had been identified as fraudulent, with no notification to investors.

## Do We Need More Lessons?

I don't know that we need new lessons, but evidently we need to dust off old ones we supposedly learned from other failures. Frankly, I've warned for years that compensating loan officers based on quantity over quality is a serious problem. We've seen many instances of bank loan officers putting big numbers on the books in one year, only to move to another institution the next. As such, there never was accountability for quality. That wasn't the case universally, and many banks have had controls such as loan review committees that must approve new bookings, especially larger ones. But often the incentives were skewed, more and more so as senior management of some firms developed a culture (as reportedly occurred at WaMu) of focusing on quantity and speed at the expense of quality.

I know firsthand of one financial services firm where years ago the idea of handsomely rewarding individuals for bringing in large new accounts was subject to review. The question posed was, "Shouldn't we better assess whether or not new business being brought to the firm is expected to be truly profitable?" The answer was a resounding "yes," resulting in a new system where executives were rewarded for conducting insightful analysis of potential profitability—even when concluding that the new business would be unprofitable or too risky and should be turned down. The result was still growth, but growth effectively managed for quality, with the business prospering going forward. Sure, this should have been an obvious part of any new business development process all along, but we know well that focus on growing the top line can spur short-sighted behavior that hurts the future bottom line.

We hear much talk about clawbacks and extended vesting periods for CEOs, to ensure actions taken on their watch to drive reported profits actually hold up in ensuing years. Well, the same concepts can, and should, be applied to employees involved in business development. It makes sense to reward personnel not only for the quantity of new business, but also the quality in terms of ultimate profitability.

Certainly internal control does matter a great deal. Companies seeking to drive up the top line without regard to quality can allow established controls to be diminished or ignored. Sometimes this is done intentionally, other times subconsciously in concert with the shortsighted push for quantity. This is where the risk officer, compliance officer, legal counsel, audit executive, audit committee, and others need to step up and do what's necessary to ensure business initiatives are well controlled—to ensure that long-term business goals are indeed likely to be met.

 ## COUNTRYWIDE FINANCIAL CORPORATION

Circumstances at this huge mortgage generator reportedly were similar to those at WaMu, so there's no need to repeat the details here. But it is worth focusing on what came out of the SEC's investigations.

To refresh memories, Countrywide's chief executive and two other senior officers were charged by the SEC with hiding risk information from investors, as well as improper sales of the company's stock. The SEC said CEO Angelo Mozilo was touting the company's loan portfolio while in private e-mails he was calling its products "toxic" and saying he "personally observed a serious lack of compliance within our origination system as it relates to documentation and generally a deterioration in the quality of loans originated." He also said internally that the company's subprime second mortgage product line was "poison," and later wrote about holding pay-option adjustable rate mortgages on the company's balance sheet: "The bottom line is that we are flying blind on how these loans will perform in a stressed environment of higher unemployment, reduced values and slowing home sales."

A couple of things are especially interesting. First is that while Mozilo as CEO expressed concerns, he wasn't willing or able to turn the direction of the company in time to avoid having to be taken over in a forced fire sale. Second, you'll remember that Jerome Kerviel of Soc Gen was motivated at least in part by his feelings about his background—he reportedly felt he didn't have the same pedigree of class stature or education that many of his colleagues had.

It seems that Angelo Mozilo suffered from a similar state of mind. Media reports say Mozilo, whose father was a butcher in the Bronx, New York, was "obsessed with wresting market share away from his buttoned-down rivals in the staid world of banking." "I run into these guys on Wall Street all the time who think they're something special because they went to Ivy League schools," Mozilo is reported to have said. "We're always underestimated. And we still are. I am. I must say, it bothered me when I was younger—their snobbery and their looking down on us."

Mozilo ultimately settled the charges with the SEC, agreeing to pay $67.5 million ($20 million by Countrywide under an indemnification agreement) and to be permanently barred from serving as officer or director of any public company.

 ## THE FORECLOSURE FIASCO

Having suffered through one of the worst times in industry history, with WaMu, Countrywide, and others brought to their knees or utterly failing, some of the big banks found themselves dealing with another fiasco. It turns out that after losing billions of dollars on bad home mortgages—in one form or another—banks found they often don't have basic documentation showing ownership of the properties on which they're trying to foreclose. One would think these financial institutions would know something about internal control, but what's transpiring causes one to seriously question that presumption.

Adding insult to injury, reports indicate that statements by bank officials in legal proceedings, saying loan files were reviewed and required documents in good order, often simply were not true. With banks' foreclosure processes on hold, homeowners who defaulted on mortgages remain in their houses and buyers aren't able to complete transactions, causing the entire housing market to remain on shaky ground.

### Problems Surface

According to reports, the problem first came to widespread light when GMAC announced it was withdrawing affidavits in pending court cases and suspending certain foreclosures to give it time to investigate its procedures. Soon afterwards JPMorgan Chase suspended foreclosures in the 23 states requiring court approval in order to determine whether the documentation meets legal standards. Bank of America then said it would "amend all affidavits in foreclosure cases that have not yet gone to judgment." And of course that wasn't the end, with JPMorgan Chase subsequently expanding the scope of its review of foreclosure documents to 41 states. Bank of America then suspended the foreclosure process in all 50 states, but after its review of documentation and saying it found no problems, it restarted the process again in the first 23 states.

Some other big banks may have issues, but at the time of this writing one of the big players, Citigroup, had not taken similar action—it didn't suspend foreclosures, saying it began a review of loan servicing processes about 18 months before in anticipating a huge increase in foreclosures. Wells Fargo initially and adamantly said its foreclosure processes were accurate and had no need to suspend them, but soon afterward said it would correct and refile documents in approximately 55,000 cases, adding its employees didn't "strictly adhere" to its own procedural requirements. With enough evidence to indicate widespread industry problems, the attorneys general of all 50 states launched an investigation into foreclosure practices.

## Why It Happened

The current mess in which banks find themselves began years ago when home prices were soaring and the banks were writing mortgages with lightning speed. It seems that the banks looked first at raking in the dollars while paying insufficient attention to mortgage servicing, including collecting and processing monthly payments from homeowners and maintaining basic ownership records.

A report in the *New York Times* said:

> Banks spent billions of dollars in the good times to build vast mortgage machines that made new loans, bundled them into securities and sold those investments worldwide. Lowly servicing became an afterthought. Even after the housing bubble began to burst, many of these operations languished with inadequate staffing and outmoded technology, despite warnings from regulators. When borrowers began to default in droves, banks found themselves in a neverending game of catch-up, unable to devote enough manpower to modify, or ease the terms of, loans to millions of customers on the verge of losing their homes.[2]

One regulator, FDIC chair Sheila Bair, who during the financial system's near meltdown generally was ahead of the curve on major issues, lamented "We waited and waited and waited for wide-scale loan modifications [but] they never owned up to all the problems leading to the mortgage crisis. They have always downplayed it."

## How It Happened

The topic at hand in this chapter is the category of internal control called operations controls, which as noted involve what a company does to make its business more effective and efficient in achieving its basic business objectives, including meeting performance and profitability goals and safeguarding its resources. This of course includes protecting assets such as mortgage loans and underlying collateral and related income streams. (Note that some controls are in place to accomplish objectives in multiple categories.)

With that in mind, let's look at some of the transgressions. Reports say the following:

- There were problems with notarizations on mortgage assignments, where documents transferring ownership of the underlying note from one institution to another were faulty. Notarizations predated preparation of legal documents or occurred in different geographical locations from those where the documents were signed—both of which indicate notaries didn't do what they attested to doing.
- The veracity of original documents compiled as part of the foreclosure process is questionable and asserted to be flawed.
- Officials at mortgage servicers who attested to reviewing loan files for accuracy and completeness sometimes signed hundreds of documents on one day, indicating such reviews had not actually taken place. These officials were dubbed "robo-signers." One said he was instructed to sign at least 350 per hour, and put his signature on 4,000 a day.

One could reasonably ask, how could this have happened? Here's what's been uncovered in media reports:

- At JPMorgan Chase, the mortgage servicing department was staffed with what became known as "Burger King kids"—"walk-in hires who were so inexperienced they barely knew what a mortgage was."
- At Citigroup and GMAC, "dotting the i's and crossing the t's on home foreclosures was outsourced to frazzled workers who sometimes tossed the paperwork into the garbage."
- At a mortgage servicing arm of Goldman Sachs, "employees processed foreclosure documents so quickly that they barely had time to see what they were signing." One deposed staffer reportedly said, "I don't know the ins and outs of the loan, I'm not a loan officer."

Citigroup, GMAC, and other banks outsourced much of the foreclosure effort to law firms later accused of shoddy work. One firm in turn outsourced the work to firms in Guam and the Philippines. A law firm employee said in a deposition that "the girls would come out on the floor not knowing what they were doing. . . . Mortgages would get placed in different files. They would get thrown out. There was just no real organization when it came to the original documents." Another testified that she and other employees of a law firm were trained to forge signatures and did the forging repeatedly.

And then there's the matter surrounding the Mortgage Electronic Registration Systems (MERS), set up by the banking industry to facilitate the securitizing of mortgages, with an ancillary benefit of letting banks avoid paying local registration fees each time a mortgage changed hands. Reportedly at least half of mortgages in the United States are recorded as owned by MERS but it actually owns none. What's been done through MERS could cause major problems going forward in the foreclosure process, with the courts viewing MERS with skepticism or worse. A federal judge blocked a bank trying to foreclose, saying the borrower was likely to win, arguing use of MERS invalidated the mortgage. Media reports highlight work of two academicians who say that MERS recording mortgages in its own name could violate precedents barring separating the mortgage from the underlying note. They point to no less than a Supreme Court decision going back to 1879, saying "the assignment of the note carries the mortgage with it, while the assignment of the latter alone is a nullity." The report notes that if assignment is a nullity, the mortgage can no longer be enforced.

State courts are taking a stand. Media reports note that "the Arkansas Supreme Court ruled last year that MERS could no longer file foreclosure proceedings there, because it does not actually make or service any loans."[3] A Utah judge "made the no-less-striking decision to let a homeowner rip up his mortgage and walk away debt-free. MERS had claimed ownership of the mortgage, but the judge did not recognize its legal standing." And back to the federal judge, it's clear he recognizes the implications of his decision, saying "This court does not accept the argument that because MERS may be involved with 50 percent of all residential mortgages in the country, that is reason enough for this court to turn a blind eye to the fact that this process does not comply with the law." Where other courts will ultimately come out is unknown at the moment, but what's happened thus far does not bode well for the comfort of bank shareholders.

After the beating the banks have taken for their roles in causing the mortgage mess and near financial system meltdown in the first place, it seems incredulous that they could have allowed this next fiasco to occur. But reports based on interviews with bank executives, other employees, and federal regulators indicate that the mess "was years in the making and came as little surprise to industry insiders and government officials." As noted, the banks were writing and selling mortgages so fast that normal processing controls took a back seat.

## Basic Internal Controls

One can only wonder how these banks dealt with the basics of internal control over their operations. It's certainly fair to ask about their attention to matters central to the control environment, such as commitment to competence, organization structure, management protocols, human resource standards, and assignment of authority and responsibility. Other obvious questions: Where was the identification and analysis of risk—the risk of significant numbers of foreclosures, and that reliable documents would be needed in the foreclosure process? Where were the control activities to ensure document processing was accurate and complete, with files intact and readily accessible when needed? Where was accountability for carrying out control procedures established and monitored?

And where was the due diligence in selecting and using outsourcing firms? A company's internal control system extends to service providers acting on behalf of the company, making it critically important that an outsourcer's control system meets the company's standards. We could go on and on, but it seems the answers to these and related questions are self-evident.

There is little doubt that the focus of attention from high-level management on down was to reap the immediate rewards of generating and selling mortgages, with document processing a low priority. And then when it came time to bring forth documentation in the foreclosure process, once again it seems the focus was on speed and quantity rather than accuracy.

Some bank officials have called the problem simply a "technicality." Well, we know that fortunes have been lost on what may be called a technicality. Internal controls can be called technical or many other things, but we know they are extremely important—especially when billions of dollars are at stake.

## Implications

Skeptics have asked whether the banks' handling of the foreclosure process did any widespread, significant harm. Well, here's food for thought: First, the foreclosure process has slowed to a crawl, with distressed properties—many of which are in foreclosure—reportedly making up about one third of all home sales. As such, buyers of these homes are on hold, awaiting title resolution, and some who already have closed on homes find they might not have true ownership. One title company stopped issuing title insurance policies on one company's foreclosed properties until further notice.

As for the banks' bottom lines, the time and effort needed to deal with this problem are not insignificant. According to one analyst, "The moratorium won't last that long but the problem will last at least four or five years, maybe a decade [and] in the short term it could easily cost $1.5 billion per quarter." Another analyst sees the foreclosure issue costing the banking industry $6 billion to $10 billion. He estimates that "each month's delay cost the banks $1,000 per home loan, so if there was a three-month delay on the roughly two million homes currently in foreclosure, that translated into a $6 billion hit."

There are further implications going beyond foreclosures, back to the original lending activities, focusing on whether the loans packaged and sold to investors adhered to the stated underwriting standards. One observer notes that, "If it turns out that mortgages were bundled together and sold improperly, more holders could sue the banks and force them to buy back tens of billions in mortgage-backed securities." This could well be the case for Bank of America, where one hedge fund suggested that the bank is potentially exposed to "more than $70 billion in losses from mortgage securities that it may have to repurchase from Fannie Mae and Freddie Mac as well as private investors." Early in 2011 the bank paid Fannie and Freddie slightly more than $2.5 billion to settle claims involving only Countrywide, with other claims still open. The two government-backed mortgage companies reportedly have already received $9 billion in repurchase claims while looking to collect $10 billion more from the likes of Wells Fargo, Citigroup, and JPMorgan Chase's Washington Mutual. When claims from insurance companies and private investors are included, analysts say the industry as a whole could be subject to losses estimated at from $20 billion to as much as $179 billion.

The lawsuits of course already have begun. Allstate, for instance, after initiating a suit against Bank of America, took similar action against JPMorgan Chase for mortgage-backed securities it bought from since-acquired Washington Mutual and Bear Stearns, reportedly saying the sellers "lied to rating agencies" while "knowing the underlying load pools were toxic." Investors and insurers may be further aided by a recent Ambac Assurance lawsuit charging that Bear Stearns not only knew early on of significant problems with loans it was packaging and selling, but it actually received settlement payments from loan originators. According to reports, Ambac says Bear Stearns years ago took the "early-default-payment settlements," but simply kept the money rather than applying it back to the investors. And there are indications that other major banks may also have done the same, providing additional impetus for buybacks. Also, AIG reportedly retains the right to sue the major banks for more than $40 billion in mortgage bond purchases, and is planning to do just that—based on the assertion that the banks made misleading statements about the quality of the underlying mortgages.

Back to the foreclosure issue, mentioned earlier was that all 50 state attorneys general are investigating what happened, which may cause more headaches for the banking industry. A media columnist recently outlined why the coming headaches might turn into painful migraines. Foreclosure is a state matter, not a federal one, he says, so the Office of the Controller of the Currency and Office of Thrift Supervision, which previously acted in favor of the large banks, can no longer intervene. And under the Dodd-Frank Act, "states can enforce their own state consumer laws against nationally chartered banks—even when those laws are stronger than any parallel federal law." Further, state attorneys general have received from officials establishing the new Consumer Financial Protection Bureau assurances that the AGs have the right to enforce the Bureau's coming rules and regulations. And that's not all—the Financial Fraud Enforcement Task Force, a coalition of federal agencies and United States attorney's offices, has announced that this foreclosure issue is its "priority No. 1."

In addition to the coalition, individual states have taken direct action, with Arizona and Nevada filing a lawsuit against Bank of America, charging "widespread fraud" and "false promises" in connection with borrowers' efforts to modify mortgage terms. A media report highlights the charges, including that the bank was "assuring customers that they would not be foreclosed upon while they were seeking loan modifications, only to proceed with foreclosures anyway; of falsely telling customers that they must be in default to obtain a modification; of promising that the modifications would be made permanent if they completed a trial period, only to renege on the deal; and of conjuring up bogus reasons for denying modifications." Present or former employees reportedly added fuel to the fire, with one saying "The main purpose of the training is to teach us how to get customers off the phone in less than 10 minutes." Another added, "When checking on a borrower's status, I often found that the modification request had not been dealt with or was so old that the request had become inactive. Yet, I was instructed to inform borrowers that they were 'active and in status.' One time I complained to a supervisor that I felt I always was lying to borrowers." No doubt there's more to come.

More state courts are making a statement, with the Supreme Judicial Court of Massachusetts, the state's highest court, ruling that Wells Fargo and U.S. Bancorp didn't have the appropriate documentation when they foreclosed, and the court returning the properties to the borrowers. More cases are likely to follow. And New York State's chief judge, noting, "It's such an uneven playing field [where] banks wind up with the property and the homeowner winds up over the cliff [not serving] anyone's interest, including the banks," set forth procedures to ensure all homeowners facing foreclosure have legal representation. Not only might other states become more pro-active, but no less than three federal government agencies have begun investigations—the Department of Justice's Executive Office for U.S. Trustees, the Federal Housing Administration, and the Federal Reserve.

The injustice and impact in human terms is well illustrated by recent reports of how JPMorgan Chase harassed a U.S. Marine Corps captain on active duty, including 3 A.M. calls threatening foreclosure. Well, it turns out the bank got it wrong in the case of the captain, along with 4,000 other military personal on active duty who were overcharged. There's something called the Service-members' Civil Relief Act that allows mortgage rate reductions and outlaws foreclosures. The bank apologized for what reportedly was a failure to "adjust its records," and now at least one more lawsuit is on its way, led by a former prosecutor driving a class action. In a similar case, a federal judge ruled that Morgan Stanley's Saxon unit broke the law in foreclosing on and selling the home of a serviceman who was on active duty, ordering the jury to decide on damages. The case recently was settled, with terms undisclosed but the serviceman and his family "well pleased." The bank then made a statement that's truly difficult to ignore: "As we have said previously, Saxon is always willing to make reasonable accommodations to amicably resolve a matter, especially for our service men and women." To me, this statement is another prime candidate for inclusion in Chapter 2's discussion of how attempts at public relations "spin" are seen for what they are, and fool no one.

None of this is lost on the aforementioned coalition of state attorneys general, which recently presented the five largest banks with a set of game-changing demands. Reports say these include prohibition against beginning foreclosure proceedings while a borrower is actively seeking loan modification, a requirement that a borrower making three payments under a temporary loan modification agreement be granted a permanent modification, modifica-tion turn-down subject to automatic review by an ombudsman or independent review panel, compensation programs that reward employees for pursuing loan modification rather than foreclosure, curtailing of late fees, and, where banks engage in misconduct, compensation to borrowers from a preestablished fund, with mortgage balances subject to reduction. While some analysts say these changes would drag out the foreclosure process and delay stabilization of the housing market, this attorneys general plan is reportedly supported by the newly formed Consumer Financial Protection Bureau, along with the Depart-ments of Treasury, Justice, and Housing and Urban Development, as well as the Federal Trade Commission.

And still more regulators have gotten into the act. The Offices of the Comptroller of the Currency and of Thrift Supervision, along with the Federal

Reserve Board and Federal Deposit Insurance Corporation, having investigated the actions of 14 banks—among them Bank of America, Citibank, GMAC, JPMorgan Chase, and Wells Fargo—and their use of third parties, uncovered significant deficiencies in foreclosure processes that they say caused violations of state and local laws and regulations. According to reports, consent orders have been signed requiring the financial institutions to make fundamental changes in operations and controls. They would, for instance, have to set up a single contact point within the organization so that homeowners can avoid what's often a maze of different departments, take steps to ensure there will be no action to foreclose while borrowers are pursuing loan modifications, improve training of staff handling foreclosures, establish more layers of management oversight over the process, and engage an independent consultant to review foreclosures over the past two years and compensate homeowners who were treated improperly. But some in Congress aren't satisfied even with this, and a ranking member of the House Committee on Oversight and Government Reform plans to introduce legislation that would go further, requiring lenders to evaluate homeowners for modifications before initiating foreclosure, create an appeals process for those who are denied modifications, place limits on foreclosure-related fees, and require servicers to prove they have the legal right to foreclose. And of course the state attorneys general are continuing to move forward pushing for their strict standards as well.

We said in Chapter 3 that when someone, in this case millions of borrowers, has been damaged, law and regulation will follow. It may be difficult to find a more direct correlation between the two than what's happening in reaction to the foreclosure fiasco.

* * *

So, does internal control really matter? You bet it does.

In the next chapters, we look at the challenges boards of directors are dealing with, and how some of the more effective ones are carrying out their responsibilities. We also address how boards and managements interface in making the governance process more effective.

 ## NOTES

1. *Corporate Board Member*, First Quarter 2011.
2. *New York Times*, October 13, 2010.
3. *New York Times*, March 6, 2011.

# Boards of Directors' Focus

WHEN THE SARBANES-OXLEY ACT became law, boards and audit committees scrambled to deal with the new rules, and soon after faced new exchange listing standards and related pressures from institutional investors to enhance corporate governance. You may remember efforts to update charters, develop or amend codes of conduct, and establish whistleblower procedures. You probably looked at whether your board had the right expertise, was appropriately independent, and regularly held executive sessions. You designated an audit committee financial expert, focused on the effectiveness of internal control over financial reporting, looked closely at your company's financial disclosures—including earnings releases, pro forma financial information, and guidance to analysts—codified record retention policies, and initiated board and committee assessments.

You also may have established communications channels for shareholders, posted public filings on your web sites, and accelerated filing of material events with the SEC. As a member of the board and one or more of its committees—whether audit, compensation, nominating/governance, or other—you probably focused on requirements and marketplace expectations associated with your role, attended conferences or a directors' college, and might have had a case of eye strain from reading published reports and articles on the topics of governance, compliance, ethics, and risk management.

More recently you've had to deal with a host of governance-related rules issued by the SEC, calling for extensive disclosures to provide more information to investors. As such, attention has been given to such matters as the relationship of a company's compensation policies and practices to risk management, the background and qualifications of directors and director-nominees, how the board or its nominating committee considers diversity when identifying director candidates, and board leadership structure—for example, one person serving as both board chair and CEO versus split roles. You've also thought about the required disclosures about the board's role in risk oversight, and potential conflicts of interests of compensation consultants, along with revised rules for reporting stock and option awards to company executives and directors in the Summary Compensation Table. And of course, while these are put forth as disclosure rules, boards have been working diligently in considering what substantive changes to board structure and protocols would be useful to the board in carrying out its responsibilities.

And now we have the financial regulatory reform law known as Dodd-Frank, which goes further to empower shareholders. Say-on-pay votes for shareholders are required, and while voting results aren't binding, the measure is viewed as a long-desired step forward, extending to severance payments as well as more routine executive compensation. The law sets in motion requirements for additional independence standards for compensation committees and for engaging compensation consultants. It mandates new disclosures on the relationship between compensation and company performance and on the ratio of compensation paid to the CEO and median pay for all other employees. Additionally, the law contains clawback provisions that go beyond those in Sarbanes-Oxley—misconduct won't be a prerequisite for a clawback—and new disclosure requirements on hedging of company equity securities, among other rules. And new whistleblower provisions take hold.

But the biggest prize in Dodd-Frank, straight from the top of the shareholder wish list, is none other than shareholder access to the proxy statement. The law gives the Securities and Exchange Commission direct authority to adopt rules letting shareholders include nominees in the company's proxy materials, which it did soon after Dodd-Frank was signed into law, though is currently on hold while a court considers a legal challenge from the U.S. Chamber of Commerce and Business Roundtable. This has been institutional shareholders' dream for years—the right to nominate directors without incurring the significant costs of a proxy fight—and goes well beyond voting on such matters as compensation, whether advisory or otherwise, to having a direct say in who sits at the board table! And even where they don't use this new ability to nominate directors, there's little doubt that large shareholders will use this new power to push boards to deal with matters on shareholders' agendas.

Is all of this a further federalization of corporate governance requirements, once the almost sole purview of the states, with Delaware taking the lead? You bet it is. Whether that's positive or not is an open question. In any event, as a corporate director or officer working with the governance process you're likely well into deciding how to deal with these requirements in the context of myriad new rules being and to be issued by the SEC.

 ## A FOCUS ON THE RULES

For years after SOX was signed into law, boards of directors and their audit committees were pushed into a mode of complying with the mandates. With attention shifted to compliance, considerably less attention was given by many boards to the kind of advice, counsel, and direction that brings greater value to the company and its shareholders.

For instance, after watching the spectacular failures of Enron, WorldCom, Adelphia, and others, many boards became more risk-averse. Later, other rules-based issues came to light, such as the problems of stock option backdating, where the financial media again had a field day. There were cases of executives illegally enriching themselves, misstating the financial statements, and filing improper tax returns. Whether because of a simple administrative issue such as a time delay between a board's granting an option and having paperwork completed, or management deceiving the board, directors had to pay attention to dealing with the backdating and its fallout. Related is the question of whether boards gave sufficient attention not only to the option granting process, but also to the integrity and ethical values of management and the related tone set at the top of the organization and its effect on the heart and soul of the organization, its leadership, and its people.

With boards having dealt with these kinds of issues, the pendulum began to swing back to providing value-added activities and better recognizing how to manage risk for positive gain. Of course, boards of some companies never lost their focus, but too many did. Yes, the strengthened governance requirements serve to enhance board performance, but make no mistake—the rules are simply enablers. That is, a board may comply in full with every requirement now on the books but could nonetheless provide little value, and indeed could provide negative value. By the same token some boards with what would be considered poor governance processes have provided tremendous value to shareholders. I've seen both, and you may have as well. A board adds value only when it executes its oversight responsibilities in a way that makes a sufficient positive contribution to the company's long-term growth, profitability, and return on investment.

So, while focus on the rules is a must, truly effective boards make sure they provide sufficient attention to value-added activities.

##  TRULY EFFECTIVE BOARDS

It's becoming increasingly clear that the landscape has changed—permanently. That means it won't go back to the way it was. In other words, ensuring compliance with the letter and spirit of the new requirements will continue to require attention going forward. This is not a case of "done once and forget about it." Sarbanes-Oxley, stock exchange listing requirements, SEC rules, Dodd-Frank, and other rules and expectations of investors—especially institutional investors and other major shareholders—require ongoing diligence.

But experienced directors and senior executives recognize that the requirements, for the most part, deal with issues of form, not function. Yes, they are important because they're now legal or regulatory mandates, and also can serve as enablers to effective board performance. But as noted, some boards that have always done these things still have not been very effective, while others had few of the now-mandated practices in place yet have been highly effective. What makes a board truly effective is something else entirely. Experienced directors—having spent a disproportionate amount of time on the new mandates that deal for the most part with additional disclosures to and empowering shareholders and imposing checks and balances on management—want to get back to the business of providing the chief executive and senior management team with value-added advice, counsel, and direction on critical issues facing the business.

So where is board attention needed? That will depend on each company, of course. But based on my experience, there are eight principal areas of responsibility where the value-add takes place, outlined here in high-level summary.

1. *Strategy.* Making sure the company gets strategy right is absolutely critical. Effective boards carefully analyze proposed strategy plans and

management's rationale for its recommendation. These directors bring experience and insight into the constructive debate, focusing on markets, competitors, risks, resources, and interdependencies. It is of critical importance that resource allocation, business processes, and senior executives' buy-in all are positioned to drive successful strategy execution.

2. *Risk management.* The board must be comfortable that management is identifying and appropriately responding to risk, and that the board itself is apprised of the most significant risks facing the company. To reach this comfort level, effective boards ensure that management has in place an effective risk-management process, and the directors assess whether risks are undertaken and managed consistent with the established risk appetite.

3. *Tone at the top.* Management establishes the corporate culture, but effective boards ensure that the desired integrity and ethical values are present. Of course, that includes a robust code of conduct, a whistleblower channel, feedback protocols, and related elements comprising a cohesive program, and also means the board must ensure the culture is driven not only by the words of management, but their actions as well.

4. *Measuring and monitoring performance.* The board must ensure that performance measures are linked to strategy, tactics, and the real value drivers. Metrics should balance financial performance with forward-looking, non-financial information. And performance awards should be aligned with company goals.

5. *Transformational transactions.* Directors must be truly comfortable with the business justifications for a proposed deal, whether it be a merger, acquisition, alliance partnership, or joint venture. Effective directors critically evaluate management's data, projections, and assumptions—particularly when it comes to "synergy" and integration assumptions. The board should apply lessons learned from past transactions, and should have the courage to walk away from a bad deal.

6. *Management evaluation, compensation, and succession planning.* Effective boards and compensation committees, especially under the current governance spotlight, ensure that performance criteria and targets for management are linked to strategic goals and desired behavior. Compensation should be crafted to retain the best talent while paying for performance. The best boards don't wait for signs of a departure before having succession plans in place.

7. *External communications.* Corporate boards—particularly their audit committees—continue to struggle to understand what entails "appropriate

oversight" of financial reporting and related processes. Effective audit committees ensure they have requisite information from management and auditors, and the committee members gain sufficient understanding and insight and challenge critical judgments, resulting in the necessary comfort with the reliability of financial reports, internal control, and related matters.

8. *Board dynamics.* This involves the ways in which the board itself operates. The most effective boards forge the right relationships, processes, and constructive engagement to carry out the above responsibilities effectively.

We'll expand on some of these areas of responsibilities in coming chapters. For a more extensive discussion you may want to look to *Corporate Governance and the Board—What Works Best*, a book issued by PwC that I led development of before the Enron debacle hit. At the risk of my being immodest, it was then hailed as a landmark and a seminal work, and, having stood the test of time, it continues to apply in the current environment.[1]

 ## A PUBLIC WATCHDOG?

Board responsibilities have long been established by state courts, with Delaware as a leader—actually *the* leader—and in recent years by federal law and regulation. Delaware's Chancery and Supreme Courts have handed down many decisions dealing with director responsibilities in carrying out their duties of loyalty and care, and acting in good faith using the business judgment rule. The resulting case law provides significant insight into effecting those responsibilities.

A few years ago I read with dismay an article in a prestigious board journal taking a different tack, saying a public company's board of directors is a watchdog. This of course immediately brings to mind the 1984 case concerning Arthur Young (now Ernst & Young) where the U.S. Supreme Court said auditors serve a public watchdog function, owing allegiance to a corporation's creditors, stockholders, and the investing public.

But the use of the word *watchdog* in connection with boards of directors is troubling for several reasons. One is that the word has regulatory oversight implications not appropriate at the board level. Another is use of the word without reference to boards' other responsibilities ignores activities critical to meeting relevant interests of public company shareowners. And another is that the word *watchdog* carries a further connotation—specifically, it implies an ability to detect any type of wrongdoing and to ward off intruders and thus prevent harm.

While the term may be appropriate for a vigilant animal guarding a warehouse, watchdog doesn't fit the role of a corporate board of directors. In carrying out its oversight role, a board must be sufficiently knowledgeable of the company's operational activities and monitor the company's policies and processes for reliable financial reporting and compliance with laws and regulations. It must consider management's conduct, and actively challenge management and take corrective action where needed.

But a board's ability to identify wrongdoing is limited for a variety of reasons, not the least of which is that the board is a part-time body. Even those boards with requisite composition that take their monitoring responsibilities seriously cannot possibly identify everything that might go wrong at a company, whether in one center of activity or a far-flung global enterprise. Indeed, even individuals in full-time roles with compliance responsibilities—such as a chief compliance officer or chief internal auditor—are not positioned to identify every misdeed, or even every significant one.

Yes, a board's monitoring role is a critical one, and must be carried out effectively. But a board also must provide the right advice, counsel, and—where needed—direction to senior management. A board that carries out only its monitoring responsibilities is shortchanging the corporate community—management, shareowners, the investing public, and the directors themselves. Taken to an extreme, a board that doesn't give sufficient attention to the company's strategy and business operations is more likely to find that, ultimately, there's no business left to monitor.

While some boards of directors never lost a balanced perspective, for many the pendulum swung to a point where monitoring was the primary focus. Whether that was an overreaction to the new requirements, or the directors' (justified) concerns about damage to personal reputations and liability, monitoring took center stage.

Many boards have since regained a more balanced perspective, and for those that haven't, it's now time to remind themselves of the other critical role they must play. Directors aren't just monitors—they're counselors, critics, protagonists, selectors, approvers, adopters, and more. They select, evaluate, and compensate executives; they approve strategic plans; they adopt and promote policies; and more—all while demonstrating a duty of care and a duty of loyalty. The board is responsible for overseeing management's efforts to enhance shareholder value—as with many things in this world, an appropriate balance is needed.

So, with this said, I'm hopeful we won't find the word *watchdog* creeping into the vocabulary in the context of the role of boards of directors. In fact, I'd like to go so far as to respectfully request parties who write or speak on corporate governance, or are directors or influencers on governance issues, to avoid its use.

##  SOCIETAL RESPONSIBILITY

Questions often arise regarding a corporation's duty to society, with the related issue of a board of directors' responsibility in seeing that such duty is properly carried out. Many large (and not-so-large) companies have embraced a measure of responsibility for social needs, based in part on the premise that the corporation owes its existence to the state, or society, and consequently should be a good citizen. There's no question that companies must comply with applicable laws and regulations, but the issue is to what extent it is required to go beyond those mandates.

Corporate social responsibility typically begins with a focus on such things as economic, environmental, and social matters, and can extend to a wide range of corporate actions. Certainly a significant number of companies have long given attention to these matters, with an increase in recent years. There are different perspectives on the broad topic of corporate social responsibility—especially when comparing viewpoints in other parts of the world. Let's look at one subset that can be used to better understand what a company's and board's responsibilities are with regard to a broader societal role.

### Corporate Gifting

Many companies contribute to worthwhile charitable causes. Certainly this can be viewed as highly commendable. Betsy Atkins, with whom I shared the podium some years back and have from time to time since been in contact with, and whom I respect as an experienced and enlightened corporate director, had something relevant to say on the subject. As reported in the *New York Times*, Betsy explains: "The notion that the corporation should apply its assets for social purposes rather than for the profit of its owners—the shareholders—is an irresponsible use of assets." She contends that companies have an obligation to be responsible—that is, comply with all laws and regulations, create quality products that are marketed in an ethical manner, and present transparent financial information to shareholders.

Also, shareholders can, if they want, spend their own money to promote causes they believe in, she adds, but that should be an individual's choice. "I do not believe that the investing public considers their for-profit public corporation investments to be part of their social charitable causes. The concept of corporate social responsibility is one that deserves to be challenged and examined carefully."

I agree with Betsy and have been making similar statements publicly and privately for a long time. Let me elaborate. There's nothing wrong with being a good citizen, however that's defined, and indeed doing so can be important to a company's success. Producing products that have inherent value, are safe, and are embraced by the marketplace is a worthy and important goal. Today many companies are "greening" their products, often to increase sales, market share, and profitability. Safe and desirable workplaces attract sought-after workers, companies with good community relations are embraced by their local society, and companies that reduce greenhouse gas emissions and other pollutants and waste are held in high esteem, often with associated positive impacts. Investors see reduced risks in companies that provide clear and meaningful financial and related disclosures, and some in the investment community are moving to invest in green or otherwise socially responsible companies.

Certainly all these movements are positive for a number of reasons, including that socially responsible human relations, supplier relations, and environmental and other initiatives, done well, can have a positive effect on the company's bottom line.

While I don't hold myself as an expert on the subject, I believe I know something about it. For a number of years in my former firm I led a joint venture with SmithOBrien, a leading corporate social responsibility boutique firm, in providing corporate social responsibility services to our corporate clients. Smith-OBrien's CEO, Neil Smith, and I have since become good friends, and he continues to chew off my ear about why the right corporate social responsibility policies and practices make good economic sense for any company. He explains, for example, how eliminating harmful pollutants from a manufacturing process can actually lower production costs, how enhancing the workplace environment can improve worker performance, and so forth. I try to tell him that when we're enjoying some down time we can talk about other things, such as our respective favorite baseball teams, the Yankees and Red Sox, but often to no avail.

But the relevant issue here is whether a company has any responsibility to give away its assets. Like Betsy Atkins, I believe generally it does not. But there is an important exception. Where donating corporate assets is deemed to lead to more revenue or higher profits or otherwise increase shareholder returns, then I'm all for it. Whether a gift is from product inventory or cold cash, if there's going to be a positive return on that investment, then by all means go for it. And there certainly are instances where gifts will accomplish those objectives, or at least provide a reasonable likelihood of doing so. It may initially be an indirect benefit, such as to open or cement relationships that will lead to more business, or otherwise provide a real return. As such, as long as they're both legal and ethically sound, there's nothing wrong with making such gifts or, by extension, operating in a way designed to achieve societal goals.

But there are instances where a CEO or other senior manager or sometimes a director has other motives. It may be to ingratiate oneself with a particular person or otherwise move up in a social circle. It may be to establish a reciprocal relationship, where I give to your charity and you give to mine. It may be a case of simply being altruistic, helping a favored cause. Or it might be to enhance a company's reputation and general good standing in the community. It's only this last instance where a gift might be appropriate, and only where a determination is made that the enhanced corporate reputation will indeed provide a real economic shareholder benefit.

## Boards' Responsibilities

Boards of directors have a responsibility to ensure that the company's resources are used wisely, and gift giving and other corporate social responsibility activities are no exception. Often this is an area where a board needs to pay particular attention, in light of frequent requests made of senior management and the typical initial response of saying yes to what seem to be, and often are, good causes. Certainly not every nickel needs to be watched and approved. But when the dollars become significant, or when pledges are made that call for significant ongoing contributions, care must be taken.

The best practice is to have a clear, board-approved policy that details what gifts are appropriate and what gifts are not, with guidelines on dollar thresholds. As noted, it's important for corporations to be responsible citizens by complying with applicable laws and regulations. But when it comes to giving away or otherwise using the company's money, it should be done with one thought in mind: to be responsible to the right party. In this case, the responsibility is to the corporation and its shareholders. If an expenditure is likely to benefit the shareholders, then by all means open the corporate pockets. If not, then the money should be invested where there's the best likelihood of shareholder return, and leave charity and other social goals to the hearts and minds of the shareholders themselves.

There's good evidence that in the last few years many companies have begun to increasingly tie gifting to achievement of specifically identifiable corporate goals.

 **POTENTIAL PITFALLS**

For corporate boards to be well positioned to effectively carry out their responsibilities, directors must bring needed knowledge, skill, and experience to the companies they oversee. We see boards of many companies do well, for instance, in selecting a CEO and senior management team, and making sure the right strategy is in place along with organizational, financial, and human resources for effective implementation. But too many other boards have struggled to do the job, for any number of reasons.

One underlying cause is devoting insufficient time to dissecting and debating issues requiring the board's attention. Being inside boardrooms, we see some directors operate on tight schedules, leaving them unable or unwilling to give needed time and attention to board matters—and they go through the motions without proper deliberation of risks, issues, and events that drive company success or failure.

Board agendas typically are set far in advance of meetings, based on expected needs and historical patterns. Travel arrangements are made and directors schedule other commitments around the established board schedules. As such, a fixed amount of time is set aside for board business, with discussion time shoe-horned into the predetermined schedule. Of course, in times of crisis directors' commitments expand significantly, with other commitments adjusted accordingly. But too often the time set aside for board and committee meetings simply isn't sufficient, especially in light of the current regulatory environment and stakeholders' heightened expectations. Some boards find it useful to build cushions into meeting schedules to deal with matters requiring additional discussion, but this hasn't become a common practice.

Exacerbating this circumstance is the fact that demands on directors' time continue to increase, with data showing that total time devoted annually to board responsibilities has doubled in recent years to about 250 hours. Much of the additional expenditure is due to boards' expanded monitoring duties emanating from compliance-related requirements. But while the time commitment has surged, attention to critical strategic and related matters that create or destroy shareholder value has not always kept pace.

My experience is that many if not most directors of public companies not only have the requisite expertise, attributes, and characteristics commensurate with their tremendous responsibilities, they also devote the time and energy needed to drive corporate success. They extend themselves as needed to guide, counsel, and when necessary direct the CEO and senior management team toward attaining established growth and return goals. But in truth some directors fall short.

Directors must delve deeply enough into significant issues. By accepting board seats, directors already have put their reputations on the line and accepted responsibility to carry out their fiduciary duties. It behooves every board member to work with sufficient diligence to see that the company succeeds.

With that said, let's look at a number of pitfalls boards have fallen into. We'll do this in David Letterman top-10 style, finishing with those most threatening to a company's success. You'll note that there's a natural parallel to some of the eight keyboard responsibilities outlined earlier.

10. *Falling prey to governance ratings.* Boards are cognizant of scores disseminated by a number of organizations providing some sort of rating. And if the investor community sees these ratings as accurate indicators of future company performance, a good deal more attention will be paid. But such correlation has yet to be proved, and spending undue attention on ratings can be counterproductive. This is because criteria used are, with few exceptions, based on information obtained from publicly available data, rather than knowledge of what goes on inside the boardroom. Yes, some information garnered in the ratings process can in certain cases, as some suggest, serve as a window onto board effectiveness. But how well the board truly operates in carrying out its responsibilities to help grow share value is more important than driving up externally developed scores.

9. *Looking at the wrong performance measures.* Boards review data provided by management, and in many cases it's the right information to examine. But when it's not, performance too often deteriorates long before directors realize it's too late to fix what needs to be fixed and value has been eroded. Historical financial and share price data are not enough. Measures must be aligned with the company's strategy and be sufficiently forward looking—including key nonfinancial data—to enable real-time appraisal of how the company is really doing.

8. *Insufficient discipline in director selection.* Having the same directors sitting in the same board seats for a long time has its benefits, but can also have major shortcomings—board membership that might have been right for a

company years ago could be wrong for today and, more importantly, for tomorrow. But haphazard selection of new directors won't ensure the right mix—the process requires thoughtful needs analysis and skills matching. Directors will want to consider not only process in selecting new board members, but also to look around the boardroom and ask, is this the group with which I want to work, and when necessary, go to war?

7. *Preoccupation with potential liability.* Boards and individual directors today are increasingly concerned with personal liability, and justifiably so. Marketplace expectations for directors have risen dramatically, to the point where it may be impossible to satisfy them all. And with the new and still untested federal requirements, our increasingly litigious society, and limitations of many directors-and-officers insurance policies, directors should be concerned about liability. But attention must be paid to fundamental board responsibilities—making sure the company has the right strategy and implementation plan; relevant and aligned performance metrics; strategically and economically sound business partners; effective ethics, control, and compliance programs; sound financial reporting; sensible and effectively motivational compensation programs; and the like. Frankly, if the board does its job well in carrying out its core responsibilities and the company is successful, there is little likelihood of being sued in the first place.

6. *Blatantly ignoring institutional investors.* Owners of significant amounts of a company's stock increasingly want, and expect, to be heard, and boards disregarding these requests are asking for trouble. If the media get involved, the spotlight becomes bright and hot, creating headaches for the board and company that can be intense and long-lasting. Boards certainly shouldn't allow institutional investors to dictate what needs to be done, but allowing major shareowners to raise issues and offer input and suggestions—and ensuring any information provided complies with Reg. FD and other rules—enables those investors to participate in the governance process without voting with their feet.

5. *Thinking you're apprised of critical risks when you're really told about problems.* With all the talk about the importance of being risk-focused, many boards are informed of business issues after the "bad stuff" has already occurred, rather than of where the potential exists for things to go seriously wrong. You want to know—far in advance—where the dangers lie that can derail key initiatives and strategic objectives, and to make sure those risks are being identified early and properly managed.

4. *Presuming top management knows what the critical risks are.* For the board to have any reasonable chance of being informed by management of key risks

facing the company, management itself needs to have processes in place to ensure it can identify newly emerging risks. As such, effective boards ensure the company has an effective risk management process where each level of management identifies, analyzes, and manages risk, and communicates upward. Only through such a process and culture can the board be comfortable that the most critical risks and related actions are presented to the board in timely fashion.

3. *Focusing too much on rules and not enough on other important responsibilities.* A tremendous amount of attention is being given to new legal requirements, the exchanges and the SEC, and ensuring compliance with these requirements is essential. But as noted, those rules tend to deal with matters of form, structure, and disclosure, and a board can follow every rule and still be ineffective. Yes, boards must carry out their responsibilities and act as an effective check and balance on management—a basic thrust behind the new rules and compliance requirements. But the board also must operate effectively as a unit, providing the needed advice, counsel, and direction to management to grow share value.

2. *Signing off on bad strategy.* Many boards do the right thing, carefully assessing strategic plans—often at an offsite retreat—reviewing market, competitive, and other relevant information before approving the company's strategy. But too many boards don't go deep enough. They don't see management's plan for implementation of the strategy and ensure that the plan is supported by the needed organizational structure, resource allocations, and buy-in of key managers who truly will make it happen—or not.

1. *Making bad decisions about the CEO.* It's fair to say that a board's most important responsibility is choosing the right chief executive. But that can also be the most difficult decision to get right. It's only after the fact that one truly knows whether the selection was good or bad. Some boards have waited too long to make a change, and some appear to have pulled the trigger too quickly. Boards that do the best jobs know their company, its needs, the environment in which it operates, and its culture and direction. They carefully identify criteria for the person needed to get the company to where it needs to be, cast a wide net internally (preferably with sound succession planning in advance) as well as externally, and—most important—they have the business acumen, instinct, and judgment to select the right individual to lead the company. And then the board puts in place the right motivations and measures, and provides the right level of oversight—neither abdication nor micromanagement—to help and allow the CEO to do the job.

So, there we have serious pitfalls boards can fall into. In the coming chapters we look more deeply into some of these, and expand on the earlier discussion of what needs to go right.

 **NOTE**

1. Copies may be available from PricewaterhouseCoopers or the Institute of Internal Auditors Research Foundation. Further discussion of board responsibilities also is available in principles set forth by the Business Roundtable, the National Association of Corporate Directors, and the New York Stock Exchange and its Commission on Corporate Governance.

# CHAPTER ELEVEN

# Overseeing Strategy and Risk Management

MOVING FROM THE AREAS that need board attention, here we look more deeply into some of those core areas of a board's oversight responsibility where it can and should add significant value to the company and its shareholders. In this chapter, we address the board's role in strategy development and risk management; in Chapter 12 we discuss CEO compensation, succession planning, and crisis management; and then in Chapter 13 we deal with measuring performance for both internal and external reporting purposes.

 ## STRATEGY

The word *strategy* pops up almost as often in boardrooms as *risk*. Directors recognize that ensuring that the company has an effective strategy in place is among their most important responsibilities, following just after selecting the right chief executive. There are almost as many variations on the strategic planning process as there are businesses, although we've seen commonalities. Numerous books and other resources on the topic are readily available, and what follows is certainly not a treatise on the subject. Rather we highlight here key elements of what works well in a board's carrying out its oversight responsibilities for strategy development, and what doesn't.

For context, it's worth noting that a majority of directors admit to shortcomings in their board's attention to strategy. The NACD's 2009 survey found strategic planning and oversight rated as the most important issue to board governance, but less than 20 percent of respondents rated their boards as highly effective in this area.

In many boardrooms the senior management team introduces a strategic plan and discusses it with the directors, with the main goal of gaining concurrence. Often strategy consultants provide expertise, with the plan sometimes based on the well-known SWOT (strengths, weaknesses, opportunities, and threats) analysis, along with relevant information on such matters as markets, competitors, economic forces, risks, and related indicators. The strategic plan is honed during a one- or two-day offsite retreat, with refinements or in some instances more substantive changes made, and ultimately a strategy document accepted as a blueprint for success.

There's nothing inherently wrong with this approach. Indeed, it often provides a basis for developing a plan that is well constructed, with the potential to truly move the company forward. We find the more effective boards, however, follow a process that goes further, focusing on additional important considerations. But first, a few potential roadblocks to avoid.

## Pitfalls

Although CEOs consistently rank strategy as a top priority, board contribution sometimes is lacking and indeed identified as an area most in need of improvement. *Corporate Governance and the Board—What Works Best*[1] describes how management–board dynamics are susceptible to a wide range of dysfunctional practices from CEOs, including:

- Setting a highly-controlled agenda for strategy discussions, creating an environment that makes it difficult for directors to raise concerns about critical issues.
- Becoming intractably committed to one strategy to the exclusion of other possibilities and impatient with directors who don't share total commitment to the chosen path.
- Reluctance to acknowledge past mistakes, hanging onto a poor strategy that results in stagnation at the company.

Directors sometimes also make negative contributions, being hesitant to aggressively and constructively challenge management-developed strategy. This may be due to directors being insufficiently prepared or being uncomfortable with the reality that management has greater understanding of the industry and company with time and resources not readily available to the board.

## Critical Success Factors

Effective strategic planning ensures clear alignment of the strategy to the company's value drivers, business plan, and implementation plan to create shareholder value. Directors need to be confident that the strategy to be adopted will result in superior shareholder value creation. The strategy should ensure the company's long-term viability or identify a potentially critical need for business combination, partnership, or other transaction. The strategic plan also should clearly define how shareholder value creation will be measured.

All this is easy to articulate, though difficult to do. But likelihood of success is enhanced by an effective working partnership with management in developing and reviewing the corporate strategy. This balance is best achieved when the board provides insight, knowledge, judgment, and analytical skill to the strategic planning process, recognizing that management ultimately owns the strategic and implementation plans, and must fully believe in them. As such, the board should foster an environment where management has the appropriate support for in-depth consideration and assessment of all significant elements relevant to devising a strategy that has a high likelihood of success within risk, growth, and return objectives. And it must engage in substantive and constructive questioning and challenge.

In deciding whether a proposed strategy makes sense for the company in the current economic and competitive environments, it can be critical to look closely at key elements sometimes overlooked. For one, effective directors focus not only on the strategy presented but also on the development process. In addition to reviewing information provided by management, they insist on getting whatever they need that's not already there. They look at such matters as critical assumptions inherent in the strategy, risk factors, major interdependencies, resources, and technology implications, and forces shaping the competitive landscape, including globalization, e-business, disruptive technologies and innovation, and convergence of industries. They zero in on the changing rules of the competitive game, understanding implications such as the worldwide regulatory environment and products and financial markets.

Importantly, they make sure they know what alternatives were discarded. That is, they probe management to learn what other strategies were considered and the rationale for their being discarded, as well as the advantages and disadvantages of those and the selected strategy and related rationale for its acceptance.

Another critical element is for management and the board to see eye-to-eye on the extent of change sought, be it incremental, substantial, or transformational. Is change to be limited to operational alignment, or will it involve repositioning the company with a new market/product focus, or encompass truly breakthrough strategy, transcending current industry practice implying an entirely new business? If management is planning one thing and the board expecting another, there's bound to be trouble.

A strategy's likelihood of success is dependent on these factors that require board attention. And there's at least one more—the plan to be used to be sure that the strategy is effectively implemented.

## Implementation and Measurement

It's well known that any strategic plan is only as good as its implementation. But unfortunately, often little attention is given in board oversight to the effectiveness of management's implementation plan. We've seen instances where boards were entirely unaware of the implementation plan or had been informed of it only in passing.

Boards need to focus as much attention on the implementation plan as they do on the strategy itself. Directors should be asking critical questions related to the plan. Does the company have the resources—financial and human—necessary to carry out the strategy? Is the company positioned and organized to successfully implement the plan? To what extent are key managers involved in the strategy development, and are they fully committed to—and capable of—successful implementation?

Also key to success is ensuring that relevant measures have been developed to gauge progress along the way. Metrics in the form of business-driver related key performance indicators or other relevant measures must be identified before implementation is begun. Those measures then are tracked by management and the board to determine whether course correction might be necessary. They also form the basis for decisions on senior management motivation, performance assessments, and compensation. In addition to traditional financial measures, performance measures should focus on operating performance, enabling ready comparison of performance to plans and budgets, in relation to past periods, peers, competitors, and other established benchmarks. Importantly, measures should include key performance indicators that are forward looking, encompassing leading indicators to provide a view to where the company is headed. More on performance measures in Chapter 12.

Again, strategy is critical, but it's useless without a realistic plan for its achievement. The board not only needs to be aware of that implementation plan, the board needs to be comfortable with it.

## Real-Time Adjustments

Another area sometimes overlooked relates to uncertainty and potential changes in the business environment. By now we should have learned that the business cycle still is with us, though now more pronounced and with longer stretches than previously. Nonetheless, it appears that most strategies today are rooted in the expectation of continuation of the current phase of the cycle.

Some companies have come to recognize the benefits of using variable strategic and implementation plans, with different courses of action geared to varying economic scenarios. But in reality, few companies' strategies are flexible, and because a strategy appropriate for a growth cycle is unlikely to work when the economy is retrenching, management must be able to quickly reconsider the strategy and revamp it as necessary. Management needs to reevaluate the competitive environment—to anticipate reactions to the downturn by customers, competitors, and key suppliers, and to consider the effect on demand, production, and service capabilities.

The boards of directors must work with management in reassessing assumptions underpinning the strategy and determining what directional change is needed. Experienced directors recognize they can offer particularly useful advice to the company's top executives, who may have served in their roles during only one phase of an economic cycle and weren't in those top jobs during another.

 ## RISK MANAGEMENT

Among the last things directors want are surprises. They want to go to sleep at night feeling comfortable that any potential icebergs are on management's radar screens, and that their corporate ship is being navigated effectively. In earlier chapters we outlined what risk management is and what it is not, and how it is implemented effectively. Here we look further at the board's responsibility in overseeing the risk management process.

Certainly board meetings don't last very long these days before the words *risk* or *risk management* or *enterprise risk management* come up. There's an unsettled feeling that if boards of major banks failed to understand and monitor risks in those organizations adequately, then other company boards probably also need to do much better in grasping a company's risks.

Unfortunately, the reality is that boards' approaches to dealing with risk often involve asking management to report on the top 5 or 10 risks facing the company. Typically a risk assessment is conducted, usually with some ranking or other prioritization designed to focus attention on the most significant issues. Knowledgeable directors, however, recognize that a risk assessment is simply a point-in-time snapshot that is soon outdated, regardless of who conducts it. They also know that hearing about the top 10 risks tells them only what senior management knows—which may well omit risks that can potentially cause tremendous damage.

Truly effective boards look to management to institute a process embedded throughout the organization to identify, analyze, manage, and report all significant risks, and to do so continuously and aggressively. It's those managers closest to the markets and customers and the supply chain, production, and other processes who are in the best positions to know what risks truly can cause major damage. Experienced directors know that while their CEO may say and even believe that an effective risk-management process is in place, a deeper look would reveal an uneven, ad hoc approach that has large holes in how risks are identified and managed.

## Asking the CEO

How does a board approach a CEO about risk management? One approach I've found that works well in terms of getting to the core issues involves asking a few simple questions.

- *What are the significant risks the company faces, and what are you and your management team doing about them?* This reasonable, straightforward question, which likely has been asked before, gets the discussion off on a positive footing, enabling a CEO to provide meaningful information on key risks and risk responses. There's usually give and take about the actions related to how the risks are best managed, with the board ultimately comfortable with the plans to address those risks.

- *How do you know you've gotten your arms around all significant risks?* This is usually where the discussion becomes more interesting, in many cases with a CEO outlining how his or her direct reports are on top of key risks and communicate effectively in how they are being dealt with. The CEO also may talk about a risk assessment by internal audit or other staff.
- *What about a particular matter that came to light late in the game that clearly was not previously identified as a risk—that is, a potential problem that indeed came to hurt us? And what about newly emerging risks—how do you know they're being timely identified?* A CEO may now become somewhat defensive—not a good sign. But he or she should be thoughtful and realistic in terms of what the company's risk identification process really is about. If there's not an effective risk management process in place, then it's difficult to maintain that there's any assurance that significant risks are and will continue to be identified in a timely manner and managed effectively.
- *How can we as a board feel comfortable that we are being apprised of all significant risks on a timely basis?* This is a reasonable question flowing from the last one, and the answer will be the same. Unless there's an effective risk management process in place in the company, the board cannot and should not feel comfortable that it's getting the information it needs. If the CEO doesn't know, it's unlikely the board will know.

## A Board's Responsibilities

Which brings us to what a board needs to do in order to carry out its oversight responsibility with respect to managing risks the company faces. In simple terms, the board needs to feel confident that the CEO and senior management team:

- Recognize their role in and responsibility for identifying, analyzing, and managing all significant risks on a timely basis
- Have put in place an effective risk management process for doing so
- Understand the board's view of what represents an acceptable risk appetite for the company and have linked it to risk tolerances in the organization
- Bring significant risks to the board, on a timely basis, with relevant information and analysis supporting decisions on how risks are being managed
- Bring to the board a portfolio view of risk

And what is an effective risk management process? There are differences of opinion, but certainly one answer is an effective enterprise risk management process, as discussed in earlier chapters. This calls for structure and discipline, with the following basics:

- A process to identify potentialities that could affect a company's ability to achieve its business objectives
- Assessing the risks in terms of likelihood of their occurring—in the short and the long term—and potential impact
- Determining risk responses in relation to risk tolerances, and executing effectively
- Taking a portfolio view of risks at the entity level
- Managing risk within the company's risk appetite
- Monitoring performance

Basically, this is it.[2] Recently we've come across writers and speakers who say the board of directors is responsible for risk management—a highly misleading statement. Yes, a board has ultimate responsibility for management of a company, but it fulfills that responsibility by hiring a CEO and providing oversight. As such, the board has responsibility for oversight—not day-to-day management—and best carries out its oversight of risk management along the lines described.

## Drucker Principles

Recently I came across an article coauthored by a colleague of mine, aimed at providing to boards of directors insight into difficulties companies have experienced with enterprise risk management. The article references principles outlined by legendary management thinker Peter F. Drucker, and describes how those principles can be applied to ERM.[3]

| Drucker Principle | Application to ERM |
| --- | --- |
| Businesses need to transcend scientific management in the Knowledge Age. | Moving from seeking to improve results through specialization, ERM calls for greater emphasis on unification—moving from separate parts to the whole. |
| Every company's enterprise view and strategy needs to start with customers. | This holds for ERM programs, which need to establish where the company intends to go and why. |
| It's important to be both holistic and systematic. | It is important to integrate people into the science, with a shared view to guide the company in continually changing environments. |

I had the great pleasure of knowing Mr. Drucker when, after my stint at the Wharton School, I was doing graduate work at NYU Graduate School of Business and was fortunate to have him as a professor in an advanced management seminar. It was evident to me even then, as a still-wet-behind-the-ears student, that Professor Drucker indeed was extraordinary, with an amazing ability to identify and articulate valuable truths about business that, while obvious after he spoke them, were previously hidden from everyone else's view.

There's no indication in the article that Peter Drucker ever spoke to ERM specifically, and to my knowledge he never did. With that said, I'd like to take the liberty of guessing what, if he were still with us, he might put forth as simple truths about enterprise risk management.

- Forget risk assessments—they have little to do with ERM.
- ERM must be embedded throughout the entirety of an organization.
- ERM isn't done by a staff function—it must be incorporated into the soul of every manager in a company.
- ERM must encompass clear responsibilities and accountability, with open and rapid communication up and down the organization.
- ERM needs to become an integral part of daily business, enhancing judgments and decision making at every level. It's not an add-on, but rather how business is conducted.

Professor Drucker, if somehow you're listening, I hope you're nodding in agreement.

## Talking Past One Another

I've seen it firsthand, and you may have as well—directors and the senior management team discussing a matter, seemingly coming to consensus, only to find that each really meant something different.

Unfortunately, ERM is rife with technical terminology, and while directors operate on a relatively high plane, it is important to be sure there's a common understanding of what's meant. We can use the terms *risk tolerance* and *risk appetite* as an example. To illustrate how even knowledgeable professionals can misspeak, I refer to a recent conversation with one such person who was a COSO board member when the ERM report was being developed.

In the conversation, confusion arose about the term *risk appetite*, which the individual used in the discussion at a lower level than appropriate—a level reserved for risk tolerance. To refresh memories, COSO ERM identifies risk appetite as "the amount of risk, on a broad level, an entity is willing to accept in pursuit of value," whereas risk tolerance relates at a lower level, being "the acceptable level of variation relative to achievement of a specific objective, and often is best measured in the same units as those used to measure the related objective." It's important to watch for circumstances where individual risks may be within a unit's risk tolerances, but taken together may exceed the risk appetite of the company as a whole.

There's more in the report making clear what each term means, but I don't want to bore you. And the point here isn't about the referenced conversation or these specific terms, but the importance of directors and management being sure to communicate effectively with one another.

## Where Board Responsibility Rests

Some boards place responsibility for oversight of risk management with the audit committee, as suggested by the New York Stock Exchange listing standards. Some have established a separate board risk committee, and some keep responsibility for the full board. There are pros and cons to each approach. As with most board issues, no one size fits all and a decision may depend on a company's industry and business, the board's organization and culture, and existing committees' current responsibilities. For instance, in a heavily regulated company or one with high-risk-based activities, a separate risk committee may be most effective.

While the audit committee might at first blush be an appropriate home for this responsibility, it's useful to first consider whether that committee already has a great deal on its plate. Some boards divide responsibility, for instance, with the risks related to financial reporting and possibly compliance with laws and regulations being overseen by the audit committee, financial risks by a finance committee, and all other risks perhaps addressed by the full board. One advantage is a sharper focus on particular categories of risk, and spreading the effort among different committees. But a disadvantage is that this system does not deal effectively with interrelated risks, and some may fall through the cracks.

My experience is that the audit committee typically is not the best place for overseeing risk management, other than dealing with financial reporting risks in connection with oversight of financial reporting and related internal control, because quite simply many audit committees already are burdened with a tremendous workload and it may not be practicable to expand its scope without shortchanging one or more of its existing responsibilities.

Often more effective is a separate risk committee to deal with risk on an enterprise-wide basis. This committee provides oversight to the company's risk management process, and it works closely with the audit committee with respect to financial reporting–related risks. With a separate risk committee, it may be useful to have one director serving on both the risk and audit committees to help ensure coordination. Thus far, few boards have gone this route—one recent study showed that only 4 percent of *Fortune* 500 boards have a separate risk committee—although that percentage will go up pursuant to Dodd-Frank's requirement for large financial institutions.

The notion of establishing separate board committees to deal with different categories of risk may be spurred by a recent legal settlement by Pfizer Corp. After the company agreed to have a subsidiary plead guilty and pay $2.3 billion to settle Justice Department criminal and civil charges of illegal marketing, Pfizer agreed to settle a derivative shareholder lawsuit accusing the board of directors and certain senior executives of breaching their fiduciary duty by failing to stop illegal off-label marketing of certain drugs. A key element is that Pfizer agreed to establish a board committee to oversee regulatory compliance, covering not only drug marketing rules, but also Medicare and Medicaid regulations, the Foreign Corrupt Practices Act, non-U.S. marketing, clinical studies and manufacturing quality control, and drug safety reporting to the Food & Drug Administration.[4] Whether a new compliance committee at this one company provides impetus for board oversight segregated by risk category remains to be seen.

A more likely approach, especially for boards with few committees that want to maintain a focus at the full board level, is to keep responsibility for overseeing the entirety of the company's risk management process for itself.

## Burying Heads in the Sand

Before we leave risk management it's useful to consider what action is needed when a risk materializes into a major problem. What information needs to be gained to help ensure the problem is fully understood—not only in order to deal with the issue at hand, but also to enhance the risk management process going forward?

An article of a few years ago, "What Organizations Don't Want to Know Can Hurt,"[5] provides a good example of what to avoid. It focuses on events surrounding the College Board when it learned of extensive errors in scoring its SAT tests. The company's president reportedly said that finding the specific cause of the failure "did not really matter," but rather what's important is to ensure that improved controls catch future problems. His position was supported by the engagement leader of a consulting firm hired by the company, saying that dissecting past problems is not necessary to ensure either that the scoring system works better in the future or that there is a good safety net to catch errors. He goes on, "You can do both without knowing whether it was rain that made the papers wet, or whether someone spilled a cup of coffee . . . [and] if we tried to brainstorm everything that could go wrong, we'd be here for years—for a lifetime. But if controls are in place to identify problems, and rescore tests that were misscored, that's what you're really looking for."

These statements are fascinating—that there's no need either to look back at why something went wrong because it's unnecessary, or to dig deeply into what could go wrong because it would take too long. It suggests that problems in test scoring—which would certainly seem to be central to the company's credibility and indeed its sustainability—are okay as long as they ultimately are found and test results rescored. Simply "catching future problems" by "rescoring tests" means that the company is satisfied with detecting major problems with scoring after they occur, rather than taking steps to prevent such problems in the first place. I wonder what users of SAT scores think about that!

If you're smiling at this you've got company. Clearly, looking neither backward nor forward is not a viable option. And doing one or the other also is not the answer. Rather, it's necessary to do both. In such circumstances, management must carefully find out what went wrong and why it went wrong in terms of the direct cause and the underlying root cause, which frequently are different. Only by getting behind what went so wrong can management feel comfortable it understands what risks continue to exist, and only then is it positioned to look at what additional risks need to be the focus of its attention going forward.

## Getting to the Bottom of a Problem

The best way to learn what went wrong does and should vary based on circumstances, although there are commonalities that serve as useful guidelines. Where a failure is due to a mistake, as appears to be the case with the College Board SAT scoring fiasco, an internal investigation, sometimes with outside help such as a qualified consulting firm, might be the best way to go. With the right techniques it should be possible to identify what went wrong and why, and position management to perform root cause analysis and determine what corrective actions are needed. Then it can employ risk management techniques to identify other significant risks that need to be managed, in the short and long term.

In circumstances where something more than a mistake appears to have occurred, it's still necessary to find out what happened, but the focus needs to be different. In most cases an independent party—typically an independent law firm, sometimes supported by investigators and other consultants—is needed to get to the bottom of a problem. If a fraud has occurred, by definition there's an intention to deceive. But even when there's no outright fraud, and the cause of the problem is simply management's not wanting to know and putting its collective head in the sand, it's often necessary to bring in independent help.

The aforementioned article points to other companies that have been in the headlines, with a common theme of management not wanting to know. Ken Lay, the former Enron CEO convicted on fraud charges and now deceased, seemed not really to want to know details of warnings brought to him by Vice President of Corporate Development Sherron Watkins. Yes, Lay instituted an investigation, but turned it over to the company's longtime law firm to look only within narrow parameters. And Merck executives reportedly failed to look further into clinical trial results showing problems with the painkiller Vioxx. There are other examples, but enough said—too often management, many times with the best of intentions but sometimes not, wants to look forward, not backward. And a desire to avoid blame and litigation can work as a powerful incentive to keep details from surfacing.

It doesn't take a genius to know that when a problem rears its ugly head it is essential to find out why. The article talks about fields like aviation and medicine that conduct investigations to find out exactly what went wrong, to learn from often deadly mistakes, and to improve processes and protocols. The National Transportation Safety Board does so by focusing primarily not on casting blame but on making things better. Similarly, many hospitals hold mortality and morbidity conferences to analyze and learn from mistakes.

Many businesses do that as well, learning from what went wrong. They don't choose between learning from the past and working to make things better. They do both, with one supporting the other. And no, it doesn't take a lifetime to find out what caused a major problem or to identify the source of the next potential disaster. Indeed, effective risk management involves analyzing and ranking risks, then dealing with those with the highest likelihood of occurring and the greatest potential impact.

No one expects any company to get into minutiae, which is neither necessary nor productive. But those companies that identify, assess, and manage risk effectively will have fewer surprises. And when a problem surfaces, they find out what went wrong and are positioned to seize greater opportunities and rewards in the future.

Many of those managers who didn't want to know learned the hard way just how costly ignorance can be—both personally and professionally, for themselves and for their companies and their stakeholders.[6]

Many boards right now are doing these things well—overseeing strategy development and implementation and risk management. And it's really not rocket science. It involves having in-depth knowledge of what the company is about, where it wants to go, how it plans to get there, and what dangers and opportunities exist. Every company's board needs to get these core responsibilities right.

 **NOTES**

1. Copies may be available from PricewaterhouseCoopers or the Institute of Internal Auditors Research Foundation.
2. Boards, of course, have considerable discretion as to how deep they want to delve into the company's risk management process. Some look into further detail, focusing on such matters as the extent to which the organization has a shared view of risk management and a common language; the process takes advantage of both related opportunities; there's a disciplined approach, aligning strategy, processes, people, technology; managers have information needed to identify and manage risks; risks are systematically identified and managed; risks openly acknowledged, discussed, with clear responsibilities for managing; risk information is communicated timely up, across, and down an organization; risks are managed not only individually, but also on an aggregate basis; and the process ultimately is a factor in allocating capital.
3. "How to Reinvent Your Company Through Better Enterprise Risk Management," *Directors & Boards' Boardroom Briefing*, 2009.
4. As reported in *Compliance Week*, February 2011. Also worth noting is the settlement's requirements that the committee work with the board's compensation committee to determine whether pay practices support the company's compliance incentives and that the company appoint an independent ombudsman to deal with employee concerns. Further required is independent funding for the committee coming from D&O policy Side A coverage, traditionally used to cover directors when a company is insolvent.

5. Karen W. Arenson, *New York Times*, August 22, 2006.

6. For additional guidance on a board's role in risk management, readers would benefit from taking a look at the National Association of Corporate Directors' 2009 report, "Blue Ribbon Commission on Risk Governance," and Wachtell Lipton's December 3, 2010 memo, "Risk Management and the Board of Directors."

CHAPTER TWELVE

# CEO Compensation, Succession Planning, and Crisis Management

A S NOTED, THERE'S NO more important board responsibility than selecting a CEO who is right for the company. Here we discuss the related and similarly relevant topic of effectively motivating and appropriately compensating the CEO, along with effective practices for succession planning. The chapter concludes with a look at the board's role in dealing with crisis.

 **CEO COMPENSATION**

Let's start with the obvious. For years now shareholders, especially large institutional activist investors, have been openly angry about the state of CEO compensation. Some can relate to the news anchor in the film *Network* screaming, "I'm mad as hell and I'm not going to take it anymore!" Others are merely ticked off. As one executive at the California Public Employee Retirement System said, "We're not against pay, but we are certainly against pay for failure, or for just showing up." Not only are shareholders upset about the relationship between pay and stock price, they point to increasing disparity between the pay of the CEO and rank-and-file employees, raising questions about its effect on employee morale as well as the broader social implications.

Recognizing the widespread attention to management compensation, evidenced not only by shareholders but also by a range of government officials and the public, directors have strived to walk the line between meaningful incentives for performance and what appear to be huge paydays for taking excessive risk or otherwise failing to achieve established corporate goals. But putting the concept of true pay-for-performance into action and avoiding short-term focus at the expense of long-term success, all while motivating and retaining good performers, is easier said than done. And with ever-expanding regulatory disclosure mandates, these decisions increasingly are made in a fishbowl environment.

Certainly there are traps to avoid. Many boards now recognize the need to understand and manage change-of-control provisions or other severance arrangements that can result in enormous CEO paydays. They watch for pay proposals where a senior manager can bet the ranch, taking risk on the basis of a coin flip: heads, the CEO wins, and tails, the shareholders lose.

But challenges remain. Among the issues boards and their compensation committees must cope with are how to align CEO and other top managers' pay with the company's strategy and ensuring the right performance measures are in place. While difficult, it's certainly achievable.

## How We Got Here

A number of assertions are put forth as to why compensation got out of control. One is that a CEO doesn't really have a boss, because boards and compensation committees have simply rubber-stamped what the CEO and the compensation consultant engaged by management say is appropriate. Underlying that is an assertion that blurry lines continue to exist between how directors are selected and treated and the power of the CEO. Another is that a tax law amendment of some years ago requiring pay-for-performance for full tax deductibility of CEO pay somehow backfired. Rather than curbing pay, it triggered a competition among CEOs to see who could outdo the other on the pay scorecard.

Moreover, a combination of factors drove CEO pay, among them extensive weight given to peer comparisons together with boards' belief that their company's CEO must be in the top half, if not upper quartile, of high performing top executives. That is, because of the well-recognized critical board responsibility to select the right CEO, if a board is doing its job, then the CEO must be a high performer. This, of course, resulted in the Lake Wobegon syndrome where every board believes its CEO is above average and must be paid accordingly, thereby continually ratcheting up CEO pay. There's also the argument that if a CEO does a truly effective job of growing shareholder wealth, that CEO deserves every dollar he or she receives.

So, when shareholders saw huge payouts of tens or even hundreds of millions of dollars as the company's share price tanked, they wanted to know how such a discontinuity was possible. They pointed to assertions noted above, but to answer the question more fully it's necessary and worthwhile to consider further relevant history.

Going back to the 1990s, institutional and other activist shareholders balked, often loudly, as CEO compensation shot up because of what they said was a broad-based rise in the stock markets. They were appalled by CEOs getting a free ride at shareholders' expense.

A number of boards listened, agreed, and acted. They took steps to decouple CEO compensation from share price at least partially, and instead identified a range of metrics and other measures to drive CEO compensation. These actions would, they posited, help to avoid the circumstances for which they previously were criticized: CEO pay rising on autopilot with bull markets.

Subsequently, however, the redesigned pay packages linked to measures other than share price resulted in compensation rising even as the market was falling, which angered shareholders once again. How, they asked, could compensation committees possibly agree to such terms? Perhaps they were forgetting the outcries of the past when compensation was linked to stock price.

Regardless, it's hard to argue that some of the anger hasn't been justified. According to an Equilar report of a few years ago, CEOs at the 10 largest financial services firms in the survey were paid a total of $320 million in the one year, while piling up $55 billion in the companies' losses and destroying more than $200 billion in shareholder value. For some companies where stock prices were actually rising, we heard echoes of earlier complaints that the price gains weren't due to outstanding CEO performance but to unrelated factors, such as oil companies reaping the benefits of the price of oil at what then was $140 a barrel.

And then there's the oft-cited case of Home Depot CEO Robert Nardelli who received a pay package of $210 million when ousted for bad performance. In this case it seems the Home Depot board learned its lesson; Nardelli's successor's pay package was much more closely tied to performance. This gets us into the whole issue of change-in-control and other severance provisions, which many experts say have gotten entirely out of hand.

At the same time, there's evidence of better alignment of shareholder interests and CEO pay. A study by consulting firm Mercer looking at a cross section of Fortune 1000 companies found a significant drop the following year, where the CEOs of 50 large U.S. companies (with median annual revenue of $66.2 billion) took a 15.8 percent cut in total direct compensation.

## CEOs as Entrepreneurs

The University of Delaware's Charles Elson, who is among the more influential voices in corporate governance, described the situation as, "We're paying executives like successful entrepreneurs, without asking them to take entrepreneurial risks." Another well-known voice on this subject is Robert Reich, the former labor secretary in the Clinton administration. In a *Wall Street Journal* opinion piece a couple of years ago, Reich noted that the pay for CEOs of *Fortune* 500 companies rose from 20 to 30 times more than average worker pay in the 1960s, to more than 364 times recently.

What may be surprising, however, is that Reich—who has long focused on issues involving labor equity—goes on to explain why this "stratospheric level of CEO pay" is actually well deserved! He says that 40 years ago a big corporation's CEO was mostly "a bureaucrat in charge of a large, high-volume production system with standardized rules, and whose competitors were docile [in] the era of stable oligopolies, big unions, predictable markets, and lackluster share performance." But a modern company operates in an environment where oligopolies have all but vanished, barriers to entry are low, and competitors lure away consumers and investors while tapping "global supply and distribution chains [that let them] access low-source suppliers from all over the world and outsource jobs abroad." And those competitors "can get capital for new investment on much the same terms."

Reich goes on to argue that the ability of a modern company to distinguish itself depends on its CEO, who has to be "sufficiently clever, ruthless, and driven to find and pull the levers that will deliver competitive advantage." With no standard CEO textbook, a small pool of proven talent, and an unwillingness to hire the wrong CEO with potentially disastrous consequences, boards are willing to pay more and more. Excepting the outliers like Nardelli, high CEO pay "is usually worth it to investors," Reich says.

## Getting to the Core

Considering the issue of CEO pay from these different perspectives, we can boil the discussion down to a few key questions.

### Are Boards Letting Chief Executives Set Their Own Pay Packages, or Are the Boards Effectively Negotiating in the Best Interests of Shareholders?

The answer depends on which company we're talking about. Yes, some boards are still mired in the past, where the chairman/CEO has undue influence on the pay package and a still too-cozy relationship between directors and the chief executive results in more of a rubber stamp than a true negotiation.

Experience shows, however, that today many and probably most public companies—and certainly the larger ones—no longer behave this way. Their boards and compensation committees are comprised of independent directors, and while they work closely with the CEO, they have an independent mind-set. They understand and embrace their duties of loyalty and care and indeed put the company's and shareholders' interests above all. But setting CEO pay is a challenge, especially when trying to lure an accomplished, successful leader from another organization. That individual needs to be persuaded to walk away from what often is a large pay package (including options that soon may be vesting) and a track record of success providing a sound basis of job security. Directors know this fact of corporate life, and they need to deal with it on a very pragmatic basis. This often requires agreeing to some type of change in control and other severance arrangement, should events fare poorly. How well boards have found the right balance is open for debate. But deal with it they must.

It's significantly easier to negotiate pay when promoting an executive from within. Other than the relatively few instances where the executive has built a strong reputation outside the organization, the compensation committee can set pay somewhere above the executive's current compensation, with appropriate incentives to align shareholder and CEO interests. The negotiation process usually is very much simplified and tends to work well for all.

Going back to the stated question: Yes, I believe that in today's environment the majority of boards and compensation committees do negotiate pay with the CEO. They are not beholden to the CEO. It's also fair to say that some do a better job than others.

### What Will Say-on-Pay Accomplish?

Several years ago I wrote that this train has already left the station and there's no turning back. One American company, Aflac, was among the first to give shareholders a nonbinding vote on executive compensation, and soon after many others followed suit. And now with Dodd-Frank, say-on-pay is here to stay.

Investors point to Britain and Australia, where say-on-pay has been common for years. Many believe those votes have helped keep CEO pay levels in check, although reports say CEO pay of the largest British companies rose 33 percent in one recent year. Certainly many shareholders fed up with escalating CEO pay embrace the ability to provide an advisory vote, with some seeing it as a first step in actually participating in determining CEO pay.

But beyond appeasing investors and letting them speak their minds, which is a good thing, I and other governance experts don't see say-on-pay as a particularly good idea. The notion that shareholders can do a better job than boards at setting CEO pay, when shareholders have limited information and a weak grasp of corporate strategy, makes little sense. Surely shareholders should have relevant information, more of which now is required, but there's no way they can make sufficiently informed judgments on compensation. This is the board's job, and the board is best positioned to do it. With that said, if there are meaningful discussions on pay issues with large shareholders who have a common base of understanding, then their input should be welcome. More on that in Chapter 16.

### Where Do We See CEO Pay Going in the Coming Years, and Does This Make Sense?

CEO compensation is likely to evolve in a number of ways. The spotlight on compensation committees certainly is having an effect on how they operate, and there now are new rules for independent committee composition, use of compensation consultants, and required disclosures. Compensation committees of many boards are doing a better job of aligning the CEO's interests with those of shareholders. They're taking greater care in developing pay packages with a better mix of components, such as restricted stock, performance options, and longer vesting periods.

No one can know whether compensation across a broad spectrum of companies will go up or down. My sense is that it will at least stabilize. But in any event we can expect to see better alignment of interests, with closer correlation of the long-term fortunes of CEOs and shareholders. Importantly, we can expect to see much greater care with change-in-control and severance provisions.

### What Can, and Should, Boards and Compensation Committees Be Doing to Do Their Jobs Right?

In my view, the answers are straightforward.

- *Real negotiation.* It is essential that pay be set through meaningful negotiation. Neither a CEO nor anyone else should be allowed to dictate or unduly influence his or her own pay. A compensation committee needs to have its own compensation consultant and be armed with information needed to act with authority. Of course these discussions should continue to be cordial—after all, the trust and working relationship between the CEO and the board needs to be maintained. But negotiation it should be. As we all know, you're not negotiating if you're not prepared to ultimately walk away from a bad deal. Discussions certainly shouldn't get to that point, but if push comes to shove, it needs to be an option.
- *True pay for performance.* Many board compensation committees have been doing a much better job at paying for real results. For the reasons described above, it's not a matter of simply tying CEO pay to stock price, or totally ignoring how the marketplace values the company's stock. Performance needs to be measured based on a number of factors specific to each company. There should be clear alignment to the strategic plan, along with forward-looking metrics that drive long-term share value.[1] And the pay package should have the right mix of components, typically including base salary and bonus but also such elements as restricted stock, performance options, and meaningful vesting schedules that truly align the CEO's and shareholders' interests and provide the right motivations and accountability for outstanding performance.

  An area requiring particularly strong focus is change-of-control and severance provisions, which must be carefully crafted to avoid some of the absurdly huge windfalls bestowed upon unsuccessful chief executives. These provisions need to undergo scenario analysis and stress testing to ensure they will appropriately fit any reasonable eventuality. At the same time, CEOs should not be disincentivized to work toward a deal that's in shareholders' interests—which, according to one study, too often is the case. An analysis of executive compensation data for the S&P 1500 (as of December 2009) by Dow Jones Investment Banker and Shareholder Value Advisors shows that 78.9 percent of CEOs would be significantly worse off—losing more than 5 percent of value—if the company were to be acquired at a 25 percent premium to shareholders. And 46 percent of the CEOs would see their wealth fall by 50 percent or more under such takeover conditions. So incentives cut both ways, and boards need to get this right.
- *Transparency.* Shareholders have a right to receive meaningful information about CEO pay, and the board and compensation committee have

a responsibility to provide it. The new Securities and Exchange Commission disclosure rules should be met with relevant information in plain English. The rules accommodate a need to avoid disclosing matters that would provide advantage to competitors, and there's room to accomplish all objectives.

## SUCCESSION PLANNING

One thing we know with certainty—every company someday will need a new CEO. Unless a CEO's mandated retirement date is approaching, a board seldom knows when that day will arrive, though for many companies it's sooner than expected. Whether performance doesn't meet expectations, a major crisis requires change at the top, or a chief executive suffers a debilitating health issue or departs voluntarily—seeking greener pastures, pursuing personal interests, or simply retiring—a board may find itself having to identify a new leader for the organization. If fortunate, a board will have the benefit of sufficient time to go through a comprehensive selection process. But it's not uncommon for a CEO's departure to come with stunning suddenness, requiring quick and decisive action.

Despite common knowledge of what's happened at other companies, too many boards simply are not prepared to deal with departure of the company's CEO, especially if it is unexpected. A recent survey shows that while 69 percent of respondents say a CEO successor needs to be ready now, only 54 percent are grooming an executive to take on the role, and 39 percent say they have zero viable internal candidates. Interestingly, the study shows boards spend an average of only two hours a year on CEO succession planning.[2]

Where does one begin? Certainly a board will want to consider who should jump into the chief executive's seat should a sudden change be needed, as well as defining a selection process when time is on the board's side. There's the issue of internal versus outside candidates, and how one is groomed and others identified. Let's take a look at what needs to be considered—now, before coming face to face with an emergency situation.

### The Sudden Departure

Every director knows that at least one individual must be identified as positioned to immediately take over as chief executive. This person might be viewed as a temporary stand-in until a more thorough search is conducted, or as the next generation of leadership.

Interestingly, when studying CEO changes at 300 companies from 2004 to 2008, search firm Spencer Stuart found "although corporate boards often turn to within their own ranks for a new chief executive officer out of desperation—when nobody else is available or groomed for the job—board members who stepped in as CEOs outperformed all other types of candidates." The firm found that executives brought in as potential CEOs after first serving as presidents or COOs performed worse when they became CEOs. It also found that a company performing well is best off promoting from the inside, whereas for a company faced with a crisis, an outsider is preferable.

This trend of boards looking toward one of their own directors to jump onto the top executive spot is supported by another survey, also showing that such appointments sometimes become permanent. Search firm Heidrick & Struggles notes that in the 15 months ending in mid-October 2010, 13 directors at *Fortune* 1000 companies were appointed permanent CEOs, compared to just 4 the year before, and three additional board members were appointed interim CEOs at their companies. In explanation, the firm says that boards want someone familiar with the company who can step in quickly. "By tapping a board member for the job—who is often a former CEO himself or herself—boards are able to move very quickly and achieve immediately results. . . . [Directors] have been sitting in the room for years debating issues," reducing risk compared with hiring externally.

Boards faced with the need to act promptly may promote someone from within, or might even have already identified an outside candidate who is quickly pursued. Whether viable alternatives are available depends on how well a board successfully carries out the succession plans described in the following paragraphs.

## The Luxury of Time

While it was once the purview of a sitting CEO to identify a successor, recent years have seen boards take direct responsibility for ensuring an effective process for succession. Certainly the CEO continues to play a key role in grooming executives capable of taking over at the top, but the full board or a committee—nominating, governance, and/or compensation—is taking charge of the process.

While there are different approaches, we can look to some commonalities that have served boards well in dealing with succession:

- The board identifies the skills, knowledge, experience, and personal attributes needed for the company—based on its industry, business, competitive and regulatory demands, consumer markets, strategy, culture, and other factors. A sharp focus is on identifying what's needed not only where the company is today, but where the strategic plan will bring the company tomorrow.

■ Responsibility rests with the current CEO to identify and groom a cadre of individuals who meet the identified criteria. This includes individual development plans ensuring that managers are given sufficient roles and responsibilities to provide the requisite experience and perspective and develop the needed knowledge and skills, and are exposed to top-level strategic and related issues. Potential candidates are coached, with the sitting CEO, head of HR, and possibly selected directors playing a role, and development progress is tracked.

■ The process cascades throughout the company, where managers at every level take similar action to recruit, develop, and assess direct reports to ensure individuals with the requisite knowledge and skills are positioned to step up as necessary.

■ The board gets to know and understand the strengths and weaknesses of potential CEO successors. This should occur naturally at board and committee meetings, dinners preceding meetings, and offline interactions where additional information or insight is obtained. Sometimes overlooked but important is learning first hand whether an individual truly wants the top spot—usually but not always the case.

■ The board's process includes identifying executives outside the company that should be considered. While direct contact typically is neither possible nor appropriate, maintaining an up-to-date list of individuals from the outside provides a useful head start when a search is initiated.

■ When it comes time to make a decision, the current CEO serves in an advisory role. The point is made well by Richard Koppes, an active director and longtime governance expert, who says that ideally, when it comes time to make decisions, the independent directors meet first with the CEO and then without him or her, because ultimately it's the board's job to decide.

Inasmuch as the CEO has responsibility for positioning future candidates, there must be associated accountability, with degree of success a factor in assessing CEO performance.

The issue of whether it's best to promote internally or go to the outside has long been debated. Certainly the answer for any company is: It depends—on factors too numerous to mention here, including the results of the study cited previously. Among the advantages to an internal candidate are knowledge of the organization and its business, operations, people, and challenges, and more modest compensation costs. An outsider brings different knowledge and perspective, and perhaps vision and skills that may be lacking internally. The list goes on, as will the debate.

One recent study concludes that internally-promoted CEOs significantly outperform those hired from the outside. One of the authors says the study found that sets of CEOs hired from within and those hired from the outside both made changes upon taking the reins. However, "CEOs from outside the firm are likely to initiate bigger changes. . . . We wanted to know whether bigger change meant better change." But the study shows it doesn't. "If a change is too big, it can take the firm away from its identity and core competencies." Findings show that although returns on assets relative to industry were similar at first, after three years, because externally hired chief executives instituted larger changes, results were worse. The author notes, "Inside CEOs, because of their deeper roots in the firm, have a better understanding of the firm's core competencies and key weaknesses. . . . They're more likely to initiate changes that complement the firm's core rather than damage it." The author surmises that outsiders might also suffer from a lack of support among employees or their executive teams.[3]

Another study supports these conclusions. Looking at American S&P 500 nonfinancial companies over a 20-year period—from 1988 to 2007—the researchers found that companies that appoint only internal candidates to the CEO position significantly outperform those that bring outsiders to the job. Having identified 36 companies that exclusively promoted CEOs from within—including the likes of Abbott Laboratories, Best Buy, Caterpillar, Colgate-Palmolive, DuPont, Exxon, FedEx, Honda, Johnson Controls, McDonald's, Microsoft, Nike, and United Technologies—the study found that these companies outperformed others across certain metrics: return on assets, equity and investment, revenue and earnings growth, earnings per share, growth, and stock-price appreciation. It also found that no nonfinancial S&P 500 company bringing in a CEO from the outside generated 20-year performance numbers equal to or better than the identified 36.

And the study's conclusions go beyond company performance. They confirm the notion that the cost of attracting an external candidate is significantly higher than that of attracting internal candidates, finding that average total compensation—salary, bonus, and equity incentives—was 65 percent higher for external CEOs. Further, "four out of 10 of CEOs recruited from outside stay in the jobs for two years or less and almost two-thirds are gone before their fourth anniversary—many taking with them hefty 'golden good-bye' payments."[4]

## Challenges

Even where clear responsibilities are established for internally based succession planning, with sitting CEOs and boards each focusing on putting in place a cadre of executives capable of taking over the top spot, it's often difficult to retain individuals with the attributes, skills, knowledge, and experience to take on the CEO role. And there are some CEOs who hide well that they simply don't want a successor waiting in the wings.

Problems in retaining key executives can surface when a company puts two or more executives in the running, inadvertently creating an unhealthy competition that negates teamwork. On the other hand, identifying one crown prince can cause other up-and-coming executives to leave for what they see as better opportunities to ultimately gain a CEO slot. Companies with a history of going to the outside for new chief executives create still different problems.

Of course, some companies will do better than others in retaining talent, often depending on corporate culture, but in any event it won't be easy.

 ## CRISIS MANAGEMENT

In a perfect world, a company that has an effective enterprise risk management process in place and operating effectively is unlikely to be faced with an unexpected event that creates havoc. But we don't live in a perfect world—and even an effective ERM process can provide only reasonable, not absolute, assurance that even risks capable of causing major damage will be mitigated.

You read the headlines and know what can and does happen, where companies' valued reputations and very survival are at stake. A crisis can result from an accident, and we need only to think of General Public Utilities' Three Mile Island, Union Carbide's Bhopal, Exxon's *Valdez*, and BP's *Deepwater Horizon*, to name just a few. Crises also can result from natural disaster, product defects, attempted hostile takeover, CEO departure, fraudulent reporting, lawsuits, regulatory investigation, deteriorated finances, and a host of other events. As shown in Exhibit 12.1, the types of crises companies face and their frequency have evolved and, as of a couple of years ago, were led by those related to white-collar crime, mismanagement, casualty accidents, consumer activism, defects and recalls, and labor disputes.

**EXHIBIT 12.1** Crisis Categories Compared (Percent of total crises each year)

| Category | 1990 | 2009 |
|---|---|---|
| Facility damage | 5.5 | 7.0 |
| Casualty accidents | 4.8 | 11.0 |
| Environmental | 7.8 | 2.0 |
| Class-action lawsuits | 2.2 | 7.0 |
| Consumer activism | 2.8 | 9.0 |
| Defects and recalls | 5.4 | 8.0 |
| Discrimination | 3.3 | 3.0 |
| Executive dismissal | 1.3 | 1.0 |
| Financial damages | 4.2 | 5.0 |
| Hostile takeover | 2.6 | 0.0 |
| Labor disputes | 10.3 | 8.0 |
| Mismanagement | 24.1 | 16.0 |
| Sexual harassment | 0.4 | 1.0 |
| Whistleblowers | 1.1 | 1.0 |
| White-collar crime | 20.4 | 18.0 |
| Workplace violence | 3.8 | 4.0 |

*Source:* Institute for Crisis Management, 2010.

## Planning for a Crisis

If there's one thing we take away from this discussion, it should be that in the absence of advance planning, a crisis that hits will not be handled well. It simply isn't possible. Events come at management and the board with such velocity and impact that being in a purely reactionary, catch-up mode can quickly turn any crisis into disaster. While it might not be possible to anticipate what type of crisis event will occur, getting crisis management pieces in place is doable and indeed essential for any company.

As with most governance-related matters, management usually should have primary responsibility for establishing, testing, and maintaining the crisis management plan, with the board or an identified committee or director providing direct oversight. Inasmuch as the plan must allow for circumstances where the CEO or other senior management team members are unable to participate when a crisis hits—or are implicated in its cause—the appointed board resources must be comfortable that the plan is sufficiently flexible to deal with such eventualities.

A crisis management plan should include:

- Identified team management members represented by a range of disciplines, along with selected board members with leadership roles and clear-cut responsibilities for execution. Legal and public relations/communications resources should be included as advisors to those on the team in decision-making roles.
- Determination of who should run the business in the event members of the current senior management are no longer able to function in their roles.
- Facilities to be used during crisis response, depending on whether regular corporate facilities are or are not available. Many plans establish a "war room" to act as response headquarters, to be housed in an offsite location if necessary. Telecommunications and IT support should be in place, along with contingency plans, and contact information and channels established and communicated to all relevant parties—including among board members, who must recognize that in a crisis availability and time commitments expand exponentially.
- An identified spokesperson for centralized and consistent messaging to other officers and directors, employees, customers, clients, lenders, investors, alliance partners, and others, and various categories of news media. Media training or a refresher is important—BP's Tony Hayward is an example of how reaction to a CEO's words can be negative and damaging.
- A specialized law firm, crisis management firm, media consultants, financial advisors, and other support lined up in advance.
- Preestablished plans for the form and content of information to be provided, and to whom, plus timing, based on the nature of a potential crisis event. Communications to emergency and regulatory authorities also should be planned.
- Means to track, monitor, and organize communications into and out of the crisis management team, for use in assessing evolving circumstances and ensuring relevant and consistent messaging. It's also useful to establish protocols for learning what is said in social networking, blogging, and other Internet-based communications, providing a basis for whatever further messaging might be helpful.

As with other emergency-based plans, this one needs to be periodically reviewed, tested, and updated. Unfortunately, other issues can take priority, and the needed review of the plan and its capabilities is often lacking. It's necessary to have predetermined checkpoints to ensure that the plan actually works when needed.

## When a Crisis Hits

With a well-established plan in place, when a crisis hits, the company needs only to carry out the plan. That may be a bit of an oversimplification, as the crisis management team will need to react quickly to fast-moving events, and no plan can account for every potentiality. But careful advance planning provides much needed direction that is critically important when having to suddenly deal with potentially disastrous circumstances.

Many experts stress the importance of the lead spokesperson, be it the CEO or a designated board member, getting out in front as much as possible in publically stating what happened, the surrounding circumstances, and what actions are being taken. A key word often used is *credibility*—with the right information put forth in the right way, there can be a justified perception by all parties that the company knows what happened, what's going on, its implications, and what needs to be done and is being done to protect all parties.

A report of the National Association of Corporate Directors's Blue Ribbon Commission, "Risk Oversight—Board Lessons for Turbulent Times," points to companies that got this right, including Ashland Oil, Johnson & Johnson, Empire Blue Cross & Blue Shield, Intel, and Lucent. It also highlights companies that "did not react in a timely fashion, and ultimately suffered for that mistake," naming Andersen, Archer-Daniels-Midland, Bankers Trust, and Exxon. We can add BP and Toyota to this list, and also the more recent events surrounding Johnson & Johnson.

As is often the case, in searching for what we should do, we can look at a list of don'ts. The NACD report includes such a list, with experienced director and Commission co-chair Norman Augustine providing the source, showing "how to turn a crisis into a catastrophe in 12 easy steps":

1. Assume that evidence of a problem must be wrong.
2. When evidence mounts, cover up the problem.
3. Let lawyers manage the response strategy: admit nothing.
4. When the problem becomes public, minimize it.
5. Never display remorse: Blame someone else, preferably the victim.
6. Take plenty of time to resolve the problem.

7. Have the highest-level responsible individual go into hiding.
8. Attack the media.
9. Anger the politicians, preferably by embracing untenable positions.
10. Shift the spotlight to the failings of the regulators.
11. Frequently reverse your position and contradict yourself.
12. Give priority to saving money: that way you can lose large amounts later.

For further information, the NACD report is worth perusing. It's also useful to keep in mind the relevance of documenting decisions, including the decision-making process, and recognizing that if the company is entering a zone of insolvency, directors' fiduciary responsibility shifts from being solely to share-holders to including creditors as well. Also, it's important to learn from a crisis with a follow-up investigation. These are topics worth researching as needed.

 **NOTES**

1. As noted, two publications provide in-depth insight and guidance on perfor-mance metrics: *Corporate Governance and the Board—What Works Best*, by PricewaterhouseCoopers, 2002, and the NACD's *Performance Metrics, Understanding the Board's Role*, 2010.
2. Heidrick & Struggles and Stanford University's Rock Center for Corporate Governance.
3. Study by Rice University associate professor of management Anthea Zhang and Nandini Rajagopalan, professor of management at the University of Southern California's Marshall School of Business, reported by CFO.com, 2010.
4. Study by the Kelley School of Business at Indiana University and A.T. Kearney, as reported by Management Issues, Ltd.

# CHAPTER THIRTEEN

# Performance Measurement and Reporting

T HE ABILITY TO EFFECTIVELY measure corporate performance is fundamental to tracking strategy implementation and CEO performance, as well other aspects of managing a business. Measures also are inherent in a company's financial reporting to the outside world. We look here at the scope of these board oversight responsibilities, and effective practices for measuring performance for these internal and external purposes.

 ## PERFORMANCE MEASURES

There's perhaps nothing more challenging to boards than ensuring the right measures are being used. As noted, performance measures are critical to tracking effectiveness of the strategy and its implementation, and motivating and fairly rewarding the chief executive and management team. Being central to these fundamental board responsibilities, performance measures can be viewed as the essential glue that holds these governance elements together.

Against a backdrop of long and loud shareholder cries for boards to pay for performance, directors are working diligently to get to the right measures.

But it's not easy, and many boards continue to struggle toward that goal. Directors are also challenged in determining how best to comply with performance-related disclosure requirements of the new Dodd-Frank law and SEC regulations.

There's substance in the oft-used phrase, "you get what you measure." Measure the wrong things, and results can be disastrous. Measure the right ones—aligned with the strategic plan and related business objectives cascading to business units throughout an organization—and managers are motivated and work together toward achieving corporate goals.

As with most governance issues, one size does not fit all, and performance measurement certainly is no exception. So, each board must determine how best to achieve its measurement objectives. With that said, experience shows that the approaches outlined here serve boards well.

## It's All about Linkage

Investors ultimately want to see a fair if not superior return on their investment, with share price typically driven by such measures as profit, earnings per share, cash flow, and assorted value added and return metrics. These financial measures are benchmarked against competitors and peers, and depending on industry and investor and analyst preferences and models, an array of additional financial metrics are used to measure corporate performance with an eye toward future prospects. These market-facing financial measures are useful to managements and boards in measuring company performance, but that's really just the starting point.

Looking beyond financial measures, some companies use any of a wide range of canned measures to assess performance. But there's another, usually more effective approach directed at the specific circumstances of a particular company. This involves beginning with what drives value for the company and linking those drivers to relevant factors, providing a foundation for forming a cohesive measurement process.

Managements and boards know what drives financial performance for their organization, focusing on such familiar metrics as revenue, sales growth, operating margin, working capital, leverage, cost of capital, and growth duration, and they ensure strategic plans are aligned with the drivers. For example, a strategy may focus on such matters as developing new products or services, opening new markets, developing new distribution channels, growth through acquisitions, production process innovation or efficiencies, enhanced sourcing, strategic alliances and partnerships, and the like.

Because strategies and performance goals must be risk-based, another step in the linkage is identifying, assessing, and managing related risks. For instance, if growth through acquisitions is a strategic initiative, attention must be given to risks related to reliability of information on targets, due diligence processes, competitors' goals and positioning, and issues surrounding synergies, cultures, and integration. Opportunities and risks are identified and dealt with to ensure strategic intent is realistically attainable with desired risk-reward relationships.

With plans for managing risks in place, performance measures can be formulated, often in context of an established categorization. For instance, one category may be the *customer*, with such performance measures as market share, on-time delivery rates, returns, customer satisfaction, existing product duration, brand awareness, and related trend lines and benchmark comparisons. *Research and development* might be another category, using measures for sales of new products, product quality, product life cycle including time to market and investment payback and duration, and innovation measured by numbers of new patents or new product pipeline. *Operations* might be another, with such measures as procurement costs, production costs, downtimes, cycle times, warehousing and distribution, related logistics costs, and so on. *Human capital* might be another category, looking at measures for recruiting, development, retention, satisfaction, percentage of jobs filled internally, workplace environment factors, and the like.

What's important here is a clear linkage to strategic initiatives and related risks. With linkage built in, measures can be established for motivating and rewarding personnel, from the CEO on down. At a top level, measures might include such financial metrics as total shareholder return, revenue growth, return on assets, but also should include a scorecard dealing with specific strategic objectives and all key responsibilities. Going downstream in the organization, measures become more granular, but always directly linked with the objectives of the business unit and overall corporate strategy.

Also of critical relevance is shaping performance measures to a company's specific culture, environment, and orientation. A large pharmaceutical company stressing new product development will want to focus on measures related to testing protocols, the FDA approval process, and timely medical professional and consumer marketplace acceptance. A company developing supplies for the office and consumer markets will measure new product development and related innovation metrics. An airline will focus on such measures as load factor, fuel costs, customer loyalty, and employee satisfaction, to name a few. And a retailer will measure satisfaction with customer service and sales from e-business.

Ultimately, there must be linkage back to the financial metrics that shareholders use to measure value. In that sense, the process comes full circle.

## A Mix of Measurement Types

In addition to measures that are both financial and nonfinancial, the measurement process must include those that are short- and long-term, absolute and relative, and quantitative and qualitative. Each serves a purpose, and a balanced mix usually is best. Measures may be put forth in a range, where a minimum represents barely acceptable performance and a maximum greatly exceeds expectations. Some measures may be adjustable, based on external economic or other factors.

Measures should be both lagging—in terms of past performance—and leading. Looking through the rearview mirror is useful in terms of accountability and reward. But measures that foretell future performance are important. This is where customer satisfaction measures—for example, repeat business, brand loyalty, cross-selling of new products, and the like—are valuable. Similarly, personnel development, evidenced by skills assessments, performance evaluations, and advancement rates are useful. Pipelines of customer orders and new products and cycle times can be used to project future accomplishments.

While having a sufficient number of targeted measures is important, some companies have fallen into a trap of measuring so many things that attention is unnecessarily diverted from truly relevant matters. It's necessary to keep the number of measures manageable.

## The Board's Oversight Role

A board is not responsible for devising either measures or the measurement process. That's management's job. But it is responsible for ensuring that management has instituted meaningful measures to enable management to track and monitor performance and take swift corrective action when necessary, and that it uses a process ensuring the types of desired linkages outlined earlier.

A board's role also includes being comfortable that it receives reliable measurement information and thereby is positioned to carry out its oversight responsibilities. A board needs to discuss with management why and how the established measures make sense for the company. A board may want to see measures in prescribed formats, with variances from targets and trend lines. Whatever the presentation, the board needs to know it gets the right information, on a timely basis, plus management's pointers as to where issues lie and what management plans to do. Where measures need refinement or replacement, the board needs to be similarly apprised. At the end of the day, the board needs to know a process is firmly in place to give directors the information they need in order to provide meaningful oversight for measuring progress toward effective strategy implementation and achievement of stated goals.

No, it's not easy. But it is a key part of the job.[1]

## FINANCIAL REPORTING

We see every day how the marketplace eagerly awaits and reacts in force to information about companies' performance and future prospects. Of course, overseeing the financial reporting process and resulting financial statements and related issuances is a key board responsibility. While financial reporting is perhaps viewed as somewhat more mundane than other board roles, certainly its importance is well understood inside and outside the boardroom.

A board's responsibility for overseeing external financial reporting has long been delegated to the audit committee, which carries out the role on behalf of the full board. In recent years, however, with evolving federalization of governance, the audit committee has become an entity unto itself, with laws and regulations outlining what it needs to do.

There's no doubt that serving as an audit committee member of a corporate board is among the most challenging roles in today's business environment. Responsibilities have expanded, market expectations have heightened, and stress levels have intensified. Ever since the Sarbanes-Oxley Act of 2002 was enacted and related SEC regulations and stock exchange listing standards were codified, audit committee members have been struggling with their elevated roles. Even experienced directors, some of whom initially surmised there would be little difficulty in audit committee service, have wrestled with issues of process and scope for the committees' activities.

Indeed, many audit committees long ago committed to practices that now are required. They ensured that all committee members have the requisite skill and independence, have seen to a whistleblower process, and have focused on the work of their companies' external and internal auditors. Some audit committees have been holding private sessions without management present for years; they engage advisors as needed and regularly assess the committee's own performance. Now that these practices are mandated by law, regulation, or rule, they've been uniformly adopted. In other words, for those audit committees that previously weren't completely *there*, they are now where they need to be; attention has been given to new mandates, with compliance considered nonnegotiable.

But experience working with audit committees shows that despite compliance with requirements, audit committee members continue to struggle with their roles—that is, there's still a lack of certainty about what they should be actually doing in the committee room. This is compounded by the fact that while most are accomplished and dedicated executives, committee members continue to be concerned about personal liability. The angst spiked when former Enron and WorldCom directors were forced to dig into their own pockets to settle legal actions against them, and it hasn't entirely dissipated.

We look here at what audit committees must do by mandate, and how the most effective committees view their roles—and where they draw the line in terms of the scope of their responsibilities.

## Scope of Responsibilities

In addition to what we can call matters of structure and form—some of which are outlined above—various rules require audit committees to devote attention to:

- Annual and quarterly financial statements
- Form 10-K's Management's Discussion and Analysis (MD&A)
- Earnings releases, including pro forma financial information
- Financial reporting and earnings guidance provided to analysts and rating agencies
- Policies on risk assessment and risk management
- Appointment, compensation, and oversight of the external auditor
- Auditor independence, including preapproval of nonaudit services, and understanding the auditing firm's quality control system and results
- Performance of the internal audit function
- Understanding key accounting policies and alternative accounting principles discussed with management, including their ramifications and the auditor's preferred treatment

This list is not exhaustive, and there are other areas that must be addressed based on a particular company's industry, business model, and exchange. The NYSE, for example, states that an audit committee's purpose includes oversight of the company's legal and regulatory compliance, without explicit limitation to financial reporting matters. And the need to discuss policies for risk assessment and risk management, despite related commentary on the rule, can be interpreted as being broad-based.

Audit committee members recognize that the committee's scope of responsibility has expanded into areas traditionally considered management's role. Appointing and compensating the external auditor, for example, now is a direct audit committee responsibility, going well beyond its traditional oversight role. The committee is charged with responsibility to establish procedures for a whistleblower process—the term in Sarbanes-Oxley is "establish," rather than oversee establishment of—although most audit committees are taking a logical approach to their involvement. In addition, there's the charge to resolve disagreements on financial reporting between management and the auditor—to "resolve," not just oversee the resolution— and to approve nonaudit services. These responsibilities have moved a part-time oversight body into management's space.

What's an audit committee to do? As might be expected, the answer to this question is multifaceted. First, most audit committees already have checked to be sure mandated compliance requirements are being fully met. These encompass the matters of structure and form, including committee composition, independence, charter, executive sessions, annual assessments, and so forth.

Second, looking at the substantive role, many audit committees find it useful to consider committee scope in four broad categories of its basic responsibilities.

1. *Financial reporting.* This includes oversight of financial reports, including the annual and quarterly financial statements, disclosures in regulatory filings, earnings releases, pro-forma information, earnings guidance, and the like.
2. *External audit.* This entails knowing the company's auditor, including the lead engagement partner and manager and other partners involved in the audit. And by *knowing,* I mean really knowing what they're doing, what their views are, and how they think. Audit committee members should be comfortable with the audit scope and approach, and should ensure effective and timely communications. This also entails confirming auditor independence, including approving appropriate nonaudit services, and dealing with related audit quality matters.
3. *Internal audit.* This category requires gaining knowledge of internal audit methodologies and audit testing plans, ensuring effective communication

channels, reviewing quality and depth of audit resources and budget, and making certain that reporting lines are appropriate and auditor objectivity protected.

4. *Internal control.* The committee's responsibilities extend to oversight of compliance with Section 404 of Sarbanes-Oxley, which represents annual reporting on the effectiveness of internal control over financial reporting, and Section 302 on quarterly reporting.

In light of what many have found to be overload, audit committee members need to ask themselves whether other responsibilities—whether specified in the committee's charter or imposed by the board—make sense in today's environment. Some audit committees have oversight responsibility for such matters as enterprise risk management and compliance with laws and regulations (as implicitly called for by the NYSE listing standards), corporate social responsibility, reliability of nonfinancial as well as financial IT systems, and the oversight of special investigations.

In connection with legal and regulatory and internal policy compliance, many audit committees have responsibility for overseeing codes of conduct—for officers, directors, and all personnel—as well as whistleblower channels. They may be asked to review the propriety of related party transactions, look at officers' perks, or monitor compliance with liquidity and collateral requirements or other contractual guarantees. And they may be expected to look beyond the reporting required by Sarbanes-Oxley on internal control over financial reporting, extending their focus to controls over company operations and compliance with laws and regulations as well.

Certainly, oversight responsibility for these matters is important at the board level. But my advice to boards is that serious consideration be given to allocating some of these responsibilities to other board committees, or keeping some for the full board itself. The best place to start is with those responsibilities not directly related to financial reporting and the related control and audit processes. For example, a number of boards have established a risk committee—now required by large financial institutions—to provide needed oversight over how the company identifies and manages a wide range of risks that can affect performance. Special investigations can be conducted by another designated committee.

The point is simple—with all the mandates for the audit committee in today's heightened regulatory environment, most audit committees have too much on their plates. To enable the committee to perform at the necessarily high level, many nonmandated responsibilities should be removed.

Relative to committee operation, the committee must be sure it obtains relevant information, and that it structures its meetings and devotes the necessary time to enable it to carry out its responsibilities effectively. Certainly, over the years audit committees have expanded the number and length of meetings, information requirements, communications with management and auditors, and off-line time devoted to committee activities, with annual calendars of a committee's activities prepared well in advance to ensure all topics are addressed. Yet it is often difficult to predict exactly how much time will be needed to discuss certain topics, or to address yet unknown events. Audit committee members know that new issues needing attention will surface, but they don't always know what they will be or when. Time for such matters needs to be built into schedules.

## Execution

My experience with audit committees shows that committee members continue to struggle with how deeply they must dive into corporate details to carry out their oversight responsibilities. Most don't want to dive too deeply—committee members recognize that theirs is an oversight role, and that getting into management's hair can be counterproductive. Yet they also recognize expectations of the marketplace, including shareowners, regulators, and the legal system.

Many committee members continue to struggle with the basic question, "How far do we need to go in understanding what's being reported to us by management, and in gaining the requisite comfort?" They know they have a critical role, but at the same time are acutely aware that they're a part-time body and are not positioned to explore the minute details on which management and auditors are focused full time. Yet the expectations are there, with very real implications—including personal reputation and liability. While of course there are no official standards or hard-and-fast rules, we can look at what many audit committees have found works best.

### Critical Perspective

Audit committee members of course are members of the board of directors, and this is critical to effective committee performance. These directors are at the board table to discuss such matters as the company's strategy and strategic implementation plan, its organization and resource allocations, performance measures, and transactions that have been consummated or are anticipated. To those ends, they receive information on current plans, performance, risks, and related actions. They understand the company's industry and business model, how the company makes money, and where the operational soft spots lie.

This information from a board-level perspective is crucial to enabling audit committee members to perform their oversight role well. It provides a basis and context for considering the content and form of financial reports prepared by management, and positions the committee to recognize what should be communicated in the company's financial reports, including what types of disclosures are needed. To be effective, committee members must keep this knowledge in the forefront of their minds and make full use of it in conducting the committee's activities.

### Challenging the Source

It's important that audit committees get information from a variety of sources. Management is, of course, the board's prime source of information, but the committee cannot—and should not—attempt to audit that information. However, committee members do need to consider the data within the context of what they know about the company and its managers, and in relation to other information sources.

■ *Management.* The committee's primary sources of information typically are the chief financial officer, finance director, chief accounting officer, and others with a clear view into the company's operations and activities and related financial data. Those executives have the depth of knowledge and insight, and are directly responsible for preparing the financial statements, related regulatory filings, pro forma information, earnings releases, and so forth. Clearly, there needs to be a high level of trust here— indeed, if the committee has concerns about the integrity of financial management, there's a much larger problem in need of immediate action.

With trust established, committee members will want to look behind the numbers and disclosures, entering into in-depth discussions that leverage a wide variety of contextual data. Experienced audit committee members know the extremes don't work—from simply asking if every- thing's okay (years ago that tack was actually taken by some committee members) to conducting confrontational interrogations. It's not enough to simply ask management if there's anything unusual or that warrants discussion. That may be a starting point, but it's only that. Some utilize a "trust but verify" philosophy, reflecting President Ronald Reagan's official stance toward the Soviets. But in this context, that might be too cynical a viewpoint, since management is on the same team as the committee, not an ideologically divergent political bloc.

A term that some years ago came into vogue among audit committee circles, *constructive skepticism*, is more appropriate. There needs to be plenty of trust in management, combined with a healthy dose of productive dialogue. Such positive interaction can help produce financial reports that reflect economic reality and contain all relevant disclosures, so that investors can make informed decisions about the company's past performance and future prospects.

After the spate of rules and regulations were handed down in the form of Sarbanes-Oxley, SEC regulations, and stock exchange listing standards, many audit committee members literally brought a checklist into the committee room—they asked their listed questions, listened to responses, and ticked the boxes. This accomplished little of substance. Certainly there's no harm in looking at a checklist during or toward the end of a meeting to ensure all key points were covered, and it's not uncommon for committees to do so, but operating purely by checklist is counterproductive.

Some committee members have been known to ask questions and then—without fully understanding the answers—simply move on, fearing their lack of knowledge will become evident by following up with another question. But pushing back is a fundamental requirement of the committee. There needs to be a dialogue, with a healthy exchange of information—for example, about how management arrived at the presented financial statements. Of critical importance is analysis of the assumptions, estimates, and judgments reflected in the financials. What support does management have for the numbers? What alternatives were considered? Is there a bias toward higher profits and earnings per share? Might different numbers better reflect the company's performance? Is there additional information, or different presentation, that better communicates economic reality? These and related questions need to be asked, and the committee should continue to ask follow-up questions until it is comfortable that the answers make full sense.

■ *External auditor.* The external auditing firm is a source of critically important information. Audit committee members will want to understand the audit methodology and approach, probing for the areas where significant attention has been given—and where it has not. Committee members should understand what challenges arose, what substantive issues caused management and auditor to differ—even if the differences ultimately were resolved—and where the difficult judgments were made.

If management and the auditor came to different conclusions on accounting principles and their application, then the audit committee needs to understand that. Audit committee members should question the auditor about whether the application fits the company's facts and circumstances and what alternative accounting principles were considered and discarded.

The committee should take full advantage of private sessions with the external auditor. These sessions present an excellent opportunity to speak frankly and fully about key issues and concerns, and to compare information obtained from management. And committee members will get a sense of how forthcoming the auditor is in communications with the committee—whether they're full and frank, or whether the committee needs to pull teeth.

■ *Internal audit.* Internal auditors also are positioned to provide the audit committee with information that may be critical to understanding financial reports, as well as operations in general. The chief internal auditor, sometimes called the chief audit executive or general auditor, will have a good sense of the control environment, encompassing the ethical values and integrity of the organization, as well as other cultural matters that serve as an underpinning to reliable financial reporting.

Here, too, there should be full and free-flowing communication. Internal audit should have full access to the company's people and activities. Indeed, a key responsibility of the audit committee is to understand internal audit's role, its capabilities, budget, scope, and the like, to ensure there are no inappropriate constraints. The audit committee should not only learn about the internal audit's findings, but also relate those findings to what the committee learned from management and the external auditor.

■ *Other sources.* Important information also can be gleaned from media coverage and reports from analysts, rating agencies, and other third parties. Those market participants have a different perspective from management and the auditors, thereby offering unique insights and perspectives worth considering while reviewing the financial information presented.

Not to be ignored is information from others in the company, and from those doing business with it. Certainly, input from help lines or whistleblower channels can be invaluable. And information—including complaints—from customers, suppliers, lenders, and regulators can be enlightening. The audit committee doesn't have the time to sort through a lot of detail here, but it should know the nature of information that might signal needed modifications to financial reports.

## Advisors

An audit committee has the right to its own advisor, and a number of committees have decided to have an advisor regularly attend meetings. There are two schools of thought on this. Some committee members, often on the advice of legal counsel, believe it's essential to have an advisor steeped in accounting principles and practices present at meetings to help ask the right questions, analyze information provided, and offer advice to the committee. Others believe this is unnecessary and, in fact, is overkill; advisors, they argue, are needed only in certain instances where a particularly difficult accounting issue is at hand.

For what it's worth, my advice to audit committees is that having an advisor on an ongoing basis generally is unnecessary and is typically not a good idea. That's because the presence of an advisor sometimes creates the tendency to leave debate and even formulating conclusions to the advisor. In addition, the audit committee already should be comprised of members who can understand and deal effectively with the issues at hand, without an advisor's prompting. If that's not the case, then committee composition should be reconsidered. And clearly many committee members are increasingly looking around the table to ensure they're comfortable that the committee indeed has the requisite skills among its membership. That doesn't mean committee members need to be accountants by training, but they need to have enough knowledge of financial reporting to be able to deal with the issues, including the identified audit committee financial expert.

Of course, bringing in an advisor can be helpful in certain situations, like those in which management and auditors disagree on a complicated accounting issue.

## The Right Balance

As with many things in life, finding the right balance is critical to success. Audit committees need to perform an important oversight role, recognizing that they do so on a part-time basis, but also that part-time board membership is taking up more and more of their time. As noted, surveys show that board service, including service on a committee, requires an average of approximately 250 hours of service per year, and that presumes no special circumstances or crises. This is approximately double the average time that was spent for board service before the last round of scandals and rule-making initiatives. And time spent on the audit committee is turning out to be more than time spent on other board committees (although the compensation committee is quickly catching up).

As a result, the audit committee must use its time wisely. It must obtain relevant information, compare it with existing knowledge and data from other sources, and challenge the information and results as necessary. But committee members must also be flexible. Committees should not fall into the common trap of setting meeting schedules and then limiting work to the allocated time. If the allotted time isn't enough to do the job correctly—if, for example, there are unusual transactions or occurrences—then the committee needs to find more time. Its responsibilities are too important, and the environment too serious, to do otherwise.

## Facilitating Audit Committee Performance

We now look at the other side of the coin: how the parties with which the audit committee deals most frequently—financial management and the external and internal auditors—can provide information and support to make the committee operate most effectively.

A couple of fundamental realities should be recognized. First, audit committees want a disciplined process for receiving and reviewing relevant information. Like most seasoned executives, committee members don't want information at the last minute, and they don't want it in a form that's unorganized, unnecessarily complicated, or poorly rationalized. Second, audit committee members don't like surprises. When a significant problem surfaces, the sooner the committee or committee chair is advised, the better.

### Management

As noted, financial management is the source of most of the audit committee's information, from financial statements and regulatory filings to pro-forma information and earnings releases. Just as the chief financial officer operates at a high level and fast pace, so do many audit committee members, who themselves may have full-time jobs or serve on multiple boards and committees. As such, they have busy schedules and set aside specific time slots to review reports, so even a short delay can throw a monkey wrench into their other scheduled business activities. Management does committee members a great service by agreeing on in advance—and keeping to—a predetermined information distribution schedule.

Providing information surrounding draft financial reports that will aid in the review process is extremely important to the committee. Managers should consider, for example, what information they used in making key decisions reflected in the financial reports, which can be critical to enabling audit committee members to effectively consider associated issues. Information about accounting principles used and, just as important, how they were applied, is essential to committee members. As such, management should provide information not only on which principles were used in the financial statements and related implications, but also alternative principles and means of application that were considered, and why they were rejected. Management also will want to inform the committee how principles used by the company compare with those of its major competitors.

Certainly audit committee members of every company, even those new to the role, understand that historical financial statements are anything but historical. They know there are myriad assumptions, estimates, and judgments about the future affecting many of the numbers. Management needs to fully disclose to the committee what is behind the numbers, and how management arrived at the amounts presented. Here, too, alternatives considered should be provided, and support for those assumptions, estimates, and judgments actually used must be available for discussion.

Also relevant is the question of what information should be provided to the committee in advance, and what should be left for discussion in meetings. The answer depends on the committee's preferences, but in general most data and related analysis should be provided ahead of meetings. That way, committee members have an opportunity to digest the information offline and understand the issues and supporting data and rationale behind the numbers, allowing use of face-to-face meetings to delve into pertinent areas in greater depth. The form of communication, whether a hard-copy board book, secure web site, or other form of electronic communication, should be mutually agreed upon by management and the committee.

As noted, an audit committee needs information from other sources, and management typically is best positioned to provide relevant information from financial analysts, rating agencies, and other external sources—warts and all—as well as information captured from customers, suppliers, and others with whom the company interacts. That information serves a valuable purpose, enabling the committee to have further context for information in financial reports. Some companies from time to time bring in well-respected investment analysts to provide additional perspective on the company's financial reporting and answer committee members' questions.

Regarding the meetings themselves, management—usually working with the committee chair—can help by setting in advance the annual meeting calendar, meeting agendas, and information requirements and timing. Depending on the company, this role may be the responsibility of the corporate secretary, a corporate governance officer, or the office of the CFO. In any event, the responsible individual will want to maintain an open communication channel with the committee chair to ensure that the committee's needs are met.

Now, there's no doubt that in light of expanded responsibilities and the environment in which committees operate, audit committees are scheduling more meetings and more time for each. No longer are meetings planned for one or two hours immediately preceding the full board meeting; adequate time is necessarily set aside with sufficient flexibility for effectively carrying out the committee's extensive responsibilities.

Another important change has occurred in how committee meetings are conducted. No longer are meetings orchestrated by financial management with most of the time spent on management's presentations. That approach, which at some companies served an unhealthy agenda by precluding sufficient discussion, has been replaced by one that facilitates full and in-depth discussions of key issues. The committee chair discusses agendas and schedules in advance with financial management, and takes charge in the committee meeting room. With management now providing relevant information in advance, along with brief and succinct presentations in meetings, the committee is positioned to delve as deeply as needed into significant matters. Management finds this approach enhances the level of comfort gained by the audit committee members, which in turn diffuses some of the tension that management and the committee members experienced in past years.

### External Auditor

With clearer and expanded responsibilities—not to mention greater accountability—audit committee members increasingly look to the external auditor as a critical support system. Audit committees expect full and free-flowing communication between auditor and committee about what is truly relevant. Having discussed technical issues with financial management, with tentative decisions reached, the auditor needs to be forthcoming in bringing those matters to the committee's attention. The discussion should be direct and frank so that the committee has a clear picture of what the challenges are and how they are being met. Timing is critical, with expectations that the information flow will occur as needed during the course of the audit engagement.

The auditor is expected to provide the firm's assessment of key accounting principles, management's related assumptions and judgments, and the adequacy of disclosures. As an independent player, the auditor must provide to the committee a sound judgment on key subjective issues. That includes whether the financial presentation not only is technically appropriate, but whether it clearly and fully discloses pertinent information in a form useful to the investing community.

The better the advance planning, the better the shared mind-set between the committee and auditor as to what is expected, in what form, and when, in order to assure the auditor carries out audit responsibilities in a manner that enables the audit committee to fulfill its mandate.

### Internal Audit

A company's internal audit function can serve as an important set of eyes and ears of the audit committee. Internal audit is present on a full-time, year-round basis, and with appropriate scope and direction can provide the committee with important information relevant to the financial reporting process. With a focus on internal control over financial reporting, internal audit's perspective can be valuable to the audit committee in considering both the strengths and weaknesses of the company's control processes as well as issues in need of attention in financial reports.

As with the external auditor, there should be clear communication between the chief internal auditor and the audit committee on internal audit's scope and testing plan. There's a wide range of potential focus, and the audit committee should be fully apprised of the extent to which internal audit is looking at financial reporting versus operational or compliance activities. In past years, many audit committee members presumed the internal audit function looked extensively at the financial reporting process, when often that was not the case. There's now usually a clearer understanding of internal audit's tasks and findings, as well as implications of those findings for the organization. Internal audit can assist the committee by clearly communicating where and how it is devoting time and resources.

Here too, timing of communication is important. I've been asked by a number of chief audit executives when they should bring to the audit committee's attention a potentially significant problem. Should they do so when the problem first is identified, when there's more clarity around the problem's scope, or after an investigation provides even greater specificity? My typical response is straightforward. First, the chief audit executive must discuss with and have a clear understanding with the committee chair in advance about when such information will be provided. Second, as a general rule, the sooner the committee chair is apprised, the better.

The vast majority of audit committee chairs with whom I've worked say they want to know about a potentially significant problem as soon as it surfaces. In addition, they want to be kept apprised as more information is obtained and an assessment is made. That way, the audit committee can concur in the approach or provide direction to internal audit as needed. If the problem turns out not to be a big deal, so much the better. So, short of an audit committee chair directing otherwise, internal audit should avoid the temptation to wait to obtain more information before raising a potentially significant issue.

An issue relevant to internal audit, as well as to each of the parties mentioned earlier, is the topic of private meetings. Experience shows that these sessions are indeed valuable, where the audit committee meets separately with management, the external auditor, and the internal auditor regularly without others present. Here, too, each party should be forthcoming, so that the audit committee members feel comfortable that they are getting relevant information without spin.

And that's the most critical way to ensure your audit committee is effective: Make sure it gets the information it needs truthfully, completely, in the right form, and in a timely fashion. Only then is the committee positioned to effectively carry out its responsibilities.

For additional information on audit committees, suggested reading is *Audit Committee Effectiveness—What Works Best*, recently updated by PricewaterhouseCoopers.[2]

 ## NOTES

1. If you're interested in digging deeper into performance metrics and their linkage to strategy, as well as to motivation and compensation, a couple of sources are worth taking a look at: PricewaterhouseCoopers' *Corporate Governance and the Board—What Works Best* and the NACD's "Performance Metrics: Understanding the Board's Role."
2. Available from the Institute of Internal Auditors, Altamonte Springs, Florida, or PricewaterhouseCoopers, LLC.

CHAPTER FOURTEEN

# Building an Effective Board

D OES YOUR COMPANY HAVE the right directors on the board? As directors look around the boardroom table, they must be confident that fellow directors are people who can successfully work together and, if necessary, go to war with, putting reputations and possibly personal assets in their hands. CEOs and senior management team members, and of course the company's shareholders, also need to be confident that the men and women providing corporate oversight do the job well.

The quality of boards of directors has for years been on the minds of Congressional leaders, regulators, shareholders, and the public, and the volume rose with the financial system's near meltdown. An article in *Newsweek* was clear in its condemnation:

> The failure of the financial system in 2008 wasn't simply a massive failure of common sense, regulation, and leadership. It was also a failure of corporate governance . . . [Boards are] supposed to be there to act almost like a governor on an engine, if it's running out of control at least to slow it down. Ideally they're supposed to monitor, advise, provide contacts to the company, and help it grow. But at the very least, they're supposed to keep it from blowing up.[1]

The article's focus turns to board composition, saying, "Unfortunately, boards are a narrow group who come from the same backgrounds as the CEOs. They tend to see the world the same way the CEOs do."

The near meltdown provides some of the impetus for the SEC rules requiring disclosure of each director's specific experience, qualifications, attributes, or skills "that led the board to conclude that the person should serve as a director for the company at the time of the filing." Also disclosed are other directorships held by each board member or director nominee during the past five years at any public company or registered management investment company, and any executive officers, directors, and director nominees who have been involved in legal actions during the past 10 years.

Basically, all this gets down to why the current or nominated board members are deemed to be right for the job. But while the increased information will allow somewhat better transparency, nobody should expect from it an ability to make a clear determination of a board's ability to perform well. Reality is that one must be inside the boardroom to make an informed judgment on how well directors are really doing.

 ## LOOKING OBJECTIVELY

Boards have long been considering their own composition, and the disclosure rules have provided somewhat further impetus for doing so, looking particularly at whether their current composition is what's needed for today's challenges. In considering who should occupy the seats at the table going forward, nominating and governance committees also are focusing on whether any directors may not be pulling their weight, and if so, how best to make necessary changes.

Many boards—74 percent of the S&P 500, according to a Spencer Stuart study—have term or age limits, forcing turnover over time. This approach is understandable, as it refreshes board composition and provides a stream of new thinking. But experience shows that this approach might not be best for a couple of reasons. First, we've seen some of the best directors cast aside simply because they've been doing the job for a long time or have reached an arbitrary age. And second, there's a tendency for board leadership *not* to remove directors who aren't cutting it, preferring to suffer with the inadequacy until term or age limits take hold.

Annual board assessments are more effective, with straightforward process that's readily implemented. Importantly, assessments are most beneficial when aimed at turning weaker directors into strong ones, enabling them to add more value at the board table. There may, however, be circumstances where a director needs to be thanked for past performance and moved off the board. And when a director is asked to move on, he or she often recognizes the reality and is comfortable leaving.

In one example, a nonexecutive chair of a large public company asked for my advice on how to change the composition of the company's board, which was overloaded with directors with similar backgrounds and narrow perspectives. We developed a supporting rationale for removing six directors. Following preliminary discussions with them, we presented the idea at a special board meeting. All six, having understood the arguments and benefits to the company, quickly agreed to the changes and tendered their resignations.

More on board assessments in a moment.

 ## A SHIFT IN DIRECTION

The aforementioned *Newsweek* article continues: "A lot of disillusioned board members . . . [say they] are completely captured by the CEO in most companies. CEOs either have selected you, or approved your being on the board. They control your renominations, your perks, your pay, almost all the information that goes to you, your committee assignments, your agendas." That's an interesting perspective, which too often was the case years ago—but we've seen that today's board dynamics generally are very different. With the vast majority of directors now being independent, along with private meetings and separation of the chair and CEO roles or putting in place a strong lead director, the dynamics have changed. Certainly in many companies the CEO-chair wields significant power, but that person no longer smacks of absolute power.

Here's one telling anecdote about how power has shifted. A nominating committee chair told me the company's board had a strict policy: Any board candidate put forth by the CEO *will be eliminated from consideration.* Yes, the names of candidates identified by the nominating committee will continue to be discussed with the CEO, but they won't be selected by him. And shareholders are pushing the point. As noted in Chapter 4, when the new CEO of HP was involved in identifying new board members, Institutional Shareholder Services objected, recommending that shareholders withhold their votes for three members of the nominating and governance committee.

In past years many large companies looked for big-name individuals, drawn from high political offices, the military, academia, and the performing arts. But just as choosing an imperial CEO has largely given way to picking seasoned and highly skilled managers, board nominating committees are looking less for the flashy name and instead focusing on director candidates who can bring the knowledge, experience, judgment, and facility to add needed value in the boardroom.

With this context, it's interesting to look a bit more deeply into what trends in board composition have developed over time. Years ago we saw many companies' board seats occupied by sitting CEOs from other companies, often hand-picked by the chief executive. And while, as suggested above, some boards were to some extent captured by a CEO, more often there were and are positives, since these directors not only understand the issues a CEO deals with, but also recognize the challenges and have the perspective and experience to provide valuable counsel. That these individuals might have long associations with the CEO can be a significant advantage in terms of fostering a good working relationship and facilitating an ability to trust one another and deal successfully with the tough issues, particularly in times of stress.

Recent years have brought significant change, for a number of reasons. Boards now have many more independent directors, with evolving rules and guidelines on what constitutes independence, and have recognized the value in bringing together different perspectives. Further, the number of CEOs on boards has diminished due to demands of CEOs' own companies, whose boards often limit the CEO to serving on perhaps one or two other company boards, since the vast majority of the CEO's time is expected to be devoted to his/her own company. A recent survey shows that over 50 percent of S&P 500 CEOs serve on no outside boards.[2]

Also, with the focus of boards several years ago changing to more of a compliance or monitoring role, many active CEOs simply haven't wanted to spend the necessary time on those kinds of matters. In many cases those board seats have been taken by heads of business units or other senior executives, where serving on an outside board offers experience in corporate governance and helps position executives to aim for the top job in their own companies.

Another factor influencing change in board composition is the burden being placed on audit committees. An audit committee financial expert is expected to be in place, and all committee members are expected to have more knowledge of financial reporting matters generally. More individuals with CFO or high-level public accounting experience have been recruited particularly for this purpose. We've seen signs of similar movement for board members with other specialized skills, such as in compensation, international business, or technology.

An increasing number of boards want to make their membership more diverse, adding important perspectives that otherwise would be absent. The result can be positive, where we've seen, for example, addition of a woman's perspective providing valuable insight into key issues faced by a company's industry, product lines, or customer base. Importantly, recent feedback from female directors indicates that they see themselves adding more value in the boardroom when there are at least two women directors to reinforce each others' thinking.

 ## BUILDING A BETTER BOARD

So how are the best boards built? In principle, what does work is pretty simple: Build a board with directors who have the knowledge, experience, and skills to understand the company's industry, business, people, and significant issues; who work collegially in providing the requisite advice, counsel, and where necessary, direction to management; and who carry out their monitoring role as well. These directors think independently, raising relevant issues, debating them fully, and working toward consensus. And they have a burning desire to see the company succeed in its mission and provide the desired growth and returns expected by shareholders. This is really a 40,000-foot perspective, and getting the right people into the board seats requires considerable thought, care, and work.

What many nominating committees do, often with outside support, is consider what criteria they want their board directors to meet, and then determine how the current directors measure up. Typically they use a matrix, with desired criteria including sought-after skill sets and other attributes—including personal and interpersonal characteristics and skills—listed in columns across the top, and current board members listed in rows down the side. Then the boxes in the matrix are filled in, either with a mark designating whether a criterion is met, or a quantitative or qualitative measure or ranking to signal relative strength in satisfying the criterion. The goal is to determine strengths and shortcomings in relation to the established categories, and to identify where enhancements are needed.

There are, however, other critical factors to include. You want to structure a board that will cooperate in providing advice, counsel, and direction to the CEO and senior management team. By no means does that mean uniform thinking, as diversity in background, perspective, and ideas is essential. But it does mean you want new board members who can enter seamlessly to provide needed strengths in a manner that promotes debate and discussion but also builds consensus for clear direction to management.

It's important to focus on the skills and attributes needed not necessarily for where the company has been or is currently, but for *where it is going based on the accepted strategic direction.* Of course there are many other factors to consider in building a board that's right for a particular company. These include the number of boards on which a candidate sits, other commitments, energy level, and so on. While there are rules of thumb for an appropriate number of boards on which a director should serve, depending on whether the director is employed full-time or otherwise retired, exceptions always crop up. Several months ago a friend of mine, who is a CEO actively running a company, mentioned he was going to join his fourth public company board, adding to his two private company boards. Unfortunately, I've not been successful in changing his mind!

Certainly one size does not fit all, and each board must carefully tailor its makeup to best handle the company and its circumstances, management, and needs. At the same time certain principles generally apply. For those of you on board nominating committees or otherwise influencing your company's board composition, here are some things some boards have struggled with that you'll want to watch out for.

- ▪ *Constituent boards.* I first used this term years ago when working with the board of directors of a bank whose directors were appointed by constituent ownership bodies. Despite legal requirements to the contrary, these directors acted in what they thought were the best interests of their constituent groups. They seemed to like each other and got along well, but couldn't agree on key business issues. The result was lack of direction to management on critical matters, ranging from strategic direction to dealing with the bank's regulators. Ultimately the bank was under severe stress and merged into another organization.

  Another example is a large organization whose directors are elected by constituent bodies or appointed by senior state officials. If you want the poster child for a dysfunctional board, this is it. Not only do these board members speak to the microphone—all board meetings are open to the public and the proceedings are taped for subsequent publication—they, like the bank board, fiercely support the positions of their constituents. An all-too-frequent result is finger pointing—literally as well as figuratively—and shouting matches during board meetings. This organization has generally done well, despite what happens in the boardroom rather than because of it, but recently it has taken a hit in earnings and is the subject of a regulatory investigation.

- *Dissident director.* We've seen instances where a board finds itself laden with one or two directors who bring a specific agenda. This arrangement sometimes can cure a clearly identified company ill, and such directors might be able to get a disorganized board back on track. Too often, however, these directors focus solely on their one issue, causing the board to take its collective eye off the real issues that need to be addressed. A typical corollary result is unnecessary discord and conflict, precluding the board from providing clear direction to management.

- *Family domination.* I worked with a reasonably large public company that continued to have more than half its board seats occupied by founding family members. The company was doing well, with over-whelming market share in its industries, but the board simply was too insular to provide the far-reaching perspective necessary for long-term sustainability and growth. In this case, the nonexecutive chair, a family patriarch, identified the problem and asked how to manage a change in a way that wouldn't alienate the family. After engaging boardroom discussion of why a change would benefit the company, family directors genuinely accepted the need to restock the board, and this story had a happy ending.

- *The paper board.* We've seen boards comprised of directors with great pedigrees and well-recognized names, but who don't really connect with the company's needs or with each other. These directors typically will do what we might call a fly-by to board meetings, without being engaged in the company or its issues. At best, some of these boards simply don't get in the way of management; at worst, they fail to recognize serious problems in need of quick and decisive action.

- *Venture-dominated board.* Companies that are about to go public or have recently done so typically change the composition of the board to gain the balance and skills needed in the next stage of the company's life cycle. Sometimes, however, a board may continue to be dominated by venture capitalists. This has both good and bad consequences. On the plus side, there are directors with intimate knowledge of the company's manage-ment, needs, and issues and a very significant stake in the company's success. The downside can include a focus different from that of other shareholders, and depending on where the company is in the process, an eye on short-term exit strategy.

## BOARD ASSESSMENTS

Important to ensuring that a board continues to be comprised of directors who individually and collectively have the skills and attributes to be effective, and operates as such, is a process for periodical assessment. Today 96 percent of S&P 500 boards conduct annual evaluations.[3] Some do so as a result of New York Stock Exchange requirements. Others are driven by the guidance of shareholder advisory organizations, by perceptions of governance best practice, or simply by a desire to bring more value to the company and its shareowners. Whatever the reason, periodically evaluating the performance of the board and its committees is a good thing—if done well, the process can make the board stronger and more effective in carrying out its critical oversight responsibilities.

Note the caveat, *if done well.* When it comes to board assessment, a number of different approaches are being taken, with some significantly more effective than others. First and foremost, it's important that the assessment process be viewed as positive and constructive, in order to build a better board. If one director isn't doing the job as effectively as needed, the process should enable the person to become a better director. With that said, there are instances where a change in board composition is deemed desirable, either because of shortcomings in a director's performance or a need for different attributes and skills necessary for effective board performance.

Among the more common assessment approaches are:

- *Boardroom discussion.* This involves simply setting aside time at a board meeting for discussion among the directors on how the board is doing. The discussion typically is led by either the board chair, the lead director if there is one, or the chair of the nominating/governance committee. The discussion may be unstructured, allowing directors to articulate how they each view the performance of the board and its committees, and how they believe performance can be improved. In other cases, a discussion agenda is prepared in advance, enabling the directors to focus attention on specific performance factors.
- *Survey questionnaire.* Typically this involves development of one questionnaire for the board as a whole and another, or a supplement, for each board committee. Content usually is provided by the general counsel or corporate governance officer and is reviewed prior to distribution with board and committee leadership, or sometimes all directors. The questionnaire is forwarded either electronically or in hard copy to the directors who provide

their written assessments, usually anonymously. The results are then compiled and provided to the board for discussion.

■ *Interview-based evaluation.* Using an interview guide that has been reviewed in advance with board members and leadership, each director is interviewed by board leadership or a supporting consultant, with input obtained on each of the identified topics. Conversations are conducted privately, on an anonymous basis. Results are compiled, and are then presented to and discussed with the board. In this approach, usually an action plan is developed, where the board determines what modifications are to be made going forward.

These are the most common assessment options, although there also are corollary approaches where a board combines elements of the three methods.

## Advantages and Shortcomings

As with most processes, there are pros and cons that apply to each board assessment method.

■ *Discussion.* The key advantage of the boardroom discussion approach is that it's simple—the conversation is straightforward, takes little advance preparation, and requires virtually no offline time commitment from the directors. But there's a price to pay with the discussion approach—namely, insufficient open and unguarded debate. Although directors are accomplished individuals and not shy about speaking their minds, many will not raise issues in the boardroom about deficiencies in how the board operates. Experience shows that while directors willingly and openly discuss issues that are put on the table, many are hesitant to bring up sensitive matters about the board's performance.

■ *Questionnaire.* Clearly, more work is involved with this approach. A document needs to be developed, reviewed, and distributed, and the results must be collected, compiled, and ultimately discussed. Hesitancy about raising sensitive issues is somewhat mitigated by promised anonymity. Interestingly, however, is that concern on the part of directors about protection of anonymity and confidentiality often remains, causing some to avoid putting their true thoughts in writing. Concerned that their words might ultimately be read by other directors or corporate personnel—or perhaps even by outside parties—directors typically do not make full use of the questionnaire process, which makes this approach less than perfect for enhancing board performance.

- *Interviews.* Typically, there is less effort involved in developing an interview guide than a questionnaire. This is because when used by a knowledgeable interviewer the guide is less detailed, serving as a framework for conversations, as opposed to a lengthy list of specific questions. The time to schedule and conduct the interviews, however, is longer, with overall effort greater than either of the other two approaches. This approach allows the directors to talk freely, knowing that they're speaking anonymously and that their words won't be dissected by board leaders and possibly others. The usual result of the interview process is that the board hears about truly important issues that, if dealt with, can make a meaningful difference in the board's performance going forward.

## What Works

It's fair to say there's no universally accepted best practice in this arena. Each board is unique, and considering the advantages and disadvantages inherent in the three approaches, each board must decide what makes the most sense based on their particular needs.

I do, however, believe one approach brings the greatest value, at least for boards that are prepared to put in the effort to conduct a high value-added assessment. While the other approaches will likely satisfy listing standards and governance guidelines, candidly interviewing directors in an anonymous, private setting provides a board with the most insightful, meaningful, and actionable information.

In effectively executing the interview approach, the following protocols are best followed. These can be and often are applied not only at the full board level, but also for committees, and information is gained regarding individual directors as well.[4]

- *Interview guide.* The guide should cover issues relevant to board performance, including director independence, board composition, meeting formats, committee structure, and other compliance matters. But it also should address how well the board operates as a group and how it interfaces with management, focusing on how well the board carries out its responsibilities to provide advice, counsel, and direction to the CEO and senior management. These responsibilities include such matters as oversight of management's strategy development, the tone management sets for the company, the ways in which the company manages risk, and performance metrics utilized by the organization. They also include CEO assessment and succession planning, financial and nonfinancial reports to external parties, and potential mergers and acquisitions. To be most effective, the guide should be just that—a framework, not a structured questionnaire—including what are called *points of focus* highlighting topical elements that provide a starting point enabling a director to speak freely.

- *The interview.* The interviewer should allow the director to address each of the topics, but it's important to avoid a question-and-answer approach. The most relevant information comes from a free-flowing dialogue, where the director is able to say what he or she thinks is important, elaborating and steering in new directions as desired. It's usually not terribly important to cover each of the points of focus in the guide. Rather, it's more important to extract specific issues the director believes are most critical. Any concern that outside parties might obtain the information can be dealt with through document retention protocols, which may justifiably include disposing of all interview documentation at the conclusion of the assessment process.
- *Interviewer.* The interviews can be conducted by the nominating or governance committee chair or lead director. In most cases, however, a leadership director's schedule would not accommodate sufficient time for a series of interviews. And even where such board leaders are viewed positively, directors may not be entirely forthcoming if interviewed by those individuals. At the risk of sounding self-serving, using an experienced, outside consultant to shape the interview process and conduct the interviews usually is most effective.
- *Analysis.* The resulting information must be objectively and carefully compiled, analyzed, and assembled in a form that allows the board to act. Idiosyncratic words and phrases that might be recognized as originating from a particular individual must be excluded. And information must be presented at the most appropriate level to promote understanding and positioning for decision making.
- *Action planning.* With the analysis completed, the board is positioned to consider the information and decide what modifications to board approaches, protocols, and any aspect of performance are desired. It is often effective for the individual who conducted the interviews and performed the ensuing analysis to present the analysis and lead discussion of what the board believes should be done. Sufficient time is needed to allow board members to air their views and come to agreement on an action plan.

Among the most significant benefits of this interview approach to board self-assessment is that the directors know that they and their fellow directors are putting truly relevant information on the table, and are developing their own plan for board enhancement. Actions aren't recommended by a company official or outside party; rather, the directors themselves decide what they need to do to improve the board's effectiveness and efficiency going forward. Many boards have found that the approach successfully turns what might be viewed as a compliance exercise into a truly effective process providing significant value.

 **BOTTOM LINE**

What it comes down to is that a board is best comprised of individuals with the background, knowledge, skills, experience, and other attributes to collectively position the board to provide the most valuable advice, counsel, and direction to and monitoring of the chief executive and senior management team. Board composition should reflect and be commensurate with the company's industry, business, circumstances, and needs. And directors should have the where-withal and strength of character to do the job well, especially in times of stress.

Among the critical factors is that the directors can work together cohesively and collegially—debating without rancor and ensuring effective boardroom dynamics. The directors need to work together and with management to give the company the greatest likelihood of success for all shareholders.

Getting board composition right has always been a critical element in a company's success, and today it's more important than ever. As you look around the board table from the perspective of director or management, you want to be sure the directors occupying these seats are qualified and positioned to do their job well. You, your colleagues, and shareholders deserve nothing less.

 **NOTES**

1. Daniel Gross, "Corporate Killers," *Newsweek*, February 3, 2010.
2. Spencer Stuart Board Index, 2010.
3. Spencer Stuart Board Index, 2010.
4. Spencer Stuart notes that only 26 percent of S&P 500 assessments include the individual director level.

# CHAPTER FIFTEEN

# Avoiding Board Pitfalls

OARDS OF DIRECTORS HAVE extremely challenging jobs, especially in today's highly competitive and litigious environment, with marketplace and shareholder expectations seemingly ever increasing. In this chapter, we look at pitfalls into which some company boards have fallen, the surrounding circumstances, and how similar missteps can be avoided, as well as challenging decisions every board faces.

## FOLLOWING THE HERD

This isn't necessarily about Merrill Lynch, either before or after its forced adoption by Bank of America, although what happened to Merrill is relevant to this discussion. Rather it has to do with board practices that can lead to trouble. If you've worked with senior executives and boards of directors as long as I have, you've witnessed troubling behaviors that can directly affect corporate performance. Indeed, a number of major corporate failures that captured headlines can be traced back to these behavioral characteristics, which I call *keeping up with the Joneses* syndrome, followed by two corollaries, *best practices* and *groupthink*.

We know that businesses must take risks to carry out their missions and to drive toward achieving growth, profit, and return objectives. We also know that competition is inherently good, bringing out the best in capable people and organizations. Similarly, benchmarking against high-performing organizations is a useful tool for measurement and improvement. All this is obvious.

Where organizations have failed, sometimes spectacularly, is where a healthy competitive desire turns into an obsessive need to match peer performance, regardless of extraordinarily high risk and possible ultimate cost. The result in such circumstances can mean betting the ranch and losing the bet. Examples that immediately come to mind—some mentioned in earlier chapters—can be seen in context of trying to keep up with the Joneses, with disastrous results:

■ Among the more recent is the implosion of major investment banks such as Bear Stearns, Lehman Brothers, and Merrill Lynch, among others. Among the reasons for their demise is senior executives looking greedily at the vast amounts of money being made in the collateralized debt obligation market by their competitors. When regulatory restraints were lifted and leverage soared, a seemingly insatiable appetite developed to grab, package, and resell the securitized assets. Yes, these companies used value-at-risk models and other risk-management procedures (see below for how well they were applied). But with compensation programs motivating behavior and what many are calling inadequate oversight by boards and regulators, senior managements were driving at breakneck speed toward the goal of more and more.

■ We saw similar behavior at Countrywide Financial, Washington Mutual, and other banks, mortgage brokers and others generating the so-called NINJA (no income, no job, no asset) and liar loans, and other mortgages where borrowers had little chance of keeping up with payments unless the market values of their homes continued to rise. Here greed, combined with up-front payments to these institutions and managers, was a driving force. Money was made hand over fist with little effective oversight.

■ In the early part of the decade Arthur Andersen, then one of the Big 5 auditing firms, held in high esteem both within and outside the profession, was brought to its knees and ultimately folded. The failure had many causes, but one stands out in my mind: Having lost its consulting arm in a major court case, Andersen's management was hell-bent on rebuilding the firm's advisory practice. One of management's fateful decisions was to let audit decisions be made closer to the client, in the context of developing better client relations. Then the Enron debacle came along, in which one individual—the engagement partner—overruled the better technical knowledge and business judgment of the national office, and made the final decision to approve Enron's financial statements and then engaged in the fatal document destruction.

- During the dot-com years, telecommunications companies watched in awe at WorldCom's tremendous growth. They modified their strategies to keep up, investing heavily in the quest for more broadband capacity. It turned out, however, that much of the so-called growth touted by competitor WorldCom was the result of fraudulent financial reporting. That didn't help the companies that poured their dollars into capacity nobody needed.

- More recently, managers investing college and university endowment funds were looking enviously at the returns of the likes of Harvard's and Yale's funds. Trustees and alumni were asking, "Why can't we do that?" Soon more and more of these other institutions' money was poured into a slew of alternative investments, generating higher returns but with increased risk. Many of these funds have since been devastated, and the schools now need to dramatically cut their offerings to students. The same goes for state and municipal pension funds, which also invested in higher-risk investments and are suffering extreme shortfalls.

- And of course there were those investors who saw colleagues and friends earning 10 percent to 12 percent returns or more year after year, in good markets and bad. Despite some difficulties in getting a piece of the action, they persevered and finally succeeded in gaining entre to participate in this outstanding investment vehicle. Unfortunately, the mastermind was a guy named Bernie Madoff, and we all know what happened to those investments.

While each of these situations has its particular sad details, a common thread connects all these disastrous business decisions: a driving need to keep up with competitors or friends, regardless of whether they were running like lemmings off the edge of a cliff.

## Best Practices

How can anyone argue with *best practices*? After all, isn't *best* unquestionably the ultimate? Unfortunately, this term and others like it, such as *leading* or *leading-edge practices*, too often are used to describe what really are common practices, or practices that successful organizations use with little evidence that those practices actually drive success. While following so-called best practices can be viewed as learning from the successes of others, there's also a potential trap in blindly following what others are doing.

At the risk of sounding immodest, I'll point to a book titled *Corporate Governance and the Board—What Works Best*, which I spearheaded development of back in 2000. By way of background, the project initially focused on a broad-based survey of board practices. But when I took over responsibility for the book's development, it became clear that examining what were in reality *common* practices wouldn't benefit the corporate director community. There was already too much focus on surveys and peer comparisons, so we shifted tacks. Instead, as noted in the preface, the book was:

> . . . developed with face-to-face input from some of the most experienced, savvy directors anywhere on the globe. With that, along with ideas of corporate governance thought leaders, a survey of board members and PricewaterhouseCoopers' own experience with leading companies and their boards, we've put together the best of the best. It might be called "best practice," but indeed no board, even those of successful companies with the largest capitalizations, is utilizing everything suggested here. To be clear, this report does not set a common standard, and certainly not a minimum one. It sets the bar at the highest level to make a board most effective in enhancing shareholder value. Accordingly, some boards will find they need to jump much higher to measure up, whereas the best boards can reach the goal of broad-based excellence more easily and quickly.

Indeed, this publication has stood the test of time because it was forward looking, grounded in what were truly the most successful practices and extending to what was needed to further enhance board performance.

The point here is that truly successful managements and boards, while certainly aware of what others are doing, don't fall into the trap of following the herd. They recognize common practices for what they are, and operate in more effective ways that drive success.

Consider CEO compensation. We know that many board compensation committees were following what was called a best practice but in reality was merely a common practice of using peer comparison as a central feature in determining CEO compensation. Among the outcomes was the Lake Wobegon effect, where every CEO had to be above average. The assumption was that if a board was doing its job well, then the company's CEO must by definition be above average.

While peer comparison against the right peer group can be a useful tool, the more effective boards also directly link compensation to the company's strategic plan. Relevant performance metrics motivate not short-term revenue but long-term return and shareholder value. While reflecting marketplace realities, compensation is geared toward achievement of specified performance measures, aligned with board-approved risk appetites. And of course, change-of-control and other severance arrangements are well thought out and tested in advance to avoid the kinds of outlandish payments we've seen all too often.

Similarly, years ago it was common for compensation committees to rely on compensation consultants engaged by the company's management. But even then some directors knew that it makes a lot more sense for the committee to hire its own compensation consultants, avoiding potential conflicts. What was once seen as a best practice now is shunned; the use of compensation consultants independent of management is widely viewed as superior. In these and other cases, there's little doubt that the so-called best practice sometimes is anything but the best.

## Groupthink

The other corollary to keeping up with the Joneses is *groupthink*, which also can cause boards of directors, as well as managements, to get into trouble.

Yale University economics professor Robert Shiller recently wrote about how panels of experts can make colossal mistakes, and he pointed to the 1972 book *Groupthink*, by Yale psychologist Irving Janis. The book, Shiller says, explains that people on panels constantly worry about their personal relevance and effectiveness, and believe that if they deviate too far from the consensus they won't be taken seriously. They self-censor their personal doubts if they can't express them in a way that conforms to the assumptions held by the group.

### The Financial System Crisis

The Shiller piece focuses principally on how groupthink played a major role in allowing the current financial system crisis to come to pass. He noted how former Fed Chairman Alan Greenspan acknowledged to Congress that he had been wrong in thinking the financial markets would properly self-regulate, with no idea that a financial disaster was about to occur. Perhaps most interesting, Greenspan contended that neither the Fed's own models nor economic experts forecasted the crisis, implying at least to some that no one could possibly have predicted it.

That premise, however, contradicts many who indeed did warn of a bubble that soon would burst, Shiller among them. And we've seen other reports of how numerous prominent individuals sounded the alarm. As noted earlier, Charles Bowsher, when he served as U.S. comptroller general more than a decade ago, spoke of the dangers of the fast-growing derivatives markets, and how a sudden failure of any of the large U.S. dealers could cause liquidity problems in the markets and pose risks to federally insured banks and the entire financial system.

Several years later Brooksley Born, chairwoman of the Commodities Futures Trading Commission, said unregulated derivatives trading "threatens our regulated markets or, indeed, our economy without any federal agency knowing about it." She planned to take regulatory action until, reports say, Greenspan and other officials convinced Congress to freeze the CFTC's regulatory authority. And as noted, Felix Rohatyn called derivatives "potential hydrogen bombs," and Warren Buffett referred to them as "financial weapons of mass destruction, carrying dangers that, while now latent, are potentially lethal."

Getting back to Shiller, he points to his membership on the economic advisory panel of the New York Federal Reserve Bank, where he himself felt the need to be restrained. "While I warned about the bubbles I believed were developing in the stock and housing markets, I did so very gently, and felt vulnerable expressing such quirky views. Deviating too far from consensus leaves one feeling potentially ostracized from the group, with the risk that one may be terminated."

## Groupthink in the Boardroom

Those of you who serve on boards of directors know well that the concept of groupthink can be all too real and have a dramatic effect on individual and group behavior. I've seen firsthand how directors, especially those new to a particular board, often are extraordinarily cautious in expressing a viewpoint that differs from the positions of board members in leadership roles or who otherwise have greater stature.

New directors sometimes are told in orientation sessions that they would be wise not to speak for the first year of their tenure; rather, they should listen and get a feel for the dynamics of the boardroom. But that advice is somewhat misguided. Certainly new directors are wise not to shoot off their mouths early on, but they are fiduciary equals at the table, and indeed have a responsibility to do their best to carry out their duty of care.

Beyond how newer directors operate is the central notion that when a consensus seems to be forming, groupthink can rear its head. Yes, there are time constraints and appropriate protocols in the boardroom. But critical issues need the benefit of healthy discussion and debate to ensure that different perspectives and positions are brought to bear.

One of the tactics a director can successfully use to ensure his or her views are truly heard is to first have offline conversations with other board members to test positions and determine whether there would be support in the boardroom. At one time deemed inappropriate, such private discussions now are accepted as a positive way to engage fellow directors and ensure the board is positioned to consider ideas that might not immediately be seen as mainstream.

Truly successful boards avoid groupthink, allowing individual directors to express their thinking and make a case for alternative actions. Importantly, major issues are discussed over the course of several meetings so that all sides of an issue can be thoughtfully considered. This contrasts with some boards we've seen with extremely tight agendas, where key decisions were made quickly, leaving some directors frustrated and too often arriving at misguided decisions, which came back to haunt and later needed to be undone.

## Management Is Not Immune

For those of you in management roles, how often do you witness people who you know have a divergent view, but who refrain from voicing their position? For example, I can recall a professional services firm manager who came out of a meeting furious with the decision reached but couldn't explain why, despite the opportunity, he didn't express his view in the group setting.

A particularly good example of groupthink occurred at a meeting with a major financial services company's CEO and his direct reports. After a brief discussion, the CEO presented his position and was ready to move on. Body language and other indicators, however, clearly suggested that at least some of the participants weren't convinced that the stated position was best for the organization, but they didn't feel sufficiently comfortable going against their boss. As an advisor, I was well positioned to bring forth an opposing viewpoint. After pushing back on the initial position, explaining the ethics surrounding the issue and probable adverse consequences of going down the identified path, a long silence followed. Ultimately, the general counsel was first to speak in favor of a new course, with others and then the CEO coming to agreement on the new direction. Rejection of groupthink resulted in more thoughtful discussion and ultimately a successful conclusion.

Certainly, in many companies we've seen compliance officers, risk officers, audit executives, and others not hesitating to say the emperor has no clothes or point out dangers that need to be addressed. These individuals are trained to go upstream as necessary to find the right management (or board) level and speak out where appropriate. But unfortunately we've seen too many instances where valid viewpoints that may well have helped shape a better business decision were simply left unspoken.

Yes, managers need to be team players and stand behind decisions once they are reached. The relevant issue here, however, is whether the right forum exists to hear divergent views, so that good ideas can come forth before a final decision is reached.

 ## OBTAINING CRITICAL INFORMATION

Every corporate director knows he or she needs relevant information to carry out oversight responsibilities effectively. But it's not easy to know exactly what that information should be, the form it should take, or where it should come from. Unfortunately, too often boards of directors don't sufficiently focus on these issues, and they get caught by surprise and pay a steep price.

For board members as well as corporate officers and staff working with boards it's worth looking at how to ensure effective communication of genuinely important information. There are different perspectives: boards worry about whether they are *receiving* proper information, and the senior executives are concerned about whether they are *sending* the right information. They are two sides of the same coin, and one cannot work without the other. We'll begin with board members' perspective.

### Through Directors' Eyes

Directors obtain the most relevant information from the CEO and senior executives in direct discussions in the boardroom and offline. Yes, they get important information from written materials presented in board books in advance of meetings, preferably with clear signs directing attention to critical issues. But unfortunately, it's not uncommon for written information to be less than adequate. Several boards I've worked with—for example, one in the utility industry, another in transportation—had been receiving board books that didn't provide needed analysis instead of just data, didn't translate technical jargon, and didn't clearly highlight related relevant issues requiring board attention.

While written information should meet directors' needs and expectations, it's the direct face-to-face discussions, questions, and challenges that provide the opportunity to evoke the requisite high-level insight from management into what's really behind the presented information and truly matters to decision making.

Every board, and indeed each director, gets a sense of the quality of information provided by management. There's seldom an issue regarding management's integrity, which is usually and appropriately taken as a given. But with that said, directors need to recognize that information provided to them might not be all that it seems, or should be. That can happen for several reasons.

Phil Lochner, a former SEC commissioner and current member of several boards, recently pointed out that even a straight-shooting CEO might not have the numbers, facts, and other information directors need to know. And a CEO may be misled by his or her staff, intentionally or otherwise. Further, Lochner notes, senior management might consist of "optimists who, in complete good faith, somehow always see the glass as half full when in fact it's cracked and leaking fast."

Seasoned directors know they can reasonably expect the company's CEO to be honest in dealings with the board, but can also expect a natural tendency to try to gain the board's support for a pending initiative or decision. As noted earlier, directors expect not only honesty but also candor—that is, communication that is direct and free from prejudice or bias. And they want management to be forthcoming—not only honest and candid, but providing a full and balanced picture.

Experienced directors have sometimes encountered situations where a senior manager hesitates to tell the whole story, leading to uncertainty and doubt. Directors and any business executive, for that matter, don't want to have to figure out every question that needs to be asked. We want people to tell us the information that they know and that we need to know. We want them to identify clearly what is fact and opinion, and the basis for their opinion. When we communicate with someone who is forthcoming with complete, honest, and unbiased information, we immediately trust not only that information, but also the individual (or institution) with respect to information coming in the future.

Let's boil all this down a bit. Directors must be confident that they're getting accurate, relevant information, and receive a full picture of the issue at hand so they can make sound judgments. Senior executives providing information to the board should be certain they are entirely forthcoming, in order to dispel any doubts the board might have about whether the executive's information is trustworthy.

Yes, in the absence of red flags, directors are entitled to rely on information provided by management—and no, directors don't need to audit what management says. But directors must recognize that regardless of how well management communicates, they cannot take internal company input as the whole story. A board must gain information from a variety of sources so it can test and supplement the information management provides and fill in any blind spots management might have.

Before we move on to supplemental information sources, there's another management/board communication issue worth mentioning. Odd as it may sound, experience has shown that in some boardroom discussions a CEO might not be sufficiently clear as to what he or she expects of the board, be it simply for the board to be informed, or the board to provide guidance or direction on the matter. By the same token, discussions can conclude without needed clarity around whether agreement is reached or specific follow-up action needed. This basic, pragmatic stuff is easily made right.

## Where to Look

Where should directors look to be sure they know what's going on in the company, the industry, and the greater socio-political-economic environment the company operates in? Lochner put forth a list:[1]

- *Securities analysts' reports.* These reports provide an outside perspective on the company and are required reading for directors. Directors will want to get their hands on reports from "analysts of all stripes, not just those sympathetic to a single point of view."
- *Media coverage.* Here, boards can set up some neutral criteria for what they want to see, for both print and electronic media.
- *Trade publications.* Periodicals covering the company's industry often contain insights not readily available elsewhere, including relating to the company's major customers and suppliers and the overall marketplace.
- *Internet coverage.* Increasingly, interesting information can be found in online stories, chat rooms, and blogs that fall outside our traditional

concepts of the media. You can't find everything and must read with a skeptical eye, but a targeted approach can be useful.

- *Investor feedback.* Listening in on presentations to shareholders and investment bankers can be valuable, especially when focusing on how management responds to questions.
- *Communication from shareholders.* Information can be gleaned from feedback obtained at scheduled meetings with shareholders and at the annual meeting, as well as comments provided on proxy cards or other inputs.

Lochner also mentions such sources as nonprofits, industry groups, and think tanks; director education programs; guest speakers; specialized books and newsletters; information in SEC filings and other government reports in the public domain; conventions and trade shows; and customers at retail outlets.

Of course, no director has enough time to delve deeply into all these potential sources of information. But it's worth the effort to look into at least some of them to get insights into the company and the environment in which it operates. The more management is able to provide relevant information from independent sources, the better positioned directors will be to do their job well—indeed, the more likely they will appreciate management's efforts in painting a full picture of what's going on.

### Getting Outside

Increasingly, directors get information through direct contact with a range of sources. My experience working with boards shows a clear trend of directors going out to obtain input firsthand from company managers, rank-and-file employees, customers, and others with whom the company does business. One client board began modestly with plant tours in locations where board meetings are held, enabling directors to observe operations and talk directly with company personnel. Others have longstanding programs of directors going to retail outlets where the company's products are sold to talk with salespeople and customers to gain a firsthand perspective.

Here, too, directors must use their time efficiently, and going to the field should be carefully planned to gain the most benefit from the limited time available.

### Putting It Together

Directors must have sufficient, relevant information in manageable form to be positioned to successfully oversee the company. Challenging as it is, directors need to determine what they need to know—and don't yet know—and how they're going to fill in the gaps. At the end of the day, it's the board that needs to determine what additional information must be forthcoming, and take the necessary steps to be certain that it arrives in the right form and at the right time. The ability of directors to fulfill their fiduciary responsibilities depends on getting this right.

## Management's Perspective

Now the opposite side of the coin—what information chief executives and the senior management team should be providing to help directors in their oversight activities.

As noted, the most important information provided to a board comes directly from the company's CEO, in board meetings and offline. Experienced CEOs recognize that most directors are smart, skilled, insightful individuals who can recognize messages behind the words, especially since many are former or current CEOs themselves, and know well the pressures and incentives that can cloud judgment. Effective CEOs go to great lengths to ensure communications to the board are straightforward, accurate, complete, candid, and forthcoming.

Naturally a chief executive wants board approval of his or her current performance and new strategies and initiatives, and we've seen how some have fallen into a trap of putting a positive spin on their plans when the unvarnished truth is needed. Most directors see through these covert efforts, and they do little more than increase skepticism and distrust. If you've seen such sugar-coating efforts, you know they only emphasize the importance of being forthright from the start.

### Key Supporting Staff

Other senior executives work with the board and its committees as well, and have come to know what directors want in terms of accurate and relevant information: details on financial reporting, internal control, and related information for the audit committee; salary, pension, healthcare benefit data, performance assessments, and succession information for the compensation committee; risk and risk-management information for the audit or risk committee or full board; strategy information for the board; and so on. But beyond what the board *wants*, senior corporate staff must consider what the board *needs*.

That thinking should begin with the board book, which contains materials for upcoming board and committee meetings. Directors need information that provides a full picture of past and expected future performance, issues, risks, and whatever else will help the board stay informed and make wise judgments. Of critical importance, and where significant improvement often is needed, is providing a clear road map to the truly relevant issues to be considered at an upcoming meeting and beyond. Board books typically contain a great deal of data and analysis, and it's essential that attention be directed to what really matters. Corporate staff are in the best position to know and facilitate directors' focus on those issues.

### Compliance Officer

A company's chief compliance officer is usually expected to brief the CEO and the board. But too often the compliance chief is put in an untenable position—not because of the individual's shortcomings, but because of the way the compliance process is structured and responsibilities assigned.

Take the case of a compliance officer—be it the general counsel or other in-house lawyer or professional—who has responsibility for ensuring the company is in overall compliance with all relevant laws and regulations. This individual will typically sharpen the code of conduct and related policies, monitor instances of potential or actual noncompliance, and report periodically to a management committee, the CEO, and the audit committee or full board. Reports typically include information coming through whistleblower channels, new and pending legal cases, corrective actions taken, and the like.

While this information is useful to the board, a major problem, obvious to those of you who have operated in this environment, is the mistaken belief that a compliance officer can be responsible for *ensuring compliance* in an organization. The truth is that he or she can't. The compliance officer is responsible for *creating an effective compliance process*, which includes putting responsibility where it needs to be: in the line and staff leadership, cascading through the managerial structure to encompass the entirety of the organization. As such, the compliance officer enables and monitors the process, ensuring that reporting mechanisms are sending relevant information upstream through the management structure, and seeing that managers receive information on new laws and regulations and how they affect managers' scope of activity.

In this context, the CEO and board need to know the following: how the compliance process is working, how information is flowing through the managerial structure, and where bottlenecks or breakdowns might be occurring. The chief compliance office can play a pivotal role by compiling relevant information for the board, including the extent to which the line and staff management team has accepted and is carrying out its compliance responsibilities.

## Risk Officer

The approach outlined immediately above holds for a chief risk officer as well. As noted earlier, the risk officer should not be held accountable for identifying, analyzing, managing, and reporting risks. Rather, the chief risk officer is positioned to ensure *an effective and efficient risk-management process exists* in the organization. Because of the essential nature of building risk management into the fabric of a company, reporting to the board is best provided through the management structure, up to the CEO and then to the board. A chief risk officer should be positioned to monitor line and staff reporting, and where critical risks are not brought forth, that officer can and should be a fallback for reporting what the board needs to know.

As with compliance officers, the board should recognize where responsibilities lie and the sources of information it receives. But the board also needs to know how the *process* is working, and what might be necessary to get it to where it needs to be.

## Additional Relevant Information

As noted, boards not only need information about what happens within the company, they need context about their whole industry—competitors, consumers, suppliers, and the like—as well as political, social, and economic factors. This is where management, supported by a governance officer or the corporate secretary, can be of tremendous service in giving directors what they need. They can provide, for example:

- A useful cross-section of securities analyst reports, both those supportive of the company and those more critical.
- Targeted sections of trade publications providing important insights into the industry and marketplace.
- Links to those Internet sites most relevant to the company, its products, reputation, and the like.
- Communications from shareholders providing insight into matters foremost on the minds of the company's owners.

Senior executives typically know a wide range of information sources useful to directors. Senior management has a good opportunity to provide relevant information to the board, and is well served by doing so. Of course it's not quantity that matters, but rather quality with related clear direction to the critical issues.

## Letting the Board Look for Itself

More and more directors are getting outside the boardroom to gain greater firsthand knowledge about the company, and management can be a catalyst and facilitator to make the time spent most worthwhile.

There are, however, some important dos and don'ts. Avoid sending directors to parts of the company preselected to provide positive input. This is a recipe for disaster; directors will recognize it for what it is and question their trust in management.

More effective is offering a cross-section of locations within and outside the company where each director can decide for himself or herself what is most appealing for obtaining information. To the extent practicable, and while ensuring ready access, visits should be unstructured, allowing free and open and unmonitored communication with company personnel. When visiting retail outlets for the company's and competitors' products, directors often find it most effective to go incognito, getting straight talk from salespeople and customers. Whether visiting company facilities, customers, or suppliers, the goal is to enable the director to arrive with as little fanfare as possible, with ready access to individuals who will be forthcoming in answering questions and discussing issues.

The board wants desperately to be able to truly trust management, including executives' character and what they say and do. This chapter began with urging board members not to follow the herd, and now, in the context of a board's trust of a CEO and at risk of using a homonym, we know what happened to Mark Hurd at Hewlett-Packard. Suffice it to say that management is absolutely best served when it operates in a manner where such trust continues to be well deserved.

 **A LEAKY HP BOARD**

Earlier we focused on what the HP board did when it learned about CEO Mark Hurd's relationship with a consultant, and on lessons to be learned from those events. Not to be forgotten is a matter occurring a few years back, also at the HP board, providing different but equally important lessons. Here's what came out of news reports at the time.

## The Leak

To refresh memories, evidence existed that confidential information was being leaked to the media by one or more HP board members. We can point to the leak itself as the first mistake, an egregious one that led directly to other major mistakes.

We know that directors owe a duty of loyalty to the company, which in brief means they must put the interests of the company and its shareholders above their own. Directors must act in good faith. Crucial to these responsibilities is maintaining in strict confidence any information about the company obtained in one's capacity as director. Doing otherwise undermines the ability of the board to deal forthrightly with company issues and can destroy the trust among directors necessary for effective board performance. At the risk of making light of a serious matter, boards need to operate like the ads for Las Vegas: What happens in Vegas stays in Vegas!

Leaking company information could subject a company to potential liability. One issue is whether the company, and perhaps the director, can be charged with circumventing the Securities and Exchange Commission's Regulation FD, which prohibits selective disclosure of material nonpublic information. There is an exception regarding the supply of information to the media, but leaking information to one reporter is different from a press release. Certainly, common practice is to disclose information more formally, such as with a press release or on Form 8-K. In any event, a director leaking information is subject to liability if it's determined that he or she engaged in intentional misconduct or violated the law.

## The Investigation

Recognizing that a leak occurred—which, by the way, seems to be a continuation of earlier leaks that happened during the tenure of the prior Chairwoman and Chief Executive Officer Carleton (Carly) Fiorina—Chairwoman Patricia Dunn initiated an investigation. She assigned this responsibility to internal personnel, and the task was turned over to the company's director of security or general counsel; it wasn't immediately clear which. Dunn said she didn't stay closely involved, in part because she would be among the investigation's targets herself. It appears, however, that she was in contact with the company's chief ethics officer/senior counsel and other internal personnel as the investigation unfolded.

You may remember that HP personnel hired an investigation firm, which in turn hired another investigation firm, which reportedly engaged in *pretexting*, generally involving subterfuge in obtaining personal information such as telephone records. The ethics and legality of pretexting are at best questionable and possibly illegal depending on state law, with the California attorney general saying he believed a "crime has been committed." Federal law also came into play, with regulators conducting their own investigations and at least one Congressional subcommittee holding hearings on the matter.

The results of the HP investigation pointed to director George Keyworth, who reportedly admitted that he indeed was the source of the leak, although he challenged the nature of information he provided to a reporter. Dunn reported the results to the board, which requested that Keyworth submit his resignation. He refused, saying he was elected by the shareholders and would remain. A colleague and ally on the board, Thomas Perkins, outraged by the request to Keyworth, decided to resign from the board. Reports conflict as to the reason, one saying Perkins demanded of Dunn that she handle the matter privately without informing the other directors, another saying he already was aware of improper investigative techniques and was protesting their use. At this point we can safely say that any concern about the chair informing the board of the results of an investigation seems misplaced at best. It's difficult to imagine why a board should not be so informed of this type of information.

## Mistake No. 2

Although we can't know all that went on at HP inside and outside of the boardroom, there's little doubt that the investigation was handled inappropriately from the start. Why a board chair would direct internal personnel to investigate members of the board of directors is beyond comprehension. Normal practice is for a board or its governance committee or audit committee—whichever is charged by charter with the responsibility for conducting such an investigation—to initiate a probe. And one of the first things the board or committee would want to do is engage an independent law firm to do the investigating—not the general counsel or the law firm with which the company normally does business, but an independent firm. And the board or committee needs to monitor the investigation and progress. With this approach, there's comfort that the investigation will be conducted objectively, within the law, and with proper oversight.

## Are the Mistakes Done Yet?

No, probably not. It seems that the wrong director resigned. One would think, after admitting to leaking any information to the media, compounded by evidence that the information was of a confidential nature, the leaking director would walk out the door. That didn't happen, as least initially. A deal later was reached where Keyworth did in fact resign his board seat.

If that's the third mistake, then mistake 3(a) is that the other director, Perkins, did resign. Normally when a crisis or other major problem hits a company, the directors come together and work toward solving the problem and getting things back on track. There are circumstances where it makes sense for a director to resign, but this doesn't seem to be one of them.

## Could It Get Any Worse?

Unfortunately for HP, it did. Although HP filed the appropriate form with the SEC disclosing Perkins' resignation, questions surrounded whether HP provided a full and accurate explanation of the resignation.

This raises at least two problems. One is a potentially improper SEC filing. Another indicates a possible lack of proper disclosure controls and procedures. As you may remember, Sarbanes-Oxley requires controls beyond Section 404. Its Section 302 requires companies to maintain controls and procedures to help ensure information in all SEC filings is correct. One might suggest that if an improper filing did occur, such controls are suspect.

## The Aftermath

CEO Mark Hurd, of course, took over as board chair—immediately, not the following January as had been previously announced—and Dunn resigned not only her role as board chair but also as a director.

The question is, how does a board that has endured such an ordeal get its house in order? Certainly, it's difficult if not impossible for a board to be effective—providing value-added advice, counsel, and direction to and monitoring of the CEO—if mutual respect and trust among the directors is absent. One would think one of the first orders of board business would be to take stock of its membership and what changes are needed to enable it to function effectively going forward.

I've long been an advocate in most circumstances of one person wearing both the CEO and chairman hats. One of the reasons is to promote strong leadership and one point of authority, clearly understood both within and outside the company. Based on his standing with the HP board and key employees, and his excellent performance in the House subcommittee hot seat, Hurd was positioned to do just that, and notwithstanding recent events, his performance bore out his ability to do the job well.

When first speaking on these events I pointed to one caveat, saying that at the time there was little if any indication that Hurd was directly involved in the investigation or had knowledge of any illegal activity. To his credit, he apologized for what HP did, admitted that process and execution broke down, said mistakes were made and red flags overlooked, by himself among others, and emphasized that he would make sure it didn't happen again. But now there are assertions that he indeed was involved in the investigation. After his recent departure, the issue is moot.

 ## ANOTHER LEAK—WHAT WAS HE THINKING?

Or more to the point, was he thinking at all? We're talking about Rajat Gupta, operating at the highest echelons of multinational business, who recently found himself charged by the Securities and Exchange Commission with illegally passing inside information to Raj Rajaratnam—since convicted on 14 counts of fraud and conspiracy—as the Galleon Group founder was about to go on trial on charges of insider trading. Mr. Gupta, a Harvard Business School graduate and former head of McKinsey & Co., has been a board member of the likes of Goldman Sachs, Procter & Gamble, and AMR, parent of American Airlines.

What did he do? Well, of course he's innocent until proven guilty, and according to media reports, his lawyer says he has done nothing wrong. But the SEC says otherwise. It alleges Gupta gave Rajaratnam advance information about earnings at both Goldman and P&G. On top of that, the SEC maintains that Gupta called the Galleon head with the inside scoop of the Goldman board's approval of Warren Buffett's $5 billion investment in the firm. The allegations speak to multiple phone calls between the two men, enabling Galleon to reap millions in profits. What must be particularly troubling for both is that the SEC says it has records of numerous telephone conversations. One played in the courtroom early on in the Rajaratnam trial has Gupta telling Rajaratnam of details of sensitive Goldman board deliberations concerning acquisitions of such firms as Wachovia and AIG. Upon hearing the recorded phone conversation at the trial, Lloyd Blankfein, Goldman's CEO, reportedly testified that Gupta violated the firm's confidentiality policies.

Recordings are powerful evidence, and let's presume for a moment that the allegations are factual. A relevant question is, is this a black eye for the companies on whose boards Gupta sat? (By the way, the reports say he did not stand for reelection to Goldman board, and more recently resigned from the boards of P&G and AMR.) My answer, based on the information available, is "no." Certainly, if the allegations are true, a statement by SEC director of enforcement is on point: "Mr. Gupta was honored with the highest trust of leading public companies, and he betrayed that trust by disclosing their most sensitive and valuable secrets." But what could or should have been done to prevent wrongdoing at the board level?

We know well the importance of a company's board of directors keeping a close eye on what the CEO and senior management team do, and on the company's system of internal control. We recognize the importance of compliance officers, risk officers, and internal audit functions. But who keeps an eye on the board, especially when their actions are outside the inner workings of the company itself, such as is alleged to have occurred here as well as with the HP director who leaked information to the media?

There are no immediate answers, other than continuing to ensure full vetting of board candidates, knowing your fellow directors well, and maintaining effective board and internal audit processes to best identify and manage potential misbehavior. With the thousands of directors of major companies acting with extraordinary integrity and ethics and in the best interests of their companies and shareholders, I believe we don't have much to worry about. But it is worth noting that it has happened, and of course could happen again.

 **NOTE**

1. Philip Lochner, Jr., "How to Find Out What Management Isn't Telling You," *Corporate Board Member* (Third quarter, 2009).

# CHAPTER SIXTEEN

# Where the Power Lies

T'S EXTRAORDINARILY CLEAR THAT shareholders are angry. They're angry about opaque or otherwise bad financial reporting, seemingly outrageous CEO compensation, poison pills, staggered boards, and anything else that emanates from the perception that boards of directors are not doing their jobs. The underlying cause, some say, is a still too-cozy board-CEO relationship and directors who don't care about legitimate shareholder needs.

Shareholders' concerns moved from simmering to boiling over when their companies lost many billions of dollars in the financial system's near meltdown, signaling to these shareholders that the boards failed in their responsibilities to oversee what managements were doing. And many just shook their heads in dismay when the CEO of General Motors told a reporter, "I get good support from the board—we say what we're going to do, and here's the time frame, and they say 'let us know how it comes out' "!

But things have evolved, with shareholders gaining significant rights, and one might believe cool heads will prevail and a mutually beneficial understanding will emerge among shareholders, managements, boards, regulators, and others. Still, the cries for change seem to only get louder.

Make no mistake, this is about power and who wields it. Shareholders who believe boards are making decisions that cost their companies huge amounts of money, or are otherwise not seeking to maximize returns, maintain that they should have greater ability to intervene and straighten things out.

 A TUG OF WAR

The war between boards of directors and shareholders has been raging for years, heating up and cooling down based on success or failure, evolving goals and opportunities, and opponents' actions. Some might not see it as a war, instead viewing the respective roles of boards and shareholders as continuing to evolve and mature with the common purpose of enhancing share value. Probably both viewpoints are accurate, depending on one's perspective and where we are in a business cycle.

I've learned that speaking or writing about this topic is like stepping into a mine field. Knowledgeable people have strong feelings, and discussing it is like talking politics in what's supposed to be a relaxed social setting, with a high risk of igniting fireworks. Nonetheless, it's worth looking at these issues and finding out where all participants potentially can benefit.

Without getting into the long history of how power has been shared over time between shareholders, boards, and managements, suffice it to say that shareholders are the owners of a corporation, the board hires and oversees management, and management manages. Pretty simple, right? Well, it's simple as long as everything goes well. But when shareholders see what they believe to be bad things happening to their companies, they want to see action taken. Which brings us to the question of just how much a company's owners can and should be able to direct or influence what happens—including the ability to grab directors by the lapels and throw them out.

 SHAREHOLDER ACTIVISM

We've seen shareholders taking action to make things better for decades, even long before institutional investors took up the battle. Years ago I had the opportunity to spend time with the Gilbert brothers—Lewis and John—governance pioneers who worked diligently to help gain even the most basic shareholder rights. They told stories of their attendance at the first Exxon (then Esso) shareholder meeting, which took place in a garage in New Jersey with about 30 in attendance, and how poorly they were treated. Incidentally, these guys weren't gadflies, but rather were—especially Lewis—true statesmen of shareholder rights who worked the system from both the inside and out to gain badly needed reforms.

Further advances occurred over time through the legislative process, government regulation, stock exchange rulemaking, and the judicial system. Matters such as independence of board and key committee membership, private meetings of independent members with presiding directors, expanded disclosure of management's compensation, financial experts on the audit committee, board assessments, and enhanced financial reporting and other disclosures, to name just a few, have been established. These have positioned boards to provide enhanced oversight of management and help shareholders gain better insight into board processes and decision making and make boards more accountable.

But more and more was and is demanded. Shareholders now have gained greater power with access to the proxy statement, say-on-pay votes, and elimination of broker voting, and they continue to push for such matters as majority election of directors, annual elections of all directors, and dismantling takeover defenses.

While much in the way of positive improvement has been accomplished, activism sometimes appears to take on a life of its own. I believe that some activists not only have become comfortable in the limelight, they indeed thrive in the self-appointed role of spokespersons for the shareholder community. There's little if any evidence one can point to supporting this assertion, but having spent significant amounts of time with a number of these activists, I've seen not-so-subtle signs that this situation is a reality.

With that said, not all shareholders are taking the same tack. While many seem to be short-term focused, with an eye toward financial restructuring or replacing management, some seem to be taking a longer-term view. Some activist firms, who have the ability to lock up investors' money for a period of years, are keeping a low profile while working to improve strategy and business operations.

 ## RECENT ACHIEVEMENTS

Among shareholders' recent gains are new, enhanced disclosure requirements by the SEC. They relate to such matters as compensation policies and how they drive risk, director and nominee qualifications, the board's leadership structure, and potential conflicts of compensation consultants. To some extent these new proposals are part of the reaction to failures in the boardrooms of financial institutions that dragged down much of the financial system, and for the most part they are positive and widely embraced by the investor community.

Some observers have noted that these disclosures are not onerous, and companies and their general counsels, corporate secretaries, and compliance officers are positioned to get the necessary information. That may be a fair assessment for the most part, but it may cause some angst. Let's take a closer look.

## Compensation Discussion and Analysis

The scope of the Compensation Discussion and Analysis disclosure requirement is broadened to require "information about how the company's overall compensation policies for employees create incentives that can affect the company's risk and management of that risk." The SEC says such disclosure can help investors know whether a company's incentives can tempt employees to take excessive risks. Indeed, the proposal sets forth with some precision the kinds of circumstances that would need additional disclosures. Based on recent history, this rule is reasonable and makes sense. We've seen evidence that compensation policies of the major investment banks—those who have gone bankrupt or been acquired—played a role in the massive Wall Street failures.

But distinguishing drivers of failure on a conceptual basis from specific cause and effect is challenging. Were the compensation policies of, say, Merrill Lynch and Goldman Sachs so very different that they drove different behavior? Or did the executives of one of these firms have the good sense to jump off the collateralized debt obligations bandwagon soon enough, while the other firm did not? We can question whether disclosures under the proposed rules for these two firms, with diametrically opposed outcomes, would really have been very different.

What would AIG have disclosed about its London-based financial products unit that brought the company to its knees? It's interesting to wonder what the disclosure would have been, when the company itself saw little risk in the unit's activities.

With that said, I actually do believe the new rules may very well change behavior for the better. More on that in a moment.

## Enhanced Director and Nominee Disclosure

The SEC rules require disclosure of the "particular experience, qualifications, attributes, or skills" of persons nominated to the board of directors, new and incumbent directors alike. The disclosures include a nominee's particular expertise and a description of why his or her service would benefit the company. Other required disclosures include legal proceedings involving the individual for an extended period. The stated goal is to help investors determine whether a particular director and the board as a whole are appropriate for the company.

With the increasing ability of a company's owners to nominate candidates for board seats and otherwise influence who sits at the table, it makes sense for shareholders to have information necessary to make informed judgments. Nobody can reasonably question whether having more relevant information is a good thing. But we can wonder whether it's possible for any investor to know enough about an individual, based on a few paragraphs of text, to make a meaningful judgment about whether that individual should be selected to represent the investor's best interests.

A relevant analogy might be voting for your House or Senate representative based solely on a one-page description of the individual's background and skills. In such contests for political office we have debates, speeches, news reports, editorials, and commentary (not to mention political advertisements), and even then it can be challenging to determine who is the best candidate. And that begs the question of the extent to which the director election process will become politicized.

## Compensation Consultants

Another requirement relates to compensation consultants. Disclosures are expanded to include fees paid to the consultants when they're involved in additional services beyond determining or recommending executive and director compensation, along with a description of the additional services.

This relates to what the SEC describes as the "appearance, or risk, of a conflict of interest that may call into question the objectivity of the consultants' executive pay recommendations." This has long been a matter of debate, and the disclosures may well be useful. Frankly, regardless of whether questioning compensation consultants' objectivity in a particular instance is justified—my experience is that in recent years there need be little concern—I've advised board clients that it usually is best simply to avoid any problem and use different firms as needed.

## Leadership Structure

Details now need to be given about a company's leadership structure and why it's the best one for the company, along with whether and why there's a combined or separate chairman and CEO. Also called for is information about a lead director and his or her role. Interestingly, the SEC states that this requirement isn't intended to influence a decision regarding a board's leadership structure.

I'm wondering, however, how these disclosures might evolve. With tongue in cheek, I can see a statement such as: "Because our CEO was recently promoted from within, we believe he's still too green and untested to give him the chairman's title. But in a few years we will likely bestow on him the chairman's mantle as well, so we will finally get back to the point where we have one point of authority in and leadership of our fine company." No doubt you can dream up other disclosure scenarios, and it will be interesting to see what lawyers ultimately come up with.

## Board's Role in Risk Management

Now we get to some of the good stuff. The SEC's rule, making explicit reference to the "role that risk and the adequacy of risk oversight have played in the recent market crisis," requires information about the board's role in the company's risk management process. It calls for a description of how the company "perceives the role of its board and the relationship between the board and senior management in managing the material risks facing the company." Information would address such matters as whether the board carries out these responsibilities by the board as a whole or a board committee, to whom persons who manage risk report, and whether and how the board manages risk.

I believe this is the most significant element of these disclosure requirements, as it has the potential to drive behavioral change among managements and boards in how they deal with risk. Disclosure in these areas by itself provides little if any benefit. But it *is* likely to prod company leaders to consider, perhaps more seriously than ever before, what they are really doing to identify, analyze, and manage risk effectively.

Disclosing how compensation policies affect the way risk is managed in the organization requires an assessment of just what the risks are, how they are managed, and how they are linked to the company's strategy, performance measures, and management's incentives and compensation. Disclosing what the board is doing to manage risk means directors will need to dig more deeply into what management is doing to manage risk, and how the board can feel comfortable that it is truly carrying out its oversight responsibilities.

It's said that sunshine is the best disinfectant, and that's worth remembering here. While the required disclosures by themselves won't do much, they are likely to be a catalyst for management and boards to look in the mirror and more deeply into their organizations and do what needs to be done to make positive disclosures.

Of course, there's always the possibility that boilerplate language will rule the day, and no meaningful change will happen. The skeptic in me says that may occur here, but the optimist says this opportunity will be seized and risk management will be made more effective. Time will tell.

## DODD-FRANK'S PROXY ACCESS

Adding to those achievements, a number of items on shareholders' wish lists came to fruition with the coming of Dodd-Frank, including say-on-pay; broker no-vote; independence standards for compensation committees and for engaging compensation consultants; mandates for new disclosures on the relationship between executive compensation and company performance, on the ratio of compensation paid to the CEO and median pay for all other employees, and on hedging of company equity securities; and clawback provisions that go beyond those in Sarbanes-Oxley, among other rules.

Managements and boards will be challenged in dealing with these requirements in a number of areas, such as deciding what constitutes "independence" and "company performance," and which costs should be included in median pay for "all other employees." Regulations will be forthcoming, but the extent of their specificity is to be determined.

But, as noted in Chapter 10, the biggest prize inside Dodd-Frank, straight from the top of shareholder wish lists, is none other than shareholder access to the proxy statement. For some time before Dodd-Frank, the SEC considered giving shareholders proxy access. Certainly the actions (or lack thereof) of boards during the financial system near meltdown, combined with long-simmering displeasure with directors on their handling of CEO compensation, were influential in prompting the initiative. And soon after the SEC gained clear authority, it acted.

The SEC rules, should they survive a legal challenge by the U.S. Chamber of Commerce and the Business Roundtable, will allow one shareholder or a group to nominate at least one individual, and up to 25 percent of the company's board seats. The shareholder(s) must have continuous ownership of at least three years with a minimum of 3 percent of the total voting power of company securities entitled to vote in electing directors. So, a large shareholder of a company with a board with, say, 12 seats can nominate three directors to the board.

With this, many institutional investors—public and private pension plans, for example—raised their glasses in celebration!

## Shareholders' Best Interests?

If shareholders and directors could agree on any single point it should be the goal of successful long-term corporate performance. With this in mind, let's look at what's been said about proxy access:

▪ The rule "threatens destabilizing effects on corporate governance, adverse impacts that may far outweigh any possible benefits to capital formation and investor protection," according to one former SEC commissioner. He notes that the newly elected directors may owe their allegiance to the nominating shareholder, rather than to the corporation. Unions and public pension funds, for example, "often use SEC-created investor privileges in pursuit of agendas different from profit maximization."

- A Conference Board blog includes comments from lawyers active in governance saying that the rule will politicize the role of public company directors. Directors are "transformed into a specialized form of politician coping with an annual election cycle," with activists "agitating for vastly increased shareholder ability to call special meetings between annual elections, at which directors could face removal votes if they have sufficiently displeased the governance activists." Directors who would like to "continue to add value at the end of their career using business skills honed over a lifetime, now will find themselves, like Donald Trump's reality show apprentices, subject to firing in public." The individual investor "could end up taking it on the chin—and not just because generally only the biggest institutional stockholders" are positioned to take advantage of the new rules, but "because proxy access will work mostly in the shadows. Those who control voting decisions by big institutional stockholders are consumed by a corporate governance agenda often divorced from value creation for shareholders and populist in substance and tone. Moreover, many of these institutional investors are controlled by special interests—the labor unions and the politicians who run or appoint the managers of huge public employee pension plans." They won't find it hard, for example, to signal that "we'd prefer you build plants in the United States even if more expensive than overseas" or "we'd prefer you didn't take that strike" or "we'd rather you invest in more expensive green energy."

- The Business Roundtable weighs in with "far from effective reform, this ruling will allow special-interest groups to pursue narrow agendas and exacerbate the market's short-term focus, adding more uncertainty than workable solutions at a fragile time in our country's economic recovery. . . . Rather than encouraging the creation of long-term shareholder value, this new federal right will handcuff boards and directors and stifle American companies' ability to focus on long-term growth by increasing costs and creating additional uncertainty for the more than 12,000 nonfinancial publicly traded companies. As business leaders, we strongly oppose this course of action and are extremely disappointed that the first of many critical decisions around the implementation of financial regulatory reform will take our country down such a dangerous path."

- An opinion piece published in the *Wall Street Journal* calls the 3 percent ownership rule arbitrary and against the one-share, one-vote principle. It says the real beneficiaries aren't small shareholders, but rather "large public pension funds with political agendas [that] are heavily influenced by politicians and union officials who often put their narrow political interests above the overall shareholder interest." It points, for example, to CalPERS, which "used its investment in Safeway to assist a union that was striking against Safeway [where] the CalPERS chairman at the time was executive director of the union that was doing the striking." And, it notes that dissenting SEC commissioner Kathleen Casey pointed to the rule's departure from the long-held legal assumption that directors have a fiduciary duty to maximize shareholder value, whereas the new proxy process risks "pitting some directors as adversaries of management."

## All Good Intentions

Certainly there are good intentions behind the proxy access rule. We live in a democracy, and we value the benefits of democratic institutions. Why, critics ask, should boards be self-perpetuating, where the owners of a company have little practical say in deciding who should represent them on the board?

But the arguments outlined against such proxy access have merit, and their prognoses are all too realistic. I say this not only from a conceptual standpoint, but from experience. Having spent a good deal of time in corporate boardrooms, I've seen the good, the bad, and the ugly. The good wins out where a qualified and independent nominating committee identifies great directors to form a cohesive board with a range of relevant attributes and skills, which in unison provides highly effective oversight of and direction to management.

But I've also seen the ugly: boards in both the public and private sectors where directors are elected or appointed by constituent groups, with disastrous results. Those directors' actions evidence they are beholden to the group that brought them to the table, in ways seeking to carry out the constituent's will.

The reality is that boards with directors identified by constituent groups, or that otherwise focus on specific shareholder causes, often do the worst possible jobs. I've seen instances when directors elected by specific constituent groups have failed to carry out their basic fiduciary responsibilities. Directors are required to carry out a duty of loyalty: to put the interests of the company and its shareholders above their own. They have a duty to care, to be reasonably informed in decision making, with a related focus on acting in good faith and looking to the business judgment rule. But some of these directors don't seem to recognize that they have a responsibility to act in the best interests of the corporation and shareholders as a whole, rather than to drive one or two particular shareholders' issues. Where a dissident director is in place, that individual often is, at best, a thorn in the side of the other directors and the CEO, and at worst is creating turmoil and causing disruption in the boardroom and causing the board to lose focus on critical business issues.

Large shareholders made their case for proxy access and won a significant battle. And its significance goes beyond the surface, because even in circumstances where their nominees don't gain board seats, their newly granted power will be used behind the scenes in influencing boards to take actions to satisfy individual constituent goals.

Was the former system perfect? No. But the new one is even less perfect. The SEC vote was 3–2 to adopt the new rule, and perhaps clearer or more knowledgeable heads will prevail in the future. Certainly there must be a better framework for governance going forward, and I hope that the shareholder community will recognize that what truly matters is long-term value creation for all owners of the company.

In the meanwhile, boards will want to look closely at director eligibility requirements and director qualification disclosures, in light of the potentials proxy access carries. On a broader basis, however, boards will be looking at how best to form or enhance communication channels with major investors to better understand issues of particular importance. Drivers include not only the new proxy access, but also mandated say-on-pay as well as the increasing influence of proxy advisory firms. ISS, for example, reportedly successfully influenced the Disney board to drop tax gross-up provisions from employment contracts with several executives, and GE's board to put new conditions on CEO Jeff Immelt's stock options, linking vesting to additional performance measures. And reports say ISS now is taking aim at Johnson & Johnson, calling for a "no" vote on CEO William Weldon's pay package, and is joined by the American Federation of State, County, and Municipal Employees, which says that despite Weldon's efforts to remedy the product quality problems, "He's the one who got the company into these tough times."

Boards and management will reach out to shareholders perhaps as never before, recognizing the rebalancing of the playing field, and learning what concerns exist and what demands may be forthcoming, which will enable prudent and proactive action to avoid unnecessary confrontation. Some companies' boards rely on management to spearhead the effort, especially when a seasoned corporate governance officer is in place. Margaret (Peggy) Foran has long been in such a role—perhaps the first, at Pfizer years ago, where she successfully interfaced with major shareholders. Now as Prudential's chief governance officer, Foran continues to cultivate long-term relationships with the company's owners, and other companies have established similar governance officer positions, with more considering doing so. Some CEOs have jumped in as well, meeting directly with large shareholders.

Beyond communication channels with key management personnel, some companies' boards are establishing direct channels between the board and major shareholders with the aim of ensuring clear messaging. Channels will reflect the realities of time limitations as well as Regulation FD, with confidentiality agreements in place or directors in listen-only mode, but nonetheless are likely to prove positive in providing influential shareholders with an ability to communicate their concerns. Anne Sheehan of the California State Teachers Retirement System (CalSTRS) and Patrick McGurn of Institutional Shareholders Services (ISS) have said that having an open dialogue makes proxy access or other proposals less likely.

For some companies, however, time is not on their side. The California Public Employees' Retirement System (CalPERS) recently announced it has engaged a firm to identify qualified director candidates to reshape boards of what it considers to be underperforming companies.

##  WHERE TO DRAW THE LINE

Relevant here is the oft-heard saying, "Be careful what you wish for," which has great merit in this context. Shareholder activists should be extremely careful about what they wish for and are working to achieve. When we look at why corporate America has been and continues to be successful, we see that the kinds of changes some activists seek would be counterproductive.

Experience shows that companies grow and prosper under outstanding management leadership, with a similarly outstanding board of directors providing excellent advice, counsel, and direction while also carrying out its monitoring role. True, some boards haven't done a great job, especially when they had to deal with new laws and regulations that resulted in a significant focus on their compliance and monitoring duties. But boards are positioned to deal with the challenges facing a company, and most have carried out their responsibilities effectively.

In my view, we must be cautious before allowing shareholders to make decisions without the information or ability to make informed judgments. Companies and shareholders prosper when boards do the jobs they are charged with doing, and retain the power and ability to do them well. This occurs when a board is comprised of the right people, with the right backgrounds and chemistry to work collegially together and with management to drive growth and return. They use their knowledge, leadership skills, experience, and business judgment to ensure the company has the right strategy, the right leadership, and the right processes to grow share value.

As noted, we've seen circumstances where a dissident director, or one with a one-topic agenda, is thrust onto a company's board. The result often is counterproductive if not disastrous. Those boards were sidetracked, failing for long periods to provide management with the guidance and direction needed, instead peppering management with different and sometimes even contradictory voices. We need to avoid circumstances where the process for choosing directors is hijacked by minority investors with limited and personal agendas.

Even with say-on-pay in hand, we continue to see an undercurrent from some activists who want to have power over pay decisions. An obvious question is whether these decisions are best made by a company's board and its compensation committee, which are held to duties of care and loyalty and acting in good faith. The board and compensation committee look in depth at performance and motivational factors linked to the company's strategy; they recognize the realities of a competitive marketplace and are supported by qualified independent compensation experts. Are they best suited to decide issues of pay, or is a group of shareholders looking in from the outside?

Yes, there have been bad decisions and lack of meaningful negotiations on compensation on the part of some boards, and one could argue that the system was broken. Experience, however, shows otherwise and, frankly, with the spotlight on compensation and newly required enhanced disclosures, we're seeing greater diligence in the compensation-setting process. All in all, I cringe at the thought of shareholders without the requisite knowledge making these kinds of decisions, with the potential of failure to recruit or retain the best possible leader for a company. And directors are not immune to the underlying threat of a withhold vote campaign in future elections.

I'm not the first to speak out on this topic. Many knowledgeable people are doing so, and one of the most experienced voices is the well-known corporate lawyer Martin Lipton. With respect to the nominating process, he says, "The foremost criterion is competence: Boards should consist of well-qualified men and women with appropriate business and industry experience. The second important consideration is collegiality. A balkanized board is a dysfunctional board; a company's board works best when it works as a unified whole, without camps or factions and without internal divisions."

## FINDING THE RIGHT BALANCE

A recurring assertion by shareholder activists is that board members are too close to the CEO and won't make the tough calls when necessary. But reality is that even directors who have close relationships with a CEO have not hesitated to dismiss the chief executive when performance indicates a change is needed. Indeed, in recent years, across American business, CEOs turned over at a record pace—less than five years tenure in the job. Yes, shareholder-activist directors might throw the CEO out more regularly, but is that in the best interest of the company? Or is it better for the board and CEO to have a solid relationship working toward selecting the best strategy with successful implementation, where the board provides high-level advice, counsel, and when needed, direction to make the company most successful?

Without question, some boards haven't done this job. Perhaps bad judgments really were to blame. But do we truly believe having directors with specialized agendas, especially those that may be beholden to specific shareholder interests, would have done a better job? Perhaps they would have done better at cutting CEO pay or enabling greater shareholder say on key issues. But would those actions result in attracting and retaining the skills to best run the company and make the right decisions to grow share value?

As with many issues, the right answer lies in finding an appropriate balance, a theme picked up in a memo published by the Weil, Gotshal and Manges law firm.[1] I've come to know and respect two of the memo's authors, Ira Millstein and Holly Gregory, and I am encouraged to see an emerging emphasis on finding balance in shareholder rights. Key points made in the memo are worth reading.

■ Shareholder activism has provided strong stimulus for rebalancing corporate power in the past 20 years. . . . To the extent that this shift has brought governance practices more into line with the theoretical accountability of management to the board and of the board to the shareholders, it is a shift that is in the nature of a correction. . . . We caution, however, that the forces for change should abate once an appropriate balance is achieved, or a new imbalance will result. . . . Activist shareholders—and the proxy advisors they often rely on—need to respect that the corporation, by law, is "managed by or under the direction of" the board. Indeed, this legal empowerment of the board goes hand in hand with the limited liability that shareholders enjoy. . . .

■ Gone are the days when shareholders can broadly claim that boards are inactive, inattentive, and intractable or captives of management. . . . Certainly, boards and managements have come a long way in recognizing that shareholders have a very legitimate interest in how the company is governed. The quid pro quo on the shareholder side is to act as concerned and rational owners who make decisions based on knowledge of the nuances; who avoid rigid, box-ticking methods of judging good governance; who don't abdicate to proxy advisors their responsibility to use judgment; and who avoid activism for activism's sake. . . .

■ If shareholders insist on ever-greater say in corporate decision making, at what point do we need to rethink director liability? We may well miss the opportunity to achieve lasting balance in the corporate power structure if shareholders fail to recognize and respect that there are limits on the issues that are appropriate for shareholder initiatives—limits that are in keeping with both the duty of the board to direct and manage the affairs of the corporation and the limited liability that has been granted to shareholders.

I applaud these recommendations, and believe they are right on point in terms of best enabling American business to succeed going forward.

 ## WHERE WE NEED TO EVOLVE

Certainly most systems can be improved, which is likely the case with regard to the sharing of power between shareholders, the board, and management. Just where the line should be drawn is subject to honest debate.

We've seen how gains by shareholder activists can become intoxicating—the more they succeed in gaining power and basking in the limelight, the more active they become. But we haven't seen that more power in the hands of shareholders translates into better performance and greater share value. I'm convinced that the current system of board collegiality, with the right people providing the best advice, counsel, and direction to the CEO and his or her management team, provides corporate America with the greatest likelihood of continued success. We can argue exactly how those directors are chosen. But until we find a better system than the current one, we shouldn't have change for the sake of change, or in order to empower shareholders who aren't positioned to make the right choices.

 ## NOTE

1. Ira Millstein, Holly Gregory, et al., "Rethinking Board and Shareholder Engagement in 2008," a Weil, Gotshal & Manges LLP Memorandum, January 2008.

# 17

# Structural Issues at the Board

THE QUESTION OF WHETHER to combine the roles of board chair and CEO or separate them generates robust debate, visceral feelings, and often strained relations. Many institutional investors and leading governance experts, and indeed many sitting directors, argue in favor of splitting the jobs, while many CEOs holding the chairman title insist their authority and the company itself would be badly damaged should they be forced to remove one hat. Here we look at this issue, along with others—how boards provide oversight to the chief executive and matters related to how directors are paid.

 ## COMBINED VERSUS SEPARATE CHAIRMAN AND CEO

In theory, it's difficult to argue that both hats should sit on the same head. The board of directors is designed for and charged with responsibility for overseeing the corporation, including management, so it seems incredible that a CEO running a company should be overseen by himself or herself as board chair. Certainly at board meetings a joint chairman-CEO has the ability to determine or strongly influence what the agenda will look like and the direction of discussion in the boardroom.

It's worth noting how the power structure evolved, including whether the role of the board of directors has been primarily advisory or monitoring. For decades, many company boards mainly provided advice and counsel to the CEO and senior management. This was due to a number of factors, including the rise of an imperial CEO who also served as board chairman and handpicked fellow board members, many of whom were friends and themselves former CEOs. Key executives in the C-suite also had board seats as well. As such, considerable power was consolidated in the hands of the chief executive.

But that model began to evolve, and with Enron, WorldCom, and other governance failures, along with the Sarbanes-Oxley Act and investor activism and related events, the pendulum shifted. Board composition changed, monitoring management became a greater priority, and impetus for separating the chairman and CEO roles grew.

There's been a clear trend toward separation over the past decade. About 10 years ago the number of S&P companies with a separate chair and CEO stood at 21 percent, moving five years later to 29 percent, and today it's at the 40 percent level. But among the largest U.S. companies, the combined role continues to be the norm, with one survey reporting that only 9 percent of the top 100 market cap companies have a nonexecutive chairman.[1]

## Two Hats on One Head

A compelling question is whether the pendulum might be swinging too far in favor of splitting the roles, ignoring an important practical side of corporate life. Reality is that the vast majority of large public companies continue to be run by a chairman-CEO, generally with positive results. Putting authority in the hands of one individual lets an organization be more nimble and move quickly and decisively, and tells everyone inside and outside the company that there's no issue of split authority or responsibility. Many believe that when a decision is to be made, one individual at the top should be in charge, someone who can drive development of the right strategy, convince the board and senior managers of its merits, and be positioned to drive its effective implementation. Externally, one voice speaks a unified message for the enterprise.

Along with boards' sharpened attention to keeping management on the straight and narrow, a number of important changes occurred in the boardroom providing a counterbalance to the power of a combined chairman-CEO.

- Board composition has been realigned. A preponderance of directors now is independent, and key committees—audit, nominating and governance, and compensation—are comprised entirely of independent directors.
- A lead director, or in some cases a presiding director, carries out a number of board leadership responsibilities and serves as a counterbalance to a powerful chairman-CEO. This lead director has authority to set board agendas and information requirements, has a role in determining how board meetings are run, and becomes a critical focal point enabling independent directors to determine what action needs to be taken that may be counter to the wishes of the chairman-CEO.
- Independent directors hold private meetings regularly, without the CEO or other management present.
- There are new required disclosures of the company's leadership structure, including whether the company splits the roles of CEO and chairman, and why or why not.
- At the management level (with board oversight) codes of conduct and whistleblower channels are in place, and management and the external auditor report on the effectiveness of a company's internal control over financial reporting.

With these changes, the argument goes, there's no need for a nonexecutive chairman, since companies can have the best of both worlds: a strong CEO with centralized authority, along with close monitoring by an independent board of directors with its own leadership.

## Two Hats on Two Heads

Still, the pressure for separation has been increasing. It gained steam back in 2002, when an influential report by the Conference Board Blue Ribbon Commission stressed the importance of getting the CEO-board relationship right, and urged companies to carefully consider separating the offices of the chairman and the CEO. It also recognized two other alternatives, saying:

1. The roles of chairman and CEO should be performed by two separate individuals, and if the chairman is not independent according to exchange definitions, then a lead independent director should be appointed.
2. Where boards do not separate the positions, or where they are in transition to such a separation, a presiding director position should be established.[2]

Since then, many have accepted the logic that no one should ever report to one's self, especially a person running a company invested with other people's money.

It's noted that along with the trend toward separation in the United States, in a number of other countries separate chairs and CEOs is the norm. Washington has taken notice, too, with legislation put forth from time to time to require separation. Pressure also comes from a number of other sources, including some institutional investors who want to see more of a check and balance on a CEO, with a view that separation helps avoid more fraudulent financial reporting and related debacles, so-called outlandish compensation packages, and the ability of a CEO to push through a strategy or transformational transaction with possibly disastrous results.

Indeed, too much power in one set of hands carries its dangers, and certainly a powerful chairman-CEO with a flawed idea, unchecked by an independent board, is a recipe for disaster. Companies looking to improve their corporate governance rating score or lower their D&O insurance premiums also tout the benefits of the two hats not being on the same head.

Among the most outspoken advocates of separation is Ira Millstein, the experienced and highly regarded governance expert. At a roundtable recently led by Charles Elson, another leading governance expert, Millstein recited the theoretical arguments for separating the roles and spoke to his experiences as well: "I've lived in boardrooms over the past 25 years . . . and know that one thing is certain: He who sits at the head of the table runs the board meeting. If the CEO sitting at the head of the table also happens to be the chairman who is running the board meeting, the meeting will be very different than a board meeting being run by an independent chair." Millstein believes, however, there should not be mandated separation, and certainly those wearing both hats should not be stripped of one of them.

Some former chairman-CEOs of major companies also speak in favor of separation, putting forth a number of additional reasons.

- CEOs are devoting increasing amounts of their time to running the board, including eliciting directors' opinions and striving for consensus on issues. That shortchanges time allowed for running the business. One CEO reported that his company's president took over the CEO responsibilities, making clear that board chair was a full-time job.
- With an effective independent chairperson, there's an additional channel of information other directors would not have had, enabling better insight into critical issues.

- The independent chair is positioned to be a more effective sounding board to the CEO.
- The chair also can serve as an effective interface with major shareholders.

A recent study, *Bridging Board Gaps*, addresses a number of current issues surrounding board performance, including whether it's best to separate the chair and CEO roles. It concludes that the "default" option should be an independent chair, although it identifies circumstances where a combined role may be appropriate. For those interested in the rationale and discussion behind that and other recommendations, the study is definitely worth the read.[3]

## Watch Out for Pitfalls

While separating the roles offers significant benefits, there are associated dangers, some of which were articulated at the aforementioned roundtable. With an independent chair, other directors may have a tendency to sit back while the chair does the heavy lifting. One former chairman-CEO of a large company, who also served as nonexecutive chair, warns of "disenfranchising the other board members and not getting the active contribution you want from each and every director." Another says directors can become a little lazy and deferential to the chair, and less diligent. And problems may surface with two strong individuals at the top, where the CEO's authority could be undermined. The problem can be compounded when the nonexecutive chair aspires, privately or otherwise, to take over as CEO.

Another problem with separation sometimes rears its ugly head: Managers dissatisfied with their roles or how the CEO deals with certain issues might go to the nonexecutive chair describing what may be only perceived problems. As such, there can be an undercurrent of discomfort and a channel that may serve to undermine the CEO's authority.

Interestingly, virtually all of the roundtable participants stress that separation of the CEO and chairman roles should not be made mandatory. The reasons vary; some note that circumstances and personnel should drive the decision, while others point to a Senate bill with concern that federal law would take the place of state law, where any governance mandates should rest.

## The "Right" Answer

There's no right answer for all companies, but there are powerful arguments supporting the idea of an independent chair. I've long advocated the notion of one point of authority in the organization, in the form of a combined chairman-CEO. I've noted circumstances where separation makes great sense, such as with a company executive newly promoted to CEO, where some track record in the new role is useful before bestowing the chairman mantle as well. The case for not adding the chairperson title makes even more sense when a promoted individual lacks prior experience as CEO or director of a comparable company. In such cases the new CEO may have enough to learn in that job without the added responsibility of the chairmanship, and the board could use an opportunity to see how the new CEO performs. Then, over time, if it is warranted, the board might decide to put both hats on the same head.

Another circumstance is when a chairman-CEO wishes to take a step back from the day-to-day grind, and asks to be responsible only for the chair's responsibilities. Another is a turnaround situation, where often there's good reason to separate the roles. No doubt other circumstances exist as well.

As noted, we've seen great corporate success with a combined chairman-CEO model, and I've long maintained that it's important in the United States, where that model is pervasive, for both the inside and outside worlds to see the one individual as being in charge. Whether we've liked it or not, in American business there has been one image of the chairman-CEO and another of a person who has the CEO title alone. Right or wrong, the authority and, yes, the power to get things done—as viewed from within the organization and outside—have been different.

Well, my viewpoint is evolving, for a few reasons. One is that with so many U.S. companies having split the roles already, there is no longer such a stigma of a CEO not also having the chairman title. And my recent experience working with boards without a combined chairman-CEO shows that the separation indeed can work well. In one of those companies there's a long history of separation, where the CEO clearly runs the company while the chair runs the board. There's little overlap, egos are in check, and the dynamics and results are excellent. In another company, with continued strong performance, circumstances required the CEO to relinquish the chairman's title. He and the board are still defining the evolving relationships, but they are on the right track and it appears the issues can be dealt with effectively going forward.

My view also is changing as a result of having watched major financial institutions fail or be brought to near meltdown in the financial system crisis. It's evident that many companies need stronger, more capable boards of directors to carry out all their responsibilities (monitoring, advisory, and directive) effectively, and having an independent chair may well be part of the solution. I wouldn't mandate one model, but certainly the arguments in favor of the two hats being worn by two different heads have become more compelling.

Where the jobs are split, having the right people in the right roles becomes critical. Each must know his or her responsibilities, powers, and limits. Each needs to understand and trust the other. And both need to have the skills and abilities to function in their respective roles. That is, the chairman must understand that the role is not to run the company, but to run the board.

Despite pressures from a number of sources, so far lawmakers, regulators, and rule-makers have not required separation of the chairman and CEO in corporate America. Presumably, those bodies will continue to let the marketplace decide what is best, such that these decisions will continue to be made by boards of directors on a case-by-case basis, recognizing what is best for the company and shareholders they serve.

## EMPOWERING CEOS IN A SHIFTING LANDSCAPE

There's long been a tug of war between boards of directors and activist shareholders about how boards should be comprised to best carry out their responsibilities. Central to these issues is the relationship with the chief executive officer—specifically, how to provide the kind of oversight that enables the CEO to successfully run the business and achieve corporate goals.

There's little doubt that expectations of and pressures on chief executives continue to evolve, and there are real questions as to whether any CEO can satisfy all constituents' demands.

### Revolt in the Boardroom

A few years ago, the *New York Times* published a commentary on a new book by *Wall Street Journal* assistant managing editor Alan Murray that shares this section's title, *Revolt in the Boardroom*. The *Times* article highlights some of Murray's key points:

- The media may portray CEOs as the center of the corporate universe, but they are not. "In fact," Murray says, "the CEO has been greatly diminished and now shares power with an array of others—boards of directors, regulators, pension fund managers, hedge fund managers, accountants, lawyers, nongovernmental organizations—all of whom are eager to have their say in the corporation's affairs."

- Murray notes there has been a "remarkable string" of CEO departures, including a number of high-profile executives who have fallen. In each case, the departure was a sign that the board was no longer willing to turn a blind eye to the chief's failings, whether fiscal, managerial, or personal. Murray cites statistics showing that those CEO departures are part of a pervasive trend, with CEO turnover up 126 percent in the five years ended in 2005.

- Investors have become outraged by both "the disappearance of their own stock market wealth and the almost-daily reports of perfidy by executives," Murray says. Corporate directors have revolted, prompted by a realization that they could be held personally responsible for misdeeds of the CEO. Directors have been forced to wake up and recognize that board membership isn't "just a cushy honor," but rather "a heavy responsibility."

- Successful executives now act less like autocrats and more like the populist politicians answering to diverse constituencies. What Murray calls a "new power elite" has emerged, including the likes of union executives, nongovernmental organizations, hedge fund managers, and others.

- Outrage over excessive pay to CEOs, particularly those who fail, is surging among the middle class. "The attack on CEOs could be the leading edge of a much bigger and broader middle-class revolt that is only now rearing its head," says Murray.

- There's a view that the boards of public companies can be unwieldy and ineffective, which follows the assertion of former AIG CEO Maurice Greenberg that boards can't run companies. This notion is supported by the tale of Hewlett-Packard's board overthrowing Carleton Fiorina, installing nonexecutive chair Patricia Dunn, and ultimately giving CEO Mark Hurd the additional title of chairman, "ending H.P.'s experiment with a new governance structure."

Looking to the future, Murray says, "Optimists see a more responsive, more democratic, more socially responsible institution emerging from the upheaval. Pessimists fear that the very same ills that plague modern-day politics—polarization, divisiveness, and stalemate—may come to hobble corporations."

## What Does It All Mean?

Despite references to Greenberg and Hurd and what's since transpired at AIG and HP, Murray's observations are worth attention. Certainly there's been a major power shift in American corporations. The once all-powerful, imperial CEO has been transformed. The individual in that position is still the most senior officer running the company, but now he or she truly reports to the board of directors. Of course, there are as many different types of CEOs as there are companies, but certainly the power shift is real.

Also true is the fact that many company CEOs are besieged from multiple angles: boards, institutional investors, regulators, lawyers, and others. Among the most significant questions, in my view, is this: When does the chief executive find the time to run the business?

Having worked with a significant number of CEOs, I've seen many different approaches being taken. Some CEOs have turned running the day-to-day business operations over to a chief operating officer or other senior executive, with the CEO focusing on fine-tuning strategy, considering major deals, dealing with the board, and courting key new customers and relationships. Others play the role of Mr. Inside or Mr. Outside, depending on where the executive sees his or her strengths and where those interests intersect with the needs of the enterprise.

But many chief executives are spread thin, still trying to run the company while also splitting time among key parties: the board, its key committees, individual directors, institutional investors, accountants, nongovernmental organizations, and others, while also addressing legal compliance, regulatory filings (though hopefully not investigations), and the myriad other issues demanding the CEO's personal time and attention.

There's a proper balance between management, the board of directors, and shareholders. It is difficult, but attainable. And while the rise of the institutional investor may have corrected what some saw as management-heavy governance structures, we also must be careful of swinging the pendulum too far in the other direction, where CEOs are demonized and stakeholders wield the power.

## Not Killing the Golden Goose

So where do we go from here? The commentary on Murray's book calls the author "maddeningly reluctant to offer his opinion on what changes corporations ought to make in order to endure as viable institutions." Well, I offer some thoughts as to where companies can focus attention—admittedly simple in concept though challenging in implementation.

- *Adding value.* If they haven't already done so, boards of directors need to move away from their sometimes excessive focus on compliance and monitoring, and pay sufficient attention to providing value-added advice, counsel, and direction to the CEO on strategic and other critical business issues. In addition to hiring the right person to run the company in the first place, this is a primary board obligation and one that brings the most value-add to the company.

- *Setting pay.* The board and management need to agree on a compensation paradigm, one that reflects meaningful pay-for-performance metrics. This program should be tied to long-term shareholder interests of growth and return and should be designed to motivate the CEO and senior management to best achieve those objectives. Directors must ultimately ignore those shareholders who send mixed messages, complaining both when CEO compensation tied to stock price rises with broad market upswings and when CEO compensation moves with internally developed benchmarks that might not follow the company's short-term stock price. Boards need to take the time to get compensation metrics right.

- *Communicating.* Boards and managements should listen carefully to what major shareholders have to say, providing a channel for meaningful communication. But shareholders and others need to let management, with board oversight, make the business decisions that are deemed to be in the best interests of the company. They are the ones who know the business and its industry, risks, markets, products, and competitors, and are best positioned to make truly informed business decisions.

Certainly making this happen is not a simple matter, as it involves bringing together many different interests, including institutional investors, regulators, and others. But it's well worth the effort. And all parties must avoid being so internally focused on their own personal objectives and vendettas that they kill the proverbial goose that laid the golden egg.

 **DIRECTOR COMPENSATION**

While director pay is not as pressing an issue, it nonetheless is a board responsibility and, for a number of reasons, boards need to get this right. We begin here with how one successful company tried a new pay paradigm that raised more than a few eyebrows.

A few years ago Coca-Cola announced a new method for paying board members. Under the program, directors would receive $175,000 in stock each year, compared with their prior pay of $125,000 in cash and stock plus payment for committee service. The catch in the new plan was that to receive the stock award, the company's reported earnings per share had to increase at an annual 8 percent rate, compounded, for three years. At the end of that period, if per share earnings were about 26 percent higher, directors would get the cash plus amounts representing reinvestment of dividends. But if earnings were any less, the directors would get nothing. Not for meeting attendance, committee service, being a committee chair— not even a retainer. Nada. Zilch.

## The Intent

"As a shareholder, I love it. I've never seen a payment plan that more directly aligns director interests with shareholder interests." That is no less than Warren Buffett talking, not me. Mr. Buffett, by the way, had announced he was stepping down from the Coke board, but Berkshire Hathaway reportedly continued to be the company's largest shareholder.

Yes, at first glance this program makes great sense. Directors have a direct stake in the company's performance. If the company makes the grade, directors are rewarded; if it doesn't, they're not. Presumably there would be correlation between earnings per share and stock price, so the fortunes of directors would go in the same direction as those of shareholders.

## Unintended Consequences

At second glance, however, this approach carries problems. Wouldn't there be incentive, some observers asked, for the audit committee and board to do what some nefarious managements have done—stretch accounting to the breaking point to make the numbers?

Certainly with regard to an audit committee, such action would be even more subtle than instances where management fudges the numbers. The audit committee wouldn't actually be formulating the bad reports, just going with the flow. It might not even be sure bad stuff was occurring, but it would simply avoid pushing, probing, or challenging quite enough. Senior managers, who serve at the pleasure of the board, certainly would be cognizant of the threshold for director payout and might want to do their part to help out the directors.

That said, in my view this scenario is unlikely to play out at a company such as Coca-Cola, or at the majority of American public companies. I believe most directors and managements have levels of integrity and ethical values high enough that this simply would not happen. A news article reporting the new pay plan quoted the chairman of Coke's corporate governance committee as saying just that: "I'm not worried about the board all of a sudden becoming corrupt to get a $175,000 payout. It's ridiculous."

But let's presume for a moment that this pay method became the accepted model that all public companies followed. Are we to presume that no audit committee member of any company would be influenced to accept financial statements that enabled three years of pay? And let's not forget, each year starts a new three-year cycle. Interestingly, the Coke governance committee chair noted that a signing bonus might be given to a new director whose financial condition wouldn't allow him or her to work without pay. Doesn't that indicate that there are some directors, even of large companies, where monetary reward is a motivator for board service?

And with regard to the broad issue of corporate integrity and ethics, the news of stock option grant backdating and timing surfaced about the time of Coke's announcement, and that gave observers more reason to pause.

## The Critics Speak

After the announcement the media uncovered a number of critics of the director pay plan. Points made against the plan include (and I'm paraphrasing):

■ We've already seen many problems with managements manipulating earnings to receive incentive payments. If the audit committee is also focused on achieving earnings targets, then the potential exists for them to be less assiduous at detecting potential problems in financial reporting.
■ Faced with a potential merger that would depress earnings in the short term, directors might nix the deal even if the merger would have long-term benefits.
■ Directors are there partly to be advisors to management, not to act like management. It's hard to be objective if directors are continuously rewarded for blessing management's recommendations—directors are then put in the same shoes as management. They need to be objective, act as a sounding board, be a check for overly aggressive or overly conservative management, and operate above the fray.

## The Reality

The points outlined, both the pros and the cons of this type of pay program, have validity. And many would agree that eliminating things like meeting fees makes sense. Directors have an obligation to attend board meetings, and doing so should be presumed and encompassed in any pay program. Indeed, many companies have dropped meeting fees, and in time we may see such fees going the route of director pensions and other perks.

Movement from stock options to restricted stock, in my mind, also is a positive, letting directors receive the benefit of good stock price performance but also feel some real financial pain with bad performance. But getting back to Coke's pay program, doesn't it look a whole lot like an indexed stock option based on reported earnings per share? That would bring us back to sharing in the upside of performance, but not the down. True, an opportunity cost would be incurred, but the psychology isn't quite the same.

How best to achieve meaningful pay for performance is challenging, as compensation committees know well. We know that basing CEO pay on stock price has resulted in rewarding executives for broad-based market movements, whereas basing pay on internal measures has resulted in cries of executives winning while shareholders lose—and similar traps lie in wait when dealing with director pay.

## The Bottom Line on Director Pay

All in all, I'm not in favor of director pay based entirely on reported earnings. I'm not particularly worried about what would transpire in the boardrooms of most companies, as I believe the vast majority of the directors wouldn't sell their souls for monetary reward. But I am concerned about what might happen somewhere, sometime.

We know fraudulent financial reporting has occurred in the past, and I've no doubt it will happen again in the future. One of the most important internal controls in preventing bad reporting—resulting, for example, from management overriding elements of a company's internal control system—rests with the board and its audit committee. I believe directors should be as objective as reasonably possible.

So let's pay audit committee members, and indeed all board members, for doing an outstanding job. I continue to believe that in most companies directors are underpaid, based on what they earn in their other business lives, the responsibilities they take on, and the value they bring. Directors should be compensated for the significant effort and attention they expend carrying out their fiduciary responsibilities—and yes, if desired, base an element of compensation on how the company performs. But let's do it the right way, and with the right incentives for doing the job well.

I'm certainly not the only one who believes directors are underpaid. One director, William Leidesdorf, focuses in particular on the risk issue:

> You're never paid enough as a director, mainly because it's not the work, it's the implied risk. And with the federal government getting into it, that risk is taking on a different dimension. It's one thing to take on risk where you've exercised your business judgment correctly and you've gone about everything in what you think is the right way, based on Delaware law and your ethics. But you can do all of the above and if the federal government takes over, you could be at risk because what was okay yesterday changes and you become a political target. And nobody wins. All you have to do is be accused and you're destroyed. That is a grave, grave danger. So as the federal government gets more into this instead of leaving it to the SEC and to states like Delaware, which have been very good at it, I'm not sure pay is going to rise sufficiently. Clearly we're underpaid.[4]

There are some that aren't so sure. The well-known Nell Minow, editor of the Corporate Library, has said that "a board is underpaid for what it should do, and overpaid for what it does do." That's typical of her commendable wit, though I believe it oversimplifies and overstates the reality. Phil Lochner provides a more balanced assessment, noting that directors whose companies "are undergoing hostile takeovers, or enduring an assault from regulators, or trying to recover from some public relations nightmare, are doubtlessly underpaid for their long and frequent conference calls and meetings, not to mention their day-long depositions, sleepless nights and incipient ulcers." He adds that board members with leadership roles or whose efforts translate to superior performance also "may well be underpaid in proportion to their work and commitment" outside the boardroom. He adds, however, that directors who fail to read materials, or who "scan their BlackBerrys while sitting at the board table, who skip out of board meetings while they are still in progress to catch earlier flights, or who remain mute in board and committee meetings are a burden on the companies where they ostensibly serve as fiduciaries." Well said, though my experience is that those latter behaviors have become the exception rather than the rule.

And when we look at the increasing expectations of directors, shareholder demands, legal and regulatory mandates, and personal liability and reputational risk—as well as the backgrounds of board members, limitations on number of seats a director may hold, and the value they bring—it's difficult to reasonably conclude that directors as a group are overpaid. I believe it's just the opposite.

By the way, back to the Coca-Cola situation: the pay plan was since changed to no longer tie director compensation to increases in reported earnings, instead paying directors the same $175,000 amount but in cash and deferred share units based on stock price. A change for the better.

 **NOTES**

1. The Korn/Ferry Market Cap 100, November 1, 2010 and 2010 Spencer Stuart Board Index.
2. The Commission members were an all-star cast: Peter G. Peterson, chairman of the Blackstone Group, former secretary of commerce and chairman of the Federal Reserve Bank of New York; John W. Snow, chairman and CEO of CSX Corporation and former chairman of Business Roundtable; John H. Biggs, former chairman, president and CEO of TIAA-CREF; John C. Bogle, founder and former chairman of Vanguard Group, Inc.; Charles A. Bowsher, former comptroller general; Peter M. Gilbert, chief investment officer of State Employees' Retirement System, Commonwealth of Pennsylvania; Andrew S. Grove, chairman of Intel Corporation; Ralph S. Larsen, former chairman and CEO of Johnson & Johnson, former chairman of The Business Council; Arthur Levitt Jr., former SEC chairman and former chairman of the American Business Conference; Professor Lynn Sharp Paine, John G. McLean Professor of Business Administration at Harvard Business School; former senator Warren B. Rudman of Paul, Weiss, Rifkind, Wharton & Garrison; Paul A. Volcker, former chairman of the Board of Governors, Federal Reserve System.
3. *Bridging Board Gaps*, Report of the Study Group on Corporate Boards, 2011, with another all-star cast: Charles M. Elson, Edgar S. Woolard, Jr. Chair in Corporate Governance and Director of the John L. Weinberg Center for Corporate Governance, University of Delaware; Glenn Hubbard, Dean and Russell L. Carson Professor of Finance and Economics, Columbia Business School; Frank Zarb, Senior Advisor, Hellman and Friedman; the Honorable William T. Allen, Director, New York University Center for Law and Business; Richard Beattie, Chairman, Simpson, Thacher and Bartlett LLP; Kenneth A. Bertsch, President and CEO, Society of Corporate Secretaries and Governance Professionals, Inc.; Kenneth Daly, President and CEO, National Association of Corporate Directors; Richard Daly, CEO and Director, Broadridge Financial Solutions, Inc.; Jon F. Hanson, Chairman and Founder of the Hampshire Real Estate Companies; Olivia F. Kirtley, former Chair, American Institute of Certified Public Accountants; Peter Langerman, President and CEO of Franklin

Mutual Advisers; the Honorable Arthur Levitt, Senior Advisor, Carlyle Group, and former Chairman, Securities and Exchange Commission and the American Stock Exchange; Eugene A. Ludwig, Principal, Promontory Financial Group; the Honorable Paul O'Neill, Special Advisor, Blackstone, and former Secretary of the Treasury; Reuben Mark, former CEO, Colgate-Palmolive; Damon Silvers, Policy Director and Special Counsel, AFL-CIO; the Honorable E. Norman Veasey, Chief Justice (retired), Delaware Supreme Court; Paul F. Washington, Chairman of the Board, Society of Corporate Secretaries and Governance Professionals; Ralph V. Whitworth, Founder, Principal, and Investment Committee member of Relational Investors LLC; Deborah C. Wright, CEO, Carver Bancorp Inc. and Carver Federal Savings Bank; and (ex officio) David M. Becker, former General Counsel, Securities and Exchange Commission.

4. William Leidesdorf, "What Directors Think: Are You Paid Enough?" *Corporate Board Member* (fourth quarter, 2010).

# CHAPTER EIGHTEEN

# Looking to the Future

N OW WE LOOK TO what might be coming over the governance horizon. In this concluding chapter we consider how boards may look and how they'll carry out their responsibilities in the coming years. We posit how boards can capture the Holy Grail of governance and, finally, take out our crystal ball to see what governance will look like going forward.

##  NEW MODELS FOR BOARD GOVERNANCE

To say that these are challenging times to be a corporate director is an understatement. Shareholders are clamoring for greater ability to determine what happens in the boardroom and who sits in the seats; the SEC has put forth a host of new rules requiring a broad range of expanded disclosures, with many more coming down the pike; and the pace of lawsuits continues unabated. All this occurs with memories still fresh of the financial system's near collapse, against a backdrop of an economy still emerging from the Great Recession.

As if that's not enough, directors continue to struggle in their roles as monitors ensuring that management properly deals with ever-expanding legal and regulatory compliance issues and otherwise does the right thing, while focusing on company strategy and performance in a fast-changing and highly competitive environment. The need to spend increasing amounts of time on board business is exacerbated by expanding committee service, where governance/nominating, compensation, and audit committees are subject to more and more rules and taking on lives of their own. And when a regulatory action, takeover initiative, or other life-changing corporate event creates something akin to a crisis environment, the pressure and demands on directors' time can become almost unbearable.

Directors, institutional investors, and other shareholders are asking a legitimate question: With the current governance model, can boards of directors truly meet the expectations thrust upon them? An emerging view is in the negative, concluding that today's governance model of corporate America necessarily must change. There have been calls for change at the margins, such as professionalizing directorship with education, testing, and/or means for certification.

But at least three different new board models have been put forth as offering significant improvement. For what it's worth, let's take a look.

## Greater Shareholder Authority

Some would say this supposedly new model already is emerging as a reality. With rules requiring ever-expanding corporate disclosures, shareholders have greater transparency into the workings of their companies. We're seeing, for example, additional disclosures having to be provided on how compensation policies drive risk, director and nominee qualifications, the board's leadership structure, and potential conflicts of interest. And there's little doubt that proposed rules enabling shareholders to put forth director nominees will soon become regulatory requirements.

Under this model, shareholder rights would continue to expand. Carried to the extreme, we can imagine shareholders being positioned to make absolute and final determinations on such matters as strategic initiatives, management compensation, who takes on or keeps the job of CEO, and of course, who serves on the board of directors.

While it might seem appealing conceptually for a company's owners to make whatever decisions they want about how the company is governed and how it's run, reality is their decisions will have little, if any, foundation. Quite simply, shareholders do not sit in the boardroom, and regardless of the amount of paper or electronic communications, shareholders cannot be positioned to make informed judgments on what's best for the company and its owners.

Bottom line: If one wanted to ruin our economic future, this would be an effective way of doing so.

## Two Boards—One Monitoring, Another Adding Value

This approach is based on the premise that no one board of directors can reasonably satisfy both principal governance responsibilities: (1) to monitor what management is doing to keep it and the company in compliance with laws, regulations, and board policies and directives; and (2) to provide value-added advice, counsel, and direction to help drive and sustain corporate profit, growth, and return. Hence this model calls for splitting these responsibilities in two, with a monitoring board being the monitor and a performance board doing what's necessary to promote corporate success.

This too has some surface appeal. As responsibilities and expectations of directors grow but time remains limited, doubling director resources certainly would help alleviate the burden.

But this model also is flawed. For one thing, because boards use much the same information to carry out both their monitoring and value-add responsibilities, having two boards would require more of management's time and energy to deal with the two different bodies. Could this problem be alleviated by having both boards sitting at the same table at the same time? Yes, but that would result in built-in inefficiency in use of directors' time, since some of the discussion would be of little interest to the members of one board or the other.

Another problem is that management likely would look to the value-add directors as the real board, since those directors would be the ones providing needed advice and counsel, and in any event would be making final determinations on strategic and other business issues. The monitoring board would likely be viewed simply as a nuisance, to be dealt with much like a regulator.

## A Full-Time Board

Yes, there are indeed proposals for turning boards of directors into full-time positions. The argument is simple: With boards taking on more and more responsibility, and expectations rising seemingly incessantly, no longer can a board of directors do its job well if it only meets 4, 8, or 10 times a year. With board meetings, committee meetings, and work done offline, average time commitments in recent years are estimated to have doubled, from about 125 hours to a neighborhood of 250 hours per year. And this presumes absence of any kind of major transaction or what might be considered a crisis. But, the thinking goes, even the current time commitment isn't nearly enough to do the job properly, so a full-time role is the answer. Full-time boards certainly would have sufficient time to carry out their monitoring and value-add responsibilities effectively. But alas, here too we have a significant downside.

First, the quality of directors would suffer. As difficult as it now is to recruit a sitting CEO or other senior corporate executive to a company's board, under this model it would be impossible. Finding retired executives or other qualified individuals also would be a challenge, inasmuch as accomplished people who have reached retirement age typically are not interested in full-time work.

Second, management would probably find itself spending inordinate amounts of time with a full-time board. We know from experience that a director with too much time on his or her hands can get into management's hair, crossing the line from oversight to management. Just think what would result with the entire board sitting full time!

## A Solution

This heading may be misleading, as I don't purport to have an absolute solution to this problem. Here, however, are a few thoughts to consider.

One approach is simply to keep the current model. It works reasonably well—never mind the investment banks and other financial institutions where boards failed miserably; in truth, most companies did *not* crash and burn, and any change in oversight structure would require a host of changes to federal and state governance laws and regulations. And there would be no case law providing guidelines and precedent.

But frankly, we can do better than either wholesale scrapping of the system or leaving it exactly as it now exists. One approach worth considering is to maintain the existing model but further expand the time directors devote to their board responsibilities so that they can devote the needed energy and attention. This would help meet shareholder expectations and reduce potential liability. It also would call for higher compensation, and would reduce the number of board seats a director could reasonably take on.

A related alternative is to have one director—the nonexecutive chair or lead director—devote more time to the job, perhaps even moving toward a full-time role. Care would be needed to ensure the additional time is devoted to board processes and issues, and does not cross the line into management. And other directors, such as committee chairs, might find it beneficial to devote more time to their board responsibilities.

I believe these last two ideas have much merit and little downside. There might be other models with the potential of working well, and I hope they will be put forth and considered. There's little doubt directors are spread too thin and are terribly challenged to meet increasing expectations. Something has to give. One essential action is to rethink the increasing level of responsibility and expectations being heaped upon corporate directors, and determine whether or not they really make sense.

With appropriate rules and expectations in place, if change is deemed necessary, then I suggest that the powers-that-be remember that the present system, while now strained, has worked reasonably well over many years. We don't want to overreact. And whatever changes are put forth should be carefully analyzed and tested under real business conditions to ensure they truly work.

If all goes well, there will be a balancing of reasonable expectations, and additional time devoted by directors will result in better corporate performance, with a win-win all around.

## A HEALTHY GOVERNANCE ENVIRONMENT

For any new model to work, boards of directors must be able to operate in an environment that promotes rather than inhibits effectively carrying out oversight activities. Since we're looking to the future, we can identify several areas where the environment needs to evolve in order to enable and facilitate governance success.

### Shareholder Rights

Shareholders have legitimate concerns about the extent to which they can affect director elections and otherwise have a say in governance issues. At the same time neither corporate America nor shareholders will be best served if companies must endure upheaval at the board level. If the shareholder power pendulum swings too far, we may be faced with frequent turnover of directors, large numbers of dissident directors, and boards unable to come to consensus. A result may be an adversarial board-CEO relationship, distracted senior management, and disrupted corporate performance. Directors spending time campaigning or otherwise politicking and CEOs dealing with dysfunctional boards serve no good purpose, and will be both distracting and destructive.

As noted, I've seen boards where directors were selected by constituent groups, and I can assure you it's not a pretty picture. Board meetings sank into finger pointing and shouting matches, with a result of not just failing to add value but actually destroying it. In one case, the company was on the verge of failure and forced into an unwanted merger. In another, with great effort the board reformed itself and helped draw the organization back from the brink, but with lost opportunities.

Boards should be allowed to operate in an environment where institutional and other shareholders are permitted to appropriately exercise reasonable rights, but where boards are positioned to retain continuity, ensure the right mix of knowledge and skills in the boardroom, and operate so that the tough issues are debated in a collegial manner. Directors must be able to trust one another, come to consensus in monitoring corporate performance, maintain an effective working relationship among themselves, and effectively work with and oversee management.

## Exposure to Personal Liability

There are mixed views as to whether directors are susceptible to greater liability in the current litigious and enforcement environment. On the one hand, the foundational *Caremark* decision, where Delaware Chancery Court Chancellor[1] William Allen (whom I've had the privilege to spend time with) set an appropriately high hurdle for imposing liability, continues to be upheld. This occurred, for example, in the recent *Citigroup* suit alleging directors had "breached their fiduciary duties by not properly monitoring and managing the business risks that Citigroup faced from subprime mortgages and securities and ignoring 'red flags'"—where the Chancery Court "dismissed these claims, reaffirming the 'extremely high burden' plaintiffs face in bringing a claim for personal director liability for a failure to monitor business risk and that a 'sustained or systemic failure' to exercise oversight is needed to establish the lack of good faith that is a necessary condition to liability."[2] On the other hand, some observers say the legal environment is somewhat less predictable than it was a few years ago.

It certainly appears, however, supported by speeches, decisions, and my personal discussions with current and former Delaware Chancery Court judges, that the underpinnings of how director liability is viewed are on solid ground. Former Vice Chancellor Stephen Lamb recently wrote on point, referring to Chancellor William Chandler:

In the wake of the recent financial crisis, it would have been an easy matter to lay the blame for the enormous losses suffered by major financial institutions at the feet of boards of directors. After all, those directors clearly did not adequately foresee or appreciate the risks inherent in the corporation's operations. Instead, Chancellor Chandler has taken pains—and no doubt flak from some quarters—to remind us all that the decisions taken by boards of directors to engage in lines of business, especially those that result in large losses, remain business judgments even when they turn out badly. Courts applying Delaware law will never examine those decisions with hindsight bias or second-guess them. The business judgment rule, including its fundamental presumption that directors act in good faith and after adequate investigation, remains precisely to promote the risk taking that is necessary to the success of all for-profit enterprises.[3]

In a recent interview Chancellor Chandler spoke about his decision in the famed Disney case. Making the point that directors should not be held liable for not following a so-called best practice, he adds, "It would be unfair and counterproductive to hold directors to a standard of care of liability that doesn't exist at the time they make a decision. . . . Holding a director to a standard that didn't exist at the time would be a perverse rule, and no doubt would cause any rational person to reconsider serving in such a capacity."[4]

Certainly prior forecasts of widespread director resignations have not come to pass, although finding highly qualified directors can be challenging. And directors are spending more time dotting every "i" and crossing every "t" due to litigation and enforcement risks, taking valuable boardroom time away from truly substantive matters. Yes, the business judgment rule remains, but being free from liability requires, as former Vice-Chancellor Lamb said, a fundamental presumption that directors act in good faith and after adequate investigation. And of course, just being slapped with a lawsuit can cause great angst and time commitment by directors.

Although few directors have had to take money out of their own pockets as a result of being sued, it has happened and certainly can happen again. Even with well-structured directors-and-officers insurance coverage in place, many directors in the current environment continue to feel exposed. This feeling is exacerbated with the evolving federalization of governance requirements. Of course directors must be held accountable for their actions, but a disparity exists in what various groups believe is the right balance between appropriate accountability and undue liability. When this is out of balance, the societal cost in terms of unnecessary work, ineffectiveness, and inefficiency is enormous.

We need an environment in which directors satisfying the duties of loyalty and care—and applying the business judgment rule in good faith—are empowered to function without undue fear of retribution. Whether that translates into protections provided by new laws, regulations, or other provisions to prevent frivolous lawsuits, and the associated legal costs, time, and energy, remains to be seen. But stakeholders will be better served when capable, knowledgeable, and conscientious directors can focus on the substance of their board responsibilities without undue worry about legal liability.

By the way, Chancellor Chandler recently mentioned to me that he plans to step down shortly, and has since made that announcement to the media. There are a number of potential successors, although Vice Chancellor Leo Strine is seen by a number of expert observers as the favorite. The Vice Chancellor is the longest-serving judge on the current court, with outstanding credentials and widespread respect. Having had the privilege of spending a bit of time with him and following his writings, there's no doubt in my mind that, if selected, Leo Strine will do very well in filling the large shoes of William Chandler and his predecessors.

## Expanding Requirements

With the Dodd-Frank law in place the governance landscape continues to shift. In the still relatively recent financial system near-meltdown we continue to hear echoes of "where were the boards?" The new law gives shareholders significantly greater power, requires more disclosure of board governance processes, and requires compensation committee independence and, for specified firms, formation of a board risk committee with a risk expert. We have new and expanded clawback provisions and whistleblower provisions, among others. And we can expect 500 regulations affecting how the new law's provisions are to be carried out.

Yes, we've seen serious problems that needed to be corrected. But there are desired outcomes that cannot be legislated or effected through regulation. Legislating good board performance is like legislating integrity and ethical values. Well-crafted rules can serve a purpose, but there are inherent limitations.

Within the context of prudent and manageable requirements, boards must be positioned to carry out their monitoring responsibilities and provide value-added advice, counsel, and direction to management without undue constraint. Certainly shareholders should have appropriate power as owners of the business, but only the directors have the information and are positioned to make informed judgments in carrying out their fiduciary responsibilities for the long-term benefit of shareholders.

 ## BOARDS' PERSPECTIVES ON RISK

We know that a board of directors must provide oversight and be comfortable with the company's risk appetite and risk management processes. With that said, directors' perspectives on risk and how much risk their company should take have evolved over time. Some years ago in the wake of Enron, WorldCom, Adelphia, and other debacles—along with a broad range of new laws, regulations, and rules affecting boards and their committees—directors of many companies developed a laser-like focus on compliance, accompanied by what was perhaps an unconscious and unintended but real consequence: taking a more risk-averse perspective. Seeing what happened to directors of failed companies, and concerned about personal reputation and potential legal liability, board members didn't want to suffer a similar fate. Not all boards over-reacted, and the focus on compliance later became more balanced; then in recent years financial services firms certainly took on excessive risk. But at the time, an aversion to risk on the part of boards was not uncommon, affecting strategy and willingness to accept risk in pursuing opportunity.

Today it's well recognized in boardrooms that every company must accept risk in pursuit of growth, profit, and return. But the nature and amount of risk naturally vary. What has not been given attention is whether society is best served, depending on whether one takes a microeconomic or macroeconomic perspective. From a micro view—the view of one company—taking less risk conceptually may well make sense. It may be wise not only from the perspective of the directors whose reputations and personal assets may be on the line, but also from the standpoint of the company's long-term viability. That is, taking less risk might result not in the highest possible return on investment, but a sufficient return to enable the company to stay in business and sustain reasonable performance over time.

But from a macro view—that of the economy as a whole—the answer might be different. Would it make sense for each company to play it safe, or rather to make the big bets that have a better chance of providing the larger returns and with them greater benefits to society? With investments in many companies, investors might end up better off with individual companies taking greater risks—perhaps not to bet the ranch every day, but to take greater risks with the likelihood of greater results.

I'm not an economist, and others are more qualified to speak to this issue than I. (I do have a degree in economics, but it doesn't really count, as every graduate from my school received the same economics degree regardless of major!) It would be useful to find empirical evidence regarding the micro versus macro view, in terms of individual corporate performance versus that of an economy as a whole.

Without such evidence, and without accompanying change in legal mandate and liability issues, boards of directors will and should continue to make decisions on risk appetite and risk tolerance in the best interests of their company and stockholders.

##  GRASPING THE HOLY GRAIL OF GOVERNANCE

Shareholders, boards of directors, and managements should agree on one thing—the primary goal of a corporation is to add shareholder value on a sustained basis. However measured—be it profit, economic value added, stock price relative to time or other benchmarks, or return based on any of a number of denominators—adding value is the primary goal. Yes, acting with integrity and high ethical values and going beyond compliance with applicable laws and regulations are extremely important and, indeed, support the objective of adding value. Some believe that helping to satisfy the needs of other stakeholders also is an important purpose of the corporate entity. But let's focus here on the primary corporate goal: adding shareholder value.

In working with boards of directors, senior managements, and institutional investors over many years, it's become evident that while the notion of adding shareholder value is universally accepted and embraced, how companies seek to do so varies widely.

### It's All about Alignment

Please forgive the overused word *alignment*, but that's what this Holy Grail really is all about. Put simply, it's about consistency of purpose and relationship and mutual supportiveness of strategy, implementation plan, organization, resources, performance metrics, and compensation, all risk-based. In concept the idea is straightforward. In execution, it's highly challenging. You'll see here what may be viewed as a high-level summary of some of the key elements of earlier chapters of this book:

- *Strategy.* It all begins with a well-developed strategy based on a clear vision and relevant and reliable information on markets, products, economics, current and potential competitors, present and needed capabilities, and relevant risks, among other factors. An effective strategy, tied to the company's mission and supported by the board and management, is the foundation. By the way, note that we're not saying "the right strategy," because clearly there can be any of a number of strategic approaches a company may follow that can translate into successfully adding value. But an effective strategy for attaining the company's highest level goals is crucial and the starting point for all that follows.

■ *Implementation.* How many times have we seen a company with a really great strategy fall on its face in implementation? Too often what's lacking is a truly effective implementation plan consistent with and supportive of the new strategy. There needs to be a plan that translates how the strategy will be executed, risk-based and on a reasonably high level, but with sufficient specificity to provide clear direction to the next tiers of managers in the organization. Those managers, in turn, need to be sure their operating plans are aligned with the strategic implementation plan.

■ *Organization.* Organizations must be sufficiently flexible and dynamic to shift or be revamped as needed to carry out the implementation and operating plans effectively. Unfortunately, too often we see an organization design continuing in place that was originally established to support a now outdated strategy. There might have been a few tweaks, but not the meaningful changes necessary to bring about the needed alignment.

■ *Resources.* Hard assets, intellectual capital, information systems, and human resources all need to support the strategy and its plan for implementation. Here, too, experience shows that often insufficient change occurs in a company's human and other resources to allow successful strategy implementation. In some instances we've seen a clear understanding of the need for change, but execution lagged to such an extent that events overtook the ability to succeed.

■ *Performance metrics.* Measures used by corporate managements to determine success naturally vary widely, and appropriately so. But measurement systems often are not modified sufficiently or revamped as needed to match a new strategy and implementation plan and revised organization and resource deployment. While new metrics (whether they be key performance indicators, benchmarks, or other measures) may be put forth with new initiatives—such as market share, profitability, or return associated with new products, new ventures, or entry into new markets—traditional measures for other core activities tend to remain beyond their relevance.

- *Compensation.* Measures to compensate the chief executive and other senior managers may be carried forward year to year, perhaps based on contractual or otherwise long-ago-agreed-to arrangements. As an astute reader, you know what's coming. Yes, too often the motivations and rewards are not sufficiently aligned with the new strategy and plan.

So what we often see is a great strategy, developed with good data and analysis and fully vetted with the board. In the best cases, alternative strategies considered by management are discussed, with discussion of pros and cons and explanation of why they were discarded and why the chosen strategy makes sense. But we find that even where a sound strategy and plan for its implementation do exist, the other factors outlined above simply are not properly aligned.

## Benefits from Effective Alignment

You may be thinking that this discussion of alignment makes sense, but why call it the Holy Grail? For two reasons: First, it's very difficult to achieve truly effective alignment; some companies do, many do not. Second, its achievement can bring extraordinary value to the company, its people, and shareholders. Let's look at the benefits to each group:

- *Senior management.* The CEO and other senior managers have the organization and resources positioned to enable and support successful strategy implementation. The entire C-suite has bought into the plan, with executives all pulling in the same direction. And these managers know how they will be held accountable and how they will be measured, with incentives and rewards consistent with the strategy and plan.
- *Other managers.* Managers at all levels know what senior management expects and how their objectives relate to the overall corporate goals. Managers are organized and have the resources needed to promote successful strategy implementation. With proper alignment, they have clear benchmarks and measures, and are motivated to work together to achieve them.
- *Board of directors.* The board is comfortable not only with the strategy, but also with knowing that the company is truly positioned for successful implementation. The board knows that senior management is committed to the strategic and implementation plans, and also that buy-in occurs throughout the managerial ranks. Relevant measures are in place, with managers motivated to meeting established goals. And with compensation

so aligned, the compensation committee and board have comfort that pay for performance finally is achieved. There's good balance of rewards for short- and long-term performance, risk-based, with a mix of past performance and forward-looking measures, all aligned with the agreed-upon direction. Additionally, complementing relevant and effective evaluation measures for the chief executive, the board is more knowledgeable of other senior managers' performance relative to aligned metrics, providing important information for succession plans.

■ *Shareholders.* With appropriate transparency—meaningful disclosure but without giving away sensitive information that would unnecessarily aid competitors—shareholders have good knowledge of what the company seeks to achieve and how it intends to get there. As with the board, shareholders have greater comfort that true pay for performance exists. Proper alignment of compensation with strategy provides measures and appropriate rewards consistent with desired short- and long-term performance.

## The Secret Map

No doubt we all want to see the ancient parchment map showing the way to this Holy Grail, with a big "X" marked to show its location. Like most things worth attaining, however, it's not that simple. The path to getting there is as different for one company as its business, strategy, organization, and resources are for others.

Here's a head start: As noted, it all begins with an effective strategy. But to some extent it's an iterative process, because the strategy cannot ignore the current business and its organization, processes, and people. Strategy, however, should not be wedded to the current state. To the extent that a revised strategy is not supported with what now exists, there is that much more need for change to attain the necessary alignment. Beyond that, there must be a commitment and cooperation among top management, other managers at many levels, and the board. Making it happen takes a good deal of hard work, with sound conceptual thinking, leadership, and attention to detail.

So in my mind, there's good reason to term this alignment "Holy Grail." Finding it takes significant effort and isn't easy—but once found, the benefits are outstanding.

 ## WHAT THE FUTURE HOLDS

We know there are fortune tellers, soothsayers, and those who otherwise claim to be clairvoyant. Now, at the conclusion of this book, I'd like to take a crack at looking forward to the future of governance, risk management, and compliance. So, with crystal ball in hand, here's what we will see going forward.

## Shareholders Will Gain Power

The train has left the station, and more passengers are jumping on. There's something extraordinarily democratic about the idea of those who own a company being able to effect important decisions, and gains have already been made. The ability for shareholders to cast an advisory vote on executive pay, including golden parachutes and the like, is now law. Numerous disclosures of such matters as board composition, structure, and operation also are required. Most significant is shareholders' newfound ability to vote on who sits in some of the seats at the board table.

While say-on-pay won't have major impact, directors will be taking note, fearing the possibility of being subject to a future withhold vote. Proxy access will have greater effect—not so much in putting constituent directors in board seats, although that will happen in some instances—but by shareholders or groups of shareholders meeting the 3 percent threshold working behind the scenes to push personal agendas that in most instances will benefit neither the company nor broader community of shareholders.

Gains by shareholder activists can become intoxicating. The more they succeed in gaining power and basking in the limelight, the more active they become. I do believe, however, that reality will take hold before we self-destruct. While it's counterintuitive, more power in the hands of shareholders does not translate into better performance and greater share value. For the golfers out there, you understand the concept of counterintuitiveness: swinging down to hit the ball up, hitting out to hit the ball straight, and swinging easy to hit it far. So while shareholder rights will strengthen, standards setters, regulators, the judiciary, and other influencers of the process will ultimately maintain a balance and allow boards comprised of the right individuals with the right talents to make the best decisions for the company and its shareholders.

## Companies Will Be Blindsided by Unintended Consequences

One such effect will be Dodd-Frank's whistleblower provisions. While chief compliance officers have been working diligently to strengthen compliance programs, along came the new laws' good intentions with visions of early identification of future Enrons, Bernie Madoffs, and other bad actors. But unless the SEC comes up with meaningful regulations, many employees will bypass internal communication channels to run as fast as they can directly to the SEC to report perceived wrongdoing with the anticipation of lottery-size payoffs.

So, compliance and other corporate officers will struggle to deal with new laws and regulations—including an expected 500 regulations related to Dodd-Frank alone. There will be more unintended consequences, and legislators and regulators will be slow to fix them.

## Regulators Will Continue to Step Up Enforcement

Take the FCPA, for example. In 2004 the Department of Justice's actions reportedly brought in $11 million in criminal fines, and $16.5 million in 2005. But in each of the last two years the number exceeded $1 billion, and DOJ officials say enforcement is going to get more aggressive. The Justice Department's sources are expanding, with regulators of foreign countries providing significant input, and customers of suspected wrongdoers also dropping a dime on misconduct. And the DOJ is regularly seeking multiyear prison terms for offenders.

Those companies that haven't already done so will take note of DOJ officials' insistence that companies with an effective compliance program will not only help to prevent misconduct from occurring, but also improve the company's position in an investigation—and its recent publicizing of specific cases where an existing compliance program benefited companies in prosecution. Experts will continue to try to determine whether there is indeed correlation between self-reporting or good compliance processes on the one hand and regulators' compassion in enforcement on the other.[5]

But companies will work harder to strengthen compliance programs on a broad basis to help keep regulators at bay and protect reputations and revenue streams. Unfortunately, some will not succeed.

## CEO Compensation Will Get Right-Sized

Please don't be fooled by this statement—I don't necessarily mean CEO pay will be universally reduced, because I don't see that happening. What we can expect, however, is better pay for performance. That's not as easy as it might seem, but boards and compensation committees will continue to do better at establishing the right performance measures, linked to the company's strategic plan, which together with an effective reward package will motivate management actions that truly add long-term shareholder value.

I do think the Lake Wobegon effect of ratcheting CEO compensation ever higher, until everyone looks above average, will moderate. And unlike a past rule requiring increased disclosure, where CEOs used information on competitors' compensation to score raises of their own, the new SEC rules on compensation disclosure—with a focus on options values, change in control provisions, and overall better disclosure of total compensation—will bring more rational decisions by compensation committees. But I also see boards paying what's needed to attract the most qualified and capable person to run the company and paying top dollar especially when required to woo the right candidate from his or her current role in a highly desirable and top-paying organization. It will become more like the entertainment industry and major league sports, where average compensation will move modestly, while the top performers who are most likely to bring success to the venture will get the big bucks.

Overall, boards will do better in aligning pay with performance based on relevant metrics, and will rein in the potential of over-the-top severance and related payoffs.

## More Companies Will Learn How to Deal with Risk

An increasing number of companies will move from having pockets of risk management to an effective enterprise risk management process. More C-suite officers and directors will understand that risk management is not about becoming risk averse, but rather having information necessary to making informed decisions enabling new initiatives to drive growth and return. They'll grasp the notion that bigger brakes are put on race cars not so they can go slower, but so they can maintain control to go faster.

But this won't happen on a widespread basis in the next few years. In dealing with a challenging economic and increasingly competitive environment, initiatives for enhancing internal processes have been put on the back burner. So while attention will be given to the substance behind the newly required risk-related disclosures, with some companies working to strengthen processes, we won't see much short-term movement toward establishing full-blown enterprise risk management. But over a period of years, enterprise risk management will become a fundamental process inherent in most large organizations.

## There Will Be More Subprime-Like Disasters

Disaster will occur again in the foreseeable future, although we don't know exactly when or what form it will take. It will happen in part because too many businesses still don't identify, assess, and manage risk effectively. A key reason for the huge losses by AIG, Bear Stearns, Citicorp, Lehman Brothers, Merrill Lynch, Morgan Stanley, and others is that those organizations didn't fully recognize how much risk they were incurring.

Broad-based failures will happen again due to lack of knowledge or insight into the risk-reward relationship, a herd mentality—recall the savings and loan fiasco, dot-com bubble, and the more recent current subprime debacle. Whether these recipes for disaster are founded in some companies' reward systems, implicit or explicit government guarantees, or other factors, there's little doubt that it's not a question of whether, but when, disaster will strike again. Hopefully it will be mitigated by the newly enacted laws and forthcoming regulations, lessening damage to shareholders, taxpayers, and the economic system.

## Boards of Directors Will Continue to Do Better

Boards and board committees have better processes, and directors are taking their jobs very seriously. With a sharper focus on their compliance and monitoring responsibilities—that is, having better audit, compensation, and nominating and governance committee processes—boards are getting back to providing the kind of advice, counsel, and direction to management that helps drive growth and return. Fortunately, this will continue.

For the most part, highly capable individuals have not been scared off with frustration about compliance responsibilities and are remaining as directors and bringing their combined knowledge, experience, and business judgment to the table. They continue to be well aware of the risks they face regarding personal reputation and liability, but are also aware of the judiciary system upholding the "good faith" and "business judgment" standards, and further comforted with increasingly effective director-and-officer insurance coverage. We will continue to see many of the best and brightest serving on corporate boards, and shareholders will benefit from their participation.

We will also see more specific areas of expertise required of directors, beyond experts in financial reporting and risk management (now required for larger financial institutions), going to such areas as compensation, international business, technology, and industry expertise. We will see fewer former CEOs in boardrooms, and still fewer active ones, which will reduce the amount of experience and wisdom for dealing with challenging issues. This is because boards of the companies they run are demanding full attention at home, especially given the troubled economy, turbulent markets, and related changes in strategic direction. And we will see fewer so-called name directors with outstanding reputations but whose skills simply don't match a board's needs.

## The Environment in which Businesses Operate Will Continue to Be Challenging

Naturally, we operate in an increasing global environment, with the success of American business dependent on the economy—that of the United States and indeed the rest of the world. Here at home we have serious issues, including large federal deficits and a huge national debt, balance-of-payments shortfalls, and the state of the pension and health care systems—national, state, municipal, and private—to name just a few. Our country is at war, and the economic, political, and social impacts and our influence as a world leader are at stake. Capital markets can be volatile, and global competition for capital fierce. I won't even think about trying to predict how this will all go. But I do know that how we deal with these issues will have a tremendous effect on businesses and how they operate, and the predictions outlined here will be affected as well. I am an eternal optimist and believe we will find ways to deal with these issues constructively and achieve positive outcomes.

So, there we have it. We have a good sense of what's coming down the pike and how best to deal with the challenges. With continued effort, diligence, intelligence, and innovation, there's no doubt we will succeed.

 **NOTES**

1. The title Chancellor applies to the chief judge on the Delaware Chancery Court, with the other four judges on that court having the title of Vice Chancellor.
2. Wachtell, Lipton December 3, 2010 memo, *Risk Management and the Board of Directors*.
3. *Directorship*, December 2010–January 2011.
4. *Directorship*, December 2010–January 2011.
5. Thomas Green, a well-recognized white-collar-criminal-defense lawyer, takes this position: "My experience suggests that resisting the investigation almost always leads to a better result for the company than had it surrendered at the outset." For more, see *Directors & Boards*, Fourth Quarter 2010. See also discussion in Chapter 3 of this book.

# About the Author

Richard M. (Rick) Steinberg is the founder and CEO of Steinberg Governance Advisors, Inc. He is an internationally recognized expert on governance, risk, and control. He advises boards of directors of major multinational, large, and middle-market companies on board responsibilities and governance best practices, and senior managements on governance, risk management, control, and compliance. Previously he was a senior partner of PricewaterhouseCoopers (PwC) and the leader of its corporate governance advisory practice. He was also a founder of PwC's risk management and control consulting practice, and served as its global leader. In addition, he was a founder and leader of PwC's U.S. Strategic Risk Services practice, developing and implementing clients' risk management processes.

As an expert in internal control and risk management, Steinberg served as the lead project partner in developing the Committee of Sponsoring Organizations of the Treadway Commission's (COSO's) *Internal Control—Integrated Framework* and led development of COSO's *Enterprise Risk Management—Integrated Framework*, the landmark reports recognized as standards for effective internal control and risk management.

Steinberg has authored numerous highly acclaimed reports, including *Corporate Governance and the Board—What Works Best* and its companion, *Audit Committee Effectiveness—What Works Best*. He is quoted in the financial press—including *Businessweek*, *Fortune*, the *Wall Street Journal*, *Dow Jones MarketWatch*, *CNN Money*, *Institutional Investor*, *Investor's Business Daily*, and the *Financial Times*—is a monthly columnist for *Compliance Week*, and is an active and sought-after speaker by major companies and business and professional organizations. He has been featured on CNBC TV's *Morning Call* and Bloomberg TV's *On the Markets* and *The Bloomberg Report*, and has guest lectured at such leading business schools as Auburn, Columbia, Delaware, Duke, MIT, NYU, and UCLA.

Steinberg is a member of the Open Compliance and Ethics Group Executive Advisory Panel, is cofounder of the *Directors' College*, presented by PricewaterhouseCoopers and the University of Delaware Center for Corporate Governance, and served as a member of the Conference Board's Global Corporate Governance Research Center Advisory Board and as co-chair of Corporate Board Member's Academic Council.

He is a graduate of the University of Pennsylvania's Wharton School and holds an MBA from New York University's Graduate School of Business.

# Index

critical information, 238–245
follow-the-herd mentality, 231–238
groupthink, 233–235
HP board leaks, 245–249
leaks, 249–250
Pitt, Harvey, 78
Political agendas, 258
Power of shareholders vs. boards
about, 251–252
balance, 262–264
Dodd-Frank Act proxy access, 256–261
goals, 264
good intentions, 259–261
limitations, 261–262
shareholder achievements, 253–256
shareholder activism, 252–253
Presiding director, 267
Pretexting scandal, 54, 247
Preventive measures, 96
Probabilistic techniques, 90
Problem notification, 217–218
Project governance, 18
Proxy statement access, 154, 253,
257–259, 294
Public Company Accounting Oversight
Board, 127

Quality vs. quantity, 142

Rajaratnam, Raj, 249
Recalls, 25–27, 28
Refinance penalties, 60
Regulatory standards, 32
Regulatory systems, 61
Reich, Robert, 188
Reporting relationships, 37
compliance officer, 233–244
Reputation damage, 24, 27
Reputations, 29, 30
Responsibilities
of board of directors, 117, 175–176,
178–179
to borrowers, 62
of business units, 115
of chief audit executive, 116–117
of chief executive officers (CEOs), 117
of chief risk officer (CRO), 116
clarity of, 34

and compliance, 31
of enterprise risk management, 114–117
for financial reporting, 206–209
of general counsel, 116
insurance companies, 62
job, 45–46
management, 61–62
mortgage generators, 62
of operating managers, 104
operational, 35
for oversight, 169–182
rating agencies, 62
regulators, 62
and reputations, 30
for risk management, 175–176,
178–179
for risk management placement, 104
for Sarbanes-Oxley Section 404,
124–126
social, 160–162
*Revolt in the Boardroom* (Murray),
271–272
Righteous culture, 8–9
Risk. *See also* Enterprise risk management;
Risk management
about, 79–80
attending to, 78–79
betting on, 77
BP experience, 92–97
defined, 76–77
key risk indicators (KRIs), 91–92
Risk appetite
vs. risk tolerance, 177–178
setting limits to, 88
and strategy, 86
Risk assessment, 19, 120, 174
Risk avoidance, 90
Risk committee, 179, 208
Risk identification process, 175
Risk management
about, 75–76, 173–174
absence of, 67
board of directors's responsibilities,
175–176, 178–179
board of directors's role in, 157
CEO on, 174–175
communications problems, 177–178
and culture, 9